THE LAW OF INTERNATIONAL SEA PIRACY

DEVELOPMENTS IN INTERNATIONAL LAW

volume 2

1. SYMMONS, CLIVE RALPH. *The Maritime Zones of Islands in International Law.* 1979. ISBN 90-247-2171-7

2. DUBNER, BARRY HART. *The Law of International Sea Piracy.* 1980. ISBN 90-247-2191-1

THE LAW OF INTERNATIONAL SEA PIRACY

by

BARRY HART DUBNER

1980

MARTINUS NIJHOFF PUBLISHERS

THE HAGUE/BOSTON/LONDON

Distributors:

for the United States and Canada

Kluwer Boston, Inc.
160 Old Derby Street,
Hingham, MA 02043
USA

for all other countries

Kluwer Academic Publishers Group
Distribution Center
P.O. Box 322
3300 AH Dordrecht
The Netherlands

Library of Congress Cataloging in Publication Data CIP

Dubner, Barry Hart, 1940-
    The law of international sea piracy.

    Bibliography: p.
    Includes index.
    1. Pirates.   2. Maritime law.   I. Title.
JX4444.D8   341.77   79-11616

ISBN 90 247 2191 1

PRINTED IN THE NETHERLANDS

TO MY WIFE

BONNIE

PREFACE

The rapid development of technology in the economic uses of the seas has required international law to develop new legal norms in order to keep in pace. In the latter half of the century, multilateral treaties have been the accepted vehicle utilized by states in order to embody these developments in express agreement fixing new legal norms. But it takes time and much patience for such agreements to be reached and brought into force. More than a generation has elapsed since the formulation of the three "useable" conventions of the 1958 Geneva Law of the Sea Conference. Yet, the Conference States in the present perennial Law of the Sea discussions are still confronted with the problems of obtaining ratifiable agreements (consensi) for embodiment into a new multilateral treaty or treaties.

During the generation since 1958, most states have been utilizing unilateral action in order to establish new territorial limits and modify existing norms in the law of the oceans. For the moment, we are busy turning over the various informal Composite Negotiating Texts issuing from the Law of the Sea Conferences against this body for unilateral action.

The problems which Professor Dubner assesses in this accelerating unilateral and multilateral development of new legal norms in response to the new technologies is the subject of piracy on the seas. He considers that this area, only indirectly related to the major maritime economic problem areas, is being skimmed over without enough consideration. He argues "political" errors are being made for the sake of "expediency", and that, once again, history is repeating itself. When formulating the conventional rules of what the Conference States have considered a rather settled, traditional area of the law of nations, they have in particular failed to protect states from acts of piracy occurring in waters other than the high seas. This reluctance is made out as the result of their apparent belief that domestic legislation would cover the actual gaps despite the fact that they had the Harvard Research and the Conference work before them

in which the insufficiencies and inconsistencies in domestic legislation are fully evident; and that this is clear even though the states
in the discussions leading to the 1958 Geneva Conventions were
prepared to be innovative, especially in the field of aircraft piracy.

   In this provocative manuscript Professor Dubner subjects the
law of sea piracy to a close and revealing examination. He traces the
development of the orthodox and unorthodox views of the states
regarding the geographic location for piracy and the modalities for
the seizure and treatment of pirates. He stresses the fact that the
development of international law in this area came to a relative
standstill long ago even though modern communications and
advanced technology and economic activities make it imperative
that the subject be constantly re-examined in order to ascertain
whether or not an updating of the so-called "norms" in the area is
necessary. Utilizing contrasts between acts of piracy which occurred
in earlier centuries and recent incidents which have been labeled
"piracy" by certain States, Professor Dubner painstakingly sets forth
the relevant practice and thought in the area so that the reader can
judge if change is presently necessary. One question constantly
recurs: Does piracy really include modern day "terrorism" cloaked
in the word "piracy" by states simply because the act occurs on
waters, regardless of geographic location?

   This contribution is thus twofold. It seeks to set forth the
emergence and development of the law of piracy. At the same time,
it is concerned with the possible new approaches to the subject that
can be utilized by the Conference States in order to deal with the
emerging problems of piracy/terrorism. It therefore can be recommended both to practitioners, concerned with present state of the
law of piracy and the law of the sea, and to scholars, seeking to
assess the interrelationship between the development of the law of
the sea, in general, and piracy, in particular.

                                          ALBERT H. GARRETSON

ACKNOWLEDGMENTS

I wish to express my gratitude to the members of the faculty and staff of the University of Western Australia School of Law for their cooperation and support in the development of this text.

A sincere expression of gratitude is extended to my wife, Bonnie, whose enthusiasm, encouragement, and technical assistance were a major factor in the completion of my work.

A special note of thanks to my research assistant, Brian McVan, for his imagination and alacrity in helping wherever needed; and to Paula Sabino, a superb and patient typist.

TABLE OF CONTENTS

CHAPTER I

INTRODUCTION

The word *piracy* has been applied to acts of murder, robbery, plunder, rape and other villainous deeds which have transpired over centuries of mankind's history. Piracy usually conjures up in one's mind images of a flag with skull and crossbones, still used today on medicine bottles to indicate poison, and of swashbucklers, plundering ships and taking booty as prize. The following excerpt could depict a scene from a movie rather than testimony given at a trial for felony and piracy which took place in 1696:[1]

From thence they went to Bonyvis, and took in some salt; and from Bonyvis they went to the Isle of May, and there they took three English ships, and plundered them; and they took the governor aboard their own ship till they had done, (for then they could demand what victuals they had a mind to) and then they sent him away again: And from the Isle of May they went to the coast of Guinea, where they put out English colours, to make the natives come aboard to trade; and when they came aboard, they surprised them, and took their gold from them, and tied them with chains, and put them into the hold; and when they came to a place called the Island of Princes, they gave seven of them away for slaves; And then they went to Vandepoe where they cleaned their ship; and from Vandepoe they went to Cape Lopes, and from Cape Lopes to Annibo, and from Annibo about the Cape; and at Madagascar they watered their ship, and got provisions, and cows to salt up; and from thence they went to Joanna, and from Joanna they went to take a junk, and took rice out of her, and sunk her; and from thence they went to the Equinoctial line, and because they were short of water and rice, they went back again to Joanna; and the wind being contrary, they went to Commeroe; and there they met a small French vessel, and they took her, and sunk her; and then went to Joanna again, and there took in Mr. May again: and then went to Meat; and because the natives would not trade with them, they burnt their town: And then they went to Bob's Key, by the mouth of the Red Sea; but before that, they met with an English vessel, that was on the same account that we were; and we rode there a night or two; and they saw there another sail a coming, which proved to be another English vessel: And in the morning they saw two more, May, Ferrel, and Wake, were

---

[1] The trial of Joseph Dawson, Edward Forseith, William Mary, William Bishop, James Lewis, and John Sparkes, at the Old Bailey, for Felony and Piracy: 8 William III. A.D. 1696, 13 How. St. Tr. 455 (1697).

the captains: And on Saturday night all the Mocha fleet passed by: And on
Sunday morning they took another vessel, that told them the said fleet was
gone by; and so they consulted whether they should follow them or stay
there. And then they went after them and overtook them, and took one
that was about three or four hundred ton, and took gold and silver out of her.
And next day they spied another sail, and got up their anchor, and stood to
her, and took her; she was called the Gunsway; they killed several men aboard,
and when they had taken and plundered the ship, they left the men aboard to
go to Surat again. And then they went to Rachipool in the East Indies, and got
water and necessaries; and from thence to Degorees, and watered again; and
then to Dascaran, where they set about twenty-five Frenchmen ashore, and
fourteen Danes, and some English; for they were afraid, if they came to England,
and were caught, they should be hanged; and they thought themselves there
secure. From that place they went to Ascension, and then to the Island Provi-
dence in the West Indies: And then they wrote a letter to the governor, to
know if he would let them come in, and said they would present the governor
with twenty pieces of eight, and two pieces of gold, if he would let them come
in; and the captain, because he had a double share, he offered forty pieces of
eight, and four of gold; and with that they sent some men down, Adams and
others, with the letter: And they came again, with a letter, from the island,
that they should be welcome, and come go again when they pleased.

Although this testimony was elicited at a municipal trial which
occurred in the seventeenth century, it was not until the twentieth
century that certain "traditional" notions of piracy were framed
within an international convention on the law of the sea. The 1958
United Nations Conference on the Law of the Sea produced the
Convention on the High Seas[2] which incorporated eight articles
relating to piracy.[3] After reading the 1958 conventional articles,
the reader may have the impression that the significant issues in the
law of international sea piracy have been resolved.[4] However, the
contrary may be so.

During different decades of the twentieth century, certain
questions have arisen regarding piracy which can be enumerated as
follows:

[2] Convention on the High Seas, opened for signature April 29, 1958, 13 U.S.T.2312
(1962), T.I.A.S. No. 5200, 450 U.N.T.S. 82. The appropriate articles of this convention
relating to piracy have been reproduced in Appendix 1.

[3] *Ibid.*, Articles 14-21 (hereinafter referred to as the 1958 conventional articles). The
Third United Nations Conference on the Law of the Sea has left these articles unchanged
as of July 20, 1977. See: Third United Nations Conference on the Law of the Sea, *Infor-
mal Single Negotiating Text*, U.N. Doc. A/CONF.62/WP.8/Part II (1975), Articles 86-93;
Revised Single Negotiating Text, U.N. Doc. A/CONF.62/WP.8/Rev.1 and A/CONF.62/
WP.9/Rev.1 (1976), Articles 88-95; and *Informal Composite Negotiating Text*, U.N.
Doc. A/CONF.62/WP.10/CORR.1 (1977), Articles 100-107.

[4] It is interesting to note at this juncture that some of the acts alluded to in the Dawson
trial, *supra*, would not constitute piracy under the 1958 conventional articles.

1. Is piratical robbery at sea essentially different from ordinary robbery on land? (1925)[5]
2. Is the jurisdiction universal because they are *hostes humani generis*, or are they said to be *hostes humani generis* because the jurisdiction is universal? (1925)[6]
3. Does the proposition state a prerequisite or a consequence? (1925)[7]
4. Does it describe a constituent element of the offense of piracy or only a reprehensible quality or characteristic which the law attributes to pirates? (1925)[8]
5. Must piracy be committed on the high seas, or can it also be committed in the territorial sea or in ports? (1957)[9]
6. Must piracy be committed for private ends, or can it also be committed by persons acting either on behalf of a state or at least on behalf of a politically organized group for a purpose which can reasonably be described as a public purpose as opposed to a private purpose? (1957)[10]
7. Should all acts of state be exempt from universal jurisdiction? (1976)[11]
8. Should all acts of politically organized, or similar groups, and of all individuals who are not acting for personal gain, revenge, and so on, be excluded from the common jurisdiction? (1976)[12]

It should be emphasized that the eight questions presented were raised by legal publicists during different periods of this century. These questions were presented in order to attract the attention of the international community to various incidents occurring during the time periods involved (in 1925 the bootlegging of whisky during prohibition; 1932, the work of the Harvard Research Group; 1950's, the preparatory work of the International Law Commission; 1958, the Conference on the Law of the Sea; 1975, the *Mayaguez*; 1961, the *Santa Maria* and other so-called "politically motivated" incidents). If these questions appear to be similar in content it is because the various conventions and writings occurring during their span did not sufficiently respond to the issues. Indeed, as will be shown in

[5] Dickinson, *Is the Crime of Piracy Obsolete?*, 38 Harv. L. Rev. 334 (1925), p. 350.
[6] *Ibid.*, p. 351.
[7] *Ibid.*
[8] *Ibid.*
[9] Johnson, *Piracy in Modern International Law*, 43 Trans. Grotius Soc. 63 (1957), p. 68.
[10] *Ibid.*
[11] Crockett, *Toward a Revision of the International Law of Piracy*, 26 DePaul L. Rev. 78 (1976), p. 98.
[12] *Ibid.*, p. 99.

later chapters many issues raised by these and other questions were bypassed because they touched upon sensitive problem areas. Perhaps, too, it was more expedient to omit them from conventions in order to resolve the "traditional" problems relating to piracy even though the resulting 1958 conventional articles on piracy were dated and moot before their adoption at the 1958 United Nations Conference on the Law of the Sea.

Against this background, the purposes of this book are to give the reader a thorough explanation of the law relating to international sea piracy, to compile all relevant data relating to this subject, to respond to some of the questions posed by legal publicists, and, by so doing, hopefully to assist in the progressive development of international law and contribute to the common heritage of mankind.

Some of the suggestions proposed may strike the reader as rather unorthodox, at least when considering the history and development of the "traditional" terms and governing concepts of the law of the sea. However, if the reader bears in mind that one need not conceive of international political boundaries as a blockade to the development of the resources and energies of mankind (especially after considering the growing shortages of energy and food resources and the ever-increasing population), then the suggestions may not seem so unusual.

The law of the sea is not a static subject. It is, for the most part, a developing area of international law. The *Informal Composite Negotiating Text*[13] (hereinafter cited as the 1977 composite text), which is being used by representatives of the states attending the Third United Nations Conference on the Law of the Sea, contains many new areas for discussion, *inter alia*, exclusive economic zone,[14] compulsory dispute settlement,[15] and scientific research.[16] Surprisingly enough, the draft articles on piracy (contained within the composite text, Part VII on the high seas) have remained unchanged. Certain publicists believe that the 1958 conventional articles on piracy do not need revision, that these articles on piracy ". . . serve the goal of repressing *private* violence at sea."[17] The fact that the 1977 composite text contains but eight static articles pertaining to piracy continues to attest to this view.[18]

---

[13] *Op. cit.*, note 3.
[14] *Ibid.*, Part V, Articles 55-75.
[15] *Ibid.*, Part XV, Articles 279-297.
[16] *Ibid.*, Part XIII, Articles 239-266.
[17] McDougal and Burke, *The Public Order of the Oceans*, (New Haven: Yale University Press) 1962, p. 879, emphasis added.
[18] *Informal Composite Negotiating Text, op. cit.*, note 3, Articles 100-107.

It will be observed that the 1958 conventional articles and the draft articles contained in the 1977 composite text each contain an identical definition of acts constituting piracy together with a geographic limitation that these acts must occur on the high seas. The rationale for this geographic limitation has been stated:

In my view, the essential consequence of an act of piracy is the displacement of the normal rule that a ship is subject exclusively to the jurisdiction of its own state by another rule that the ship in question is subject in some measure to the jurisdiction of the coastal state as well as of the flag state, but there seems no good reason to go further than that and authorise the international community as a whole to assume jurisdiction over acts that are clearly taking place within national territory.[19]

However, even the geographic limitation has been questioned recently:

Admittedly, this aspect of the law relating to piracy may be largely academic, but if a "pirate" craft were to operate from the high seas against shipping within the territorial waters of a state which lacked the naval resources to put an end to these depredations, would the naval forces of a state, the merchant shipping of which had as yet been unmolested, have to stand helplessly by until its intervention were requested by the coastal state or by a state that had suffered damage?[20]

One need only look at the geographic locations of recent acts of piracy in order to see that this aspect of the law relating to piracy may not be academic:

Kota Kinabalu, August 8, 1977. In a drive against piracy on the high seas, still not uncommon in waters around Borneo and the southern Philippines, Malaysia is tightening control of the region's lucrative barter trading and smuggling.

To keep track of the traders, they are now allowed to deal in only three towns around Sabah's 1,500 mile coast line — Labuan in the west, Tawau and Sandakan in the east.

Soon, according to the Sabah Police Commissioner, Mr. Yussof Khan, they will be allowed to trade only in Labuan, this east Malaysian state's duty-free island port southwest of the state capital. Most of them already go there because of the variety of goods available.

To make it easier to sort out genuine traders from smugglers, fishermen, gun runners and pirates, they must now sail in three clearly-defined corridors about one mile wide — away from fishing areas. If they do not, they risk being turned back or being fired on, according to the commissioner.

He says that one result of the corridor system introduced at the beginning of the year, has been a sharp decrease in piracy.

Pirates used to hide among fishing vessels before pouncing on traders.[21]

[19] Johnson *op. cit.*, note 9, p. 71.
[20] Greig, *International Law*, 2nd ed., (London: Butterworth) 1976, p. 332.
[21] *South China Morning Post*, August 9, 1977, (Business News) p. 11. This excerpt is taken from an account of acts of piracy occurring in the territorial waters of the Philippines. A complete account of these incidents is cited in Appendix 2. See also: *The Hongkong Standard*, August 11, 1977, p. 8.

Nevertheless, the orthodox view on the subject has been that states do not need a provision regarding acts of piracy committed within their territorial seas because these acts would be committed within the municipal jurisdictional competence of nations capable of acting to suppress piracy committed for "private ends."[22]

It will also be observed that the 1958 conventional articles and the draft articles contained in the 1977 composite text state that there must be an act committed for "private ends." The act must be committed by a vessel or aircraft against another vessel or aircraft. Any violent act will do (or detention or depredation) — no "taking" is necessary. These limitations present other problems for discussion because of the difficulties that arise from what may be considered political rather than legal questions (that is, insurgency, belligerency, the granting of political asylum, the acts of states in general, and so on). Also, it will be observed that warships cannot commit acts of piracy because they are always subject to the jurisdiction of their native states.[23] The exception to this general rule is where a mutiny has occurred on board the warship and the mutineers have taken control of it.

The 1958 conventional articles and the draft articles contained in the 1977 composite text disclose a self-evident problem, namely, that they appear to be applicable to incidents and acts which constituted piracy in previous centuries. The corollary to this proposition is that the various political incidents (and the legal implications arising therefrom) which have occurred in the twentieth century (for example the *Mayaguez* incident[24] and the *Santa Maria*[25]) may not be covered by the codified 1958 conventional definition of piracy. In addition, the types of acts occurring today are more akin to acts of terrorism which may, or may not, involve insurgents, belligerents, or various liberation groups and which may be classified as acts committed for "political" rather than "private" ends.

The main argument against challenging the so-called "traditional" piracy norms seems to be that since a definition of acts constituting piracy has been agreed upon in the 1958 conventional articles, why bother to change them? At least there is one area in the law of the

---

[22] The articles heretofore cited, as well as this book, deal only with the international law of sea piracy, not with municipal laws which provide for punishing certain acts as piracy. For a discussion of this distinction see, for example, Dickinson, *op. cit.*, note 5; Joyner, *Aerial Hijacking as an International Crime*, (New York: Oceana) 1974, pp. 21-24.

[23] For this reason the law of piracy would not be applicable to an action such as the 1968 seizure of the U.S.S. *Pueblo* by Cambodian naval vessels on the high seas. See: 18 I.C.L.Q. 961 (1969).

[24] S.S. *Mayaguez* Incident, U.S. Digest, ch. 14, sectional (1975).

[25] Green, The Santa Maria: *Rebels or Pirates?*, 37 Brit. Y.B. Int'l L. 496 (1961).

sea which has universal consensus. Another argument which could be advanced is that many of these so-called "political" acts are not acts of "piracy" but rather acts falling within other definitions contained in international law such as "war." The problem is that states may label acts committed by terrorists, insurgents, belligerents, or murderers as piratical for political reasons, in order to incite and manipulate the feelings of the general public so that various consequences can be justified.[26] It is rather easy to conjure up situations or scenarios to which the current 1958 conventional articles (and the 1977 composite text) do not appear to be applicable. When most people think of piracy, they still think in terms of seventeenth-century piratical acts (that is, the swashbucklers) rather than acts which can be perpetrated as a result of vast technological advances in weapons, mass communications, and so on. Many of the changes that could be effected are stymied by political and legal considerations such as rigid adherence to the traditional principle of sovereign rights, even though the sovereign state might be aiding and abetting a person who should be considered an international criminal.

Any suggestion that is made for revising the 1958 conventional articles on piracy will have to consider all of the various possibilities which can occur between an individual and a state. Under the 1958 conventional articles on piracy, we see that an *individual* can commit any or all of the acts defined as piracy; that these acts can be "private" or committed for private ends; and, that the punishment would be prescribed by the captor or the state affected by the act under municipal law. After looking at the current incidents (for example, the *Santa Maria*) and comparing this to the swashbuckler type of piracy which occurred in earlier centuries, some of the main problems under the present 1958 conventional articles become evident. These are, *inter alia*: (a) the articles apply only to "individuals"; (b) the acts constituting piracy have been enacted mainly for the purpose of expediency; and (c), the convention assumes that the municipal law of the captor or other appropriate state will contain legislation prescribing punishment for acts of piracy committed under conventional law.

Any recommendation for change in the status quo, therefore, will have to contain different alternatives in order to make the law of piracy applicable to incidents occurring in the twentieth century. Suggestions might be made to:

---

[26] The problems inherent in distinguishing between piratical acts and acts by politically motivativated insurgents is exemplified by the *Santa Maria* incident. For an analysis see Fenwick, *Piracy in the Caribbean*, 55 Am. Jour. of Int. L. 410 (1961). For an opposing view see Green, *op. cit.*, p. 496.

1. Amend that portion of the 1958 conventional articles on piracy which relate to "private" as opposed to both private and "politically" motivated acts;

2. Amend that portion of the 1958 conventional articles dealing with the acts constituting piracy in order to broaden the definition;

3. Amend that portion of the 1958 conventional articles which restricts the geographic limitation to the high seas areas only;

4. Amend that portion of the 1958 conventional articles on piracy and hot pursuit to allow for the extension of hot pursuit into the territorial waters of the coastal state;

(a) Notify the coastal State that the alleged pirate has entered its waters, at which point the coastal State could refuse to take any action at all;

(b) Turn over the alleged pirate to the offended nation;

(c) Allow the offended nation to go into the coastal state to capture the pirates;

(d) Justify this intrusion because the coastal state is aiding, abetting and harboring a person who has allegedly committed an international crime.

5. Amend that portion of the 1958 conventional articles which deals with methods of seizure to create and develop the concept of an international zone around the alleged pirate which would extend no matter where the international criminal seeks refuge;

(a) After capture, the pirate could be placed into an international prison[27] in order to await disposition of his case;

6. Amend that portion of the 1977 composite text to provide for compulsory dispute settlement in cases of piracy:

(a) The mechanism or authority utilized would have the jurisdiction to prescribe and enforce penalties and punishment;

(b) It would take into consideration such political considerations as requests for asylum, insurgency, belligerency, and so on;

(c) It would be operating under a uniform procedure and would prevent states from making difficult political decisions or from employing their municipal legislation on piracy, if any.

In other words, we are interested mainly in seeking alternatives to the present 1958 conventional articles concerning the seizing of persons or property involved in piratical acts; the methods of seizure; the disposition of seized vessels and persons; the geographic

---

[27] Smith, *The Probable Necessity of an International Prison in Solving Aircraft Hijacking*, 5 Int. Lawyer 269 (1971). For a general discussion of the alternatives available in this area see Paust, *A Survey of Possible Legal Responses to International Terrorism: Preventing, Punishment, and Cooperative Action*, 5 Ga. J. Int. and Comp. L. 431 (1975).

location of seizure of persons and property; the effects of seizure; and the very definition of what acts should constitute piracy under conventional law. We will have to review the "traditional" approaches in order to ascertain what alterations, if any, are necessary, in order to update the law of international sea piracy. In order to define acts of piracy and to prescribe uniform penalties applicable to the incidents which can occur, we will have to review carefully the work of the Harvard Research Group[28] (hereinafter cited as the Group) and the International Law Commission[29] (hereinafter cited as the Commission) whose works led to the adoption of the 1958 conventional articles. We will see if the "traditional" meaning of piracy is suitable and if there is justification for changing the 1958 conventional articles on piracy. We will also have to determine what basis, if any, is present for states to assert a common jurisdiction over pirates.

Although the problems regarding piracy have been transpiring for centuries, the analysis contained in the literature is somewhat dated and illustrates a lack of interest and creative thinking. There are a few articles which discuss the history of piracy with a view toward setting forth approaches to the current problems;[30] but other than the writings regarding air piracy,[31] none thoroughly utilize the extensive efforts of the Harvard Research Group and the International Law Commission to propose solutions to the incidents which have occurred during the last twenty years. In addition, there are few specialized treatises which deal with law of the sea problems, exclusively. Those of Colombos[32] and McDougal and Burke[33] represent the most extensive of this group. These treatises contain limited discussions of the current incidents and problems related thereto as raised by the legal publicists in the few main articles that appear on the subject. The authors engage mainly in historical and traditional discussions, applying the orthodox views of the day.

[28] Harvard Research in International Law, *Draft Convention on Piracy with Comments,* 26 Am. of Int'l. L. 749 (1932).

[29] The International Law Commission was established pursuant to General Assembly Resolution 174 (II) dated November 21, 1947. The Commission held its first session in 1949. At that time, they prepared a provisional list of topics which they considered to be necessary and feasible. One of the topics under consideration was the possible creation of a regime of the high seas. The International Law Commission has for its object the promotion of the progressive development of international law and its codification.

[30] E.g., Crockett, *op. cit.,* note 11, pp. 92-99.

[31] See e.g., Joyner, *op. cit.,* note 22.

[32] Colombos, *International Law of the Sea,* 6th rev. ed., (New York: David McKay) 1967.

[33] *Op. cit.,* not 17.

The general international law treatises contain definitions of piracy, some of the historic problems regarding piracy and the treatment accorded to insurgents and belligerents, in general.[34]

There are many cases which were decided under English, American and other state municipal laws, but since the municipal laws on piracy vary from state to state, their usefulness as guiding lights to resolving present-day problems in an international context is rather limited.

The methodology employed in preparing this study is varied. In order to provide the reader with material which can assist in a thorough understanding of the subject matter, this study has commenced with an historic (or swashbuckler) incident in this chapter. Toward the end of this study, recent incidents will be set forth in order to illustrate the motivations which may be prevalent under current or future political scenarios. In the intervening period, the study focuses on the work of the Harvard Research Group and the International Law Commission. The Harvard Research Group published its draft convention and comments in 1932. It contained, *inter alia,* a compilation of practically all of the diverse opinions on the subject which had been published at that time. Since part of its draft convention was later adopted by the Conference States in 1958, with little or no change whatsoever, the reader is given an opportunity to review extensively the work of the Group. In addition, all of the published debates contained in the summary records reveal the practical considerations with which the International Law Commission was later confronted when preparing its report to the General Assembly of the United Nations.

This study is divided into (a) an introduction to early international acts of sea piracy; (b) a review of applicable terminology as utilized throughout the manuscript; (c) an extensive historic review of the subject matter with heavy reliance on the work of the Harvard Research Group; (d) an extensive review of the work of the International Law Commission which was framed within its report to the General Assembly and later adopted as conventional articles by the Conference States; (e) a review of the more recent politically motivated incidents of sea piracy; and (f) some suggestions for revising and updating the 1958 conventional articles on piracy.

Other approaches or forms of methodology could have been utilized in order to present the subject matter. However, it is envisaged that the approach set forth herein is the most illustrative

---

[34] For example, see Bishop, *International Law,* (Boston: Little, Brown) 1971, pp. 555-556.

and revealing for the reader. It is a difficult task to decide on the proper methodology to employ. Yet, in order to demonstrate the diverse viewpoints regarding the international law of sea piracy and to take advantage of the creative thinking of other publicists, this form of methodology will be employed throughout this study.

The contributions which this study is endeavoring to make to the literature, therefore, are to identify the current problems, to accommodate the conflicting interests of the international community, and, to set forth suggestions applicable to the law of international sea piracy.

APPENDIX 1 TO CHAPTER I

Convention on the High Seas, opened for signature April 29, 1958, 13 U.S.T. 2312 (1962), T.I.A.S. No. 5200, 450 U.N.T.S. 82

Article 14
All States shall co-operate to the fullest possible extent in the repression of piracy on the high seas or in any other place outside the jurisdiction of any State.

Article 15
Piracy consists of any of the following acts:
1. Any illegal acts of violence, detention or any act of depredation, committed for private ends by the crew or the passengers of a private ship or a private aircraft, and directed:
(a) On the high seas, against another ship or aircraft, or against persons or property on board such ship or aircraft;
(b) Against a ship, aircraft, persons or property in a place outside the jurisdiction of any State;
2. Any act of voluntary participation in the operation of a ship or of an aircraft with knowledge of facts making it a pirate ship or aircraft;
3. Any act of inciting or of intentionally facilitating an act described in sub-paragraph 1 or sub-paragraph 2 of this article.

Article 16
The acts of piracy, as defined in Article 15, committed by a warship, government ship or government aircraft whose crew has mutinied and taken control of the ship or aircraft are assimilated to acts committed by a private ship.

Article 17
A ship or aircraft is considered a pirate ship or aircraft if it is intended by the persons in dominant control to be used for the purpose of committing one of the acts referred to in Article 15. The same applies if the ship or aircraft has been used to commit any such act, so long as it remains under the control of the persons guilty of that act.

Article 18

A ship or aircraft may retain its nationality although it has become a pirate ship or aircraft. The retention or loss of nationality is determined by the law of the State from which such nationality was derived.

Article 19

On the high seas, or in any other place outside the jurisdiction of any State, every State may seize a pirate ship or aircraft, or a ship taken by piracy and under the control of pirates, and arrest the persons and seize the property on board. The courts of the State which carried out the seizure may decide upon the penalties to be imposed, and may also determine the action to be taken with regard to the ships, aircraft or property, subject to the rights of third parties acting in good faith.

Article 20

Where the seizure of a ship or aircraft on suspicion of piracy has been effected without adequate grounds, the State making the seizure shall be liable to the State the nationality of which is possessed by the ship or aircraft, for any loss or damage caused by the seizure.

Article 21

A seizure on account of piracy may only be carried out by warships or military aircraft, or other ships or aircraft on government service authorized to that effect.

APPENDIX 2 TO CHAPTER I

South China Morning Post, Tuesday, August 9, 1977 (Business News), p. 11: "Sea Corridors Curb Pirates and Smugglers," by Colin Bickler

In a drive against piracy on the high seas, still not uncommon in waters around Borneo and the southern Philippines, Malaysia is tightening control of the region's lucrative barter trading and smuggling.

To keep track of the traders, they are now allowed to deal in only three towns around Sabah's 1,500 mile coast line — Labuan in the west. Tawau and Sandakan in the east.

Soon, according to the Sabah Police Commissioner, Mr. Yussof Khan, they will be allowed to trade only in Labuan, this east Malaysian state's duty-free island port southwest of the state capital. Most of them already go there because of the variety of goods available.

To make it easier to sort out genuine traders from smugglers, fishermen, gun runners and pirates, they must now sail in three clearly-defined corridors about one mile wide — away from fishing areas. If they do not, they risk being turned back or being fired on, according to the commissioner.

He says that one result of the corridor system introduced at the beginning of the year, has been a sharp decrease in piracy.

Pirates used to hide among fishing vessels before pouncing on traders.

The corridors are well away from fishing grounds to eliminate this possibility.

The trading is worth a lot of money to Sabah. According to statistics it brings about M$48 million (US$16 million), a year to the state of about 800,000 people.

A development from decades of smuggling by traders in the southern Philippines, to which Sabah is closer than the main port areas of the northern Philippines, it has always been a legal business in Sabah. Much of it is now legal in the Philippines as well.

After years of being unable to curb the business, the Philippines set up legal barter trading areas in various southern towns, principally Zamboanga City — about 200 miles northwest of Sabah and 550 miles south of Manila.

Locals and tourists are allowed to buy limited amounts of goods there duty free, for their own use. Among the most popular are thin rice noodles known as sotanghon, which costs half the price in the barter trade areas than in Manila's supermarkets.

They also sell transistor radios, tape recorders, large numbers of China-made umbrellas, perfumes, fabrics and candy.

But the heart of the trade, as it has been for decades, are duty-exempt U.S. cigarettes which remain highly popular in the Philippines despite it being a tobacco exporting country famous for fine cigars.

It also includes several brands of Hongkong-made cigarettes, which Sabah imports especially for the Philippines trade.

The legal barter trade areas have clearly not stopped the smuggling.

Early this month, police raided a market in Angeles City, near the U.S. Clark Field base about 50 miles north of Manila.

They were after goods smuggled from the U.S. military duty-free stores. They found quite a few, but they also found thousands of pesos worth of goods that had apparently left Sabah for the southern barter trade markets but were diverted to illegal channels in the north instead.

Such goods are also on sale in the central Philippines city of Cebu.

According to Sabah police, about 1,000 boats a month arrive from the Philippines. They bring copra and similar wares to sell in Sabah and load up with luxury goods to take home.

Hongkong Standard, Thursday, August 11, 1977, p. 8: "Sabah's War on Pirates Paying Off?" by Colin Bickler

In a drive against piracy on the high seas, still not uncommon in waters around Borneo and the southern Philippines, Malaysia is tightening control of the region's lucrative barter trading and smuggling.

To keep track of the traders, they are now allowed to deal in only three towns around Sabah's 1,500 mile coast line — Labuan in the west, Tawau and Sandakan in the east.

Soon, according to Sabah Police Commissioner Yussof Khan, they will be allowed to trade only in Labuan, this East Malaysian state's duty-free island port just southwest of that state capital, to which most of them come now because of the variety of goods available there.

And to make it easier to sort out genuine traders from smugglers, fishermen, gun runners and pirates, they must now sail in three clearly-defined corridors about one mile wide — away from fishing areas — or risk the chance of at the least being turned back or at the worst being fired on, according to the commissioner.

He says that one result of the corridor system introduced at the beginning of the year, has been a sharp cutback in piracy, once rife in this area, where the Brunei and Borneo pirates were notorious to 18th and 19th century seafarers.

Previously, pirates used to hide among fishing vessels pouncing on traders. The corridors are well away from fishing grounds to eliminate this possibility.

The trading is worth a lot of money to Sabah, according to statistics it brings about 48 million ringgit ($80 million) a year to the state of about 800,000 people.

A development from decades of smuggling activities by traders in the southern Philippines, to which Sabah is closer than the main port areas of the northern Philippines, it has always been a legal business in Sabah and much of it is now legal in the Philippines as well.

After years of being unable to curb the business, the Philippines set up legal barter trading areas in various southern towns, principally Zamboanga City — about 200 miles northwest of Sabah and 500 miles south of Manila.

Here locals and tourists are allowed to buy a limited amount of goods duty free for their own use. Among the most popular are thin rice noodles known as Sotanghan, which costs half the price in the barter trade areas than in Manila's supermarkets. They also sell transistor radios, tape recorders, large numbers of China-made umbrellas, perfumes, fabrics and candy.

But the heart of the trade, as it has been for decades, are "blue seal" — named for the colour of the duty-exempt stamps of US made cigarettes which remain highly popular in the Philippines despite it being a tobacco exporting country famous for fine cigars.

It also includes several brands of Hongkong-made cigarettes, which Sabah imports especially for the Philippines trade.

The legal barter trade areas have clearly not stopped the smuggling. However early this month, police raided a market in Angeles City, near the US Clark field base about 50 miles north of Manila.

They were after goods smuggled from the US military duty-free PX stores. They found quite a few but they also found thousands of pesos worth of goods that apparently had left Sabah for the southern barter trade markets but were diverted to illegal channels in to north instead.

Such goods are also on sale in the central Philippines city of Cebu.

CHAPTER II

A REVIEW AND UPDATE OF THE APPLICABLE TRADITIONAL LAW OF THE SEA AND OTHER TERMINOLOGY RELATED TO THIS STUDY

To understand the international law of sea piracy, a general know-ledge of the law of the sea and associated terminology is required. It is appropriate at this time, therefore, to set forth the applicable 1958 conventional articles and then to discuss these concepts in the context of possible revisions which may occur under the 1977 composite text or at future law of the sea conferences. In addition, the new proposals which could affect our discussion of piracy, as set forth in the 1977 composite text, will be analyzed with a view toward their possible utilization in resolving the current dilemmas regarding piracy. For the purpose of this study, therefore, the pro-posed 1977 textual revisions regarding territorial seas, contiguous zones, high seas, dispute settlement mechanisms, and the exclusive economic zone will be discussed in order to demonstrate their utility in resolving problems related to (a) the seizing of persons or property involved in piracy; (b) the methods of seizure; (c) the disposition of seized vessels and persons; (d) the areas of seizure of persons and property; (e) the effects of seizure; and (f) the develop-ment of a new definition of elements necessary to constitute acts of piracy and uniform prescriptions therefor.

We will begin our review and update of the applicable traditional law of the sea and other terminology related to this study by setting forth the legal definition of the territorial sea.

TERRITORIAL SEA

Under the 1958 Convention on the Territorial Sea and the Con-tiguous Zone,[1] the legal definition of a territorial sea is stated in Articles 1 and 2:

[1] Convention on the Territorial Sea and the Contiguous Zone, opened for signature April 29, 1958, 15 U.S.T. 1606 (1964), T.I.A.S. No. 5639, 516 U.N.T.S. 205.

PART I: TERRITORIAL SEA

Section I: General

Article 1
   1. The sovereignty of a State extends, beyond its internal waters, to a belt of sea adjacent to its coast, described as the territorial sea.
   2. This sovereignty is exercised subject to the provisions of these articles and to other rules of international law.

Article 2
The sovereignty of a coastal State extends to the air space over the territorial sea as well as to its bed and subsoil.

What is lacking in the Articles 1 and 2 definition under the 1958 conventional articles is that there is no definite distance agreed upon as to the breadth of the territorial sea. In other words, a state could unilaterally claim a three-mile or 200-mile or any other territorial sea. As a result, there is no uniformity of distance. Under the draft articles contained in the 1977 composite text,[2] the breadth of the territorial sea is set at a uniform distance not exceeding 12 nautical miles:

Section 2: Limits of the Territorial Sea

Article 3: Breadth of the Territorial Sea.
Every State has the right to establish the breadth of its territorial sea up to a limit not exceeding 12 nautical miles, measured from baselines determined in accordance with the present Convention.

It is important to note, at this stage, that all of the topics contained in the 1958 conventional articles and the 1977 composite text articles on law of the sea interplay with each other. Therefore, if a 12-nautical-mile limit is adopted by the Conference States, this will mean that the new conventional articles on the Contiguous Zone, for example, will have to be modified to reflect the change in distance because, under the 1958 Convention on the Territorial Sea and the Contiguous Zone, the maximum extension of the Contiguous Zone is twelve nautical miles from the baselines from which the breadth of the territorial sea is measured. If pirates cannot be pursued into another state's territorial waters, it is obvious that these measurements must be known to the state giving chase.

CONTIGUOUS ZONE

Under the 1958 Convention on the Territorial Sea and the Contiguous Zone,[3] the legal definition of a contiguous zone is stated in Article 24:

   [2] Third United Nations Conference on the Law of the Sea: *Informal Composite Negotiating Text*, U.N. Doc. A/CONF. 62/WP.10/CORR. 1 (1977), Article 3, p. 21.
   [3] *Op. cit*, note 1.

1. In a zone of the high seas contiguous to its territorial sea, the coastal State may exercise the control necessary to:
(a) Prevent infringement of its customs, fiscal, immigration or sanitary regulations within its territory or territorial sea;
(b) Punish infringement of the above regulations committed within its territory or territorial sea.
2. The contiguous zone may not extend beyond twelve miles from the baseline from which the breadth of the territorial sea is measured.

It will be observed that the contiguous zone falls within the high seas which are adjacent to the coastal state. Within the zone, the coastal state has four general functional areas of regulation and control. After looking at the *travaux préparatoires* [legislative record] of the article and combining this with the application of the *inclusio unius exclusio alterius* rule, it becomes evident that the states are limited to these four functional areas and cannot carve out any other special jurisdictions on the high seas. Under the 1977 composite text, the contiguous zone may not extend beyond 24 nautical miles from the baselines from which the breadth of the territorial sea is measured.[4] It will be observed that this new figure of 24 miles is twice the distance that it was under the 1958 conventional articles. Obviously, this distance was set to coordinate the extension from the three-mile territorial sea limit (which was observed for many decades by the traditional maritime nations) to 12 miles under the 1977 composite text. In other words, the wisdom of the representatives of the Conference States was that twice the distance of the territorial sea figure would be sufficient for a contiguous zone.

HIGH SEAS

The legal definition of *high seas* is stated in Article 1 of the 1958 Convention on the High Seas:[5]

The term "high seas" means all parts of the sea that are not included in the territorial sea or in the internal waters of a State.

This provision is modified under the 1977 composite text by the parallel provision contained in Article 86:[6]

[4] *Informal Composite Negotiations Text, op. cit.,* note 2, Article 33 (21), p. 31.
[5] Convention on the High Seas, opened for signature April 29, 1958, 13 U.S.T. 2312 (1962), T.I.A.S. No. 5200, 450 U.N.T.S. 82.
[6] *Informal Composite Negotiating Text, op. cit.,* note 2, p. 56.

The provisions of this Part apply to all parts of the sea that are not included in the exclusive economic zone, in the territorial sea or in the internal waters of a State, or in the archipelagic waters of an archipelagic State. This article does not entail any abridgement of the freedoms enjoyed by all States in the exclusive economic zone in accordance with Article 58.

It should be noted at this juncture that, according to the 1977 composite text definition of high seas, all states would still enjoy the "freedoms" set forth in article 87.[7] Although the interplay of the economic zone and the high seas will be discussed later in this study (pp. 156-158), it is important to realize that, as a practical matter, geographical areas of high seas under the 1977 composite text could be greatly diminished. This could possibly justify an argument for maintaining the status quo in the 1958 conventional articles on piracy because areas of municipal jurisdiction would be greatly increased thereby reducing the geographic areas within which "traditional" acts of piracy could occur under the 1958 conventional articles and the 1977 composite text.

As will also be mentioned later in this study, (pp. 110-111) one concern today is that due to advanced technology, the definition of piracy, contained in the 1958 conventional articles and 1977 composite text, applies to acts and methods of piracy occurring in prior centuries. Perhaps modification of the definition is essential in order to conform to twentieth-century forms of piracy, for example hijacking vessels for smuggling, and/or "political" terrorism.[8]

If twentieth-century forms of piracy are occurring in coastal waters rather than on the high seas, or if certain coastal states are unable to handle effectively acts of piracy occurring in one geographic location but transgressing other traditionally recognized water boundaries as well (for example, high seas, internal waters, and so on), then another area of concern is embodied within the 1958 conventional articles dealing with the doctrine of hot pursuit,[9] which has been codified in Article 23 of the 1958 conventional articles.[10]

---

[7] *Ibid.* Article 87 mandates certain freedoms which can be exercised on the high seas by coastal and landlocked states, *inter alia*, freedoms of navigation, overflight, fishing, scientific research, and so on.

[8] One interesting question of contemporary significance involves the state's perception of jurisdiction. Professor Joyner puts the question as follows: ". . . are pirates considered pirates *jure gentium* if they descend from the high seas into the territory of a state, then return to the open waters to pursue piratical activities?" See Joyner, *Aerial Hijacking as an International Crime* (New York: Oceana) 1974, p. 29.

[9] For a comprehensive study of the subject of hot pursuit see Poulantzas, *The Right of Hot Pursuit in International Law* (Leiden: A.W. Sijthoff) 1969, pp. 345-348, and Moore, *Digest of International Law* (Washington, D.C.: Government Printing Office) 1906, vol. 2, p. 985.

[10] Convention on the High Seas, *op. cit.,* note 5. Article 23 is reproduced in Appendix 1 to this chapter.

The two most important elements concerning the right of hot pursuit for the purpose of this study deal with the embarkation point for the pursuit, contained in Article 23 (1), and the termination point for the hot pursuit prior to the entry into territorial waters of a third state – contained in Article 23 (3).[11] The applicable provisions in the 1977 composite text, that is, Article 111, Sections 1 and 3,[12] are identical to those contained in the 1958 conventional articles. These provisions could be amended in order to update the 1958 conventional articles relating to piracy as will be more fully discussed in later chapters (pp. 76-78, 163-165). At the present time, however, it is noteworthy that the informal consultative group on the regime of the high seas experienced difficulty in the past with regard to six major items. Two of these items: (a) whether hot pursuit could continue into the economic zone and (b) whether the term *high seas* should be defined to exclude the exclusive economic zone and archipelagic waters, directly affect this study and will be reviewed later.

EXCLUSIVE ECONOMIC ZONE

Provision for an exclusive economic zone was not contained in the 1958 conventional articles on the law of the sea. Part V, that is, Articles 55-75, of the 1977 composite text deals with this concept[13] although states have been declaring 200-mile limits, unilaterally, for quite a while.[14]

The Informal Consultative Group of the Whole, established to consider the question of an exclusive economic zone, held four meetings. The group's discussion started with the assumption that the coastal state has sovereign rights to the renewable and non-renewable resources in a zone extending to 200 miles from the baseline from which the breadth of the territorial sea is measured. The issues to be considered were (a) interests to be accommodated in the economic zone and the extent of those interests; (b) rights or

[11] For a good discussion of this particular aspect of hot pursuit see Joyner, *op. cit.*, note 10, pp. 33-35.

[12] *Informal Composite Negotiating Text, op. cit.*, note 2, p. 65.

[13] *Ibid.*, pp. 41-51. Articles 55-60 and 73-75 have been reproduced in Appendix 2 of this chapter.

[14] Between 1950 and 1972 the number of states claiming only three miles of territorial waters decreased from 40 to 25 while the number claiming 12 miles increased from 3 to 56 and as many as 15 states advanced claims to distances between 18 and 200 miles. Many South American nations have indicated a special desire to implement a 200-mile limit as evidenced by the Declaration of Santo Domingo of 1972, 11 I.L.M. 892. See Greig, *International Law*, 2nd ed., (London: Butterworth) 1976, pp. 194-198.

jurisdiction of the coastal state other than those related to resource exploitation; (c) coastal state rights relating to scientific research, artificial islands and installations, and other uses of the sea such as energy production; (d) navigation; and (e) other issues. However, many delegations did not follow the agreed outline and gave long dissertations on their well-known concepts of an economic zone. No decisions were reached by the group, and there are still a number of major issues of contention between the maritime powers, the developing coastal states and the landlocked and geographically disadvantaged states including (1) the extent to which a coastal state should be given jurisdiction in respect of control and abatement of pollution within its economic zone; (2) whether high seas rights should apply to navigation or whether the coastal state can exercise control over navigation other than with respect to pollution; (3) the degree of control by the coastal state of scientific research within its economic zone; (4) access to renewable and nonrenewable resources; and (5) allocation of residual rights in the economic zone. The 21 general articles on the exclusive zone in the 1977 composite text include some on fisheries and delimitation (Articles 61-68).

The reason the concept of an exclusive economic zone is mentioned in this study is that it is possible that states may declare that acts of piracy occurring within their respective economic zones fall within their exclusive jurisdictions because these acts constitute danger to commerce and navigation. In addition, it will be observed that Article 58 (2) of the 1977 composite text provides that:

Articles 88-115 [which include the articles on piracy and hot pursuit] and other pertinent rules of international law apply to the exclusive economic zone insofar as they are not incompatible with this Chapter.[15]

This economic zone has been described by Aguilar M. Andres, Chairman, Second Committee, as neither falling within the area of high seas nor the territorial sea. It is a zone *sui generis*.[16]

SETTLEMENT OF DISPUTES

There did not exist any provision for the settlement of disputes under the 1958 conventional articles.[17] At its 71st plenary meeting on August 2, 1976, the conference authorized the president to pre-

---

[15] *Informal Composite Negotiating Text, op. cit.*, p. 42.

[16] "*Sui generis* is a Latin term denoting one of a kind." Joyner, *op. cit.*, p. 25, note 25.

[17] The development of a dispute settlement mechanism acceptable to the Conference States was a complicated process. For an account of the evolution of the draft articles see Adede, *Settlement of Disputes Arising Under the Law of the Sea Convention*, 69 Am. J. of I.L. 798 (1975), and Sohn, *Settlement of Disputes Arising Out of the Law of the Sea Convention*, 12 U. of San Diego L.R. 495 (1975).

pare a revised single negotiating text on this subject, which would have the same status as parts I-III of the *Revised Single Negotiating Text*.[18]

Concerning the dispute settlement mechanism, it should be noted that in the past there developed among the Conference States two main trends of thought. First, a general approach was envisioned whereby states would move towards settlement through special procedures or a conciliation process before submitting the dispute to a judicial body for settlement. States would have a choice, when ratifying the convention, of accepting the jurisdiction of either the International Court of Justice, an arbitral tribunal composed in accordance with procedures laid down in an annex to the convention, a new law of the sea tribunal, or all three. There was, within this general approach, a division as to substantive areas in which compulsory settlement would be applicable. At one extreme, some states thought that there should be no room for exceptions to this jurisdictional competence; whereas, at the other extreme, a number of states considered that compulsory settlement should not be applied to disputes arising in maritime zones within national jurisdiction. However, most states which favored no exceptions, conceded, in an effort to achieve agreement, that limited specific exceptions would have to be permitted. Similarly, a number of those states which proposed that compulsory settlement should not apply in areas of national jurisdiction suggested a system whereby states would declare, when ratifying the convention, in which areas they would accept compulsory settlement. Second, a number of states favored a functional approach based on reference to specific categories of disputes and to special procedures of settlement. Thus,

---

[18] Third United Nations Conference on the Law of the Sea, *Revised Single Negotiating Text*, U.N. Doc. A/CONF.62/WP.8/Rev.1 and A/CONF.62/WP.9/Rev.1 (1976). Basically, in Section I (Articles 1-6) there is imposed upon the states an obligation to settle disputes by peaceful means, etc. Section II is devoted, *inter alia*, to procedural aspects. Annex I deals with the topic of conciliation and Annex II creates a statute of the law of the sea tribunal which includes Section I that deals with the organization of the tribunal (e.g. election and composition of tribunal); Section II, the competence of the tribunal, Section III, procedure; Section IV, amendment. Annex III deals with arbitration provisions and Annex IV with special arbitration procedures. This text was presented as a further stage in the work of the conference and did not enjoy any status other than that of serving as a basis for continued negotiation. In other words, it was a procedural device used to carry forward the process of negotiation in the expectation that it would help toward the attainment of general agreement. It will be recalled that the *RSNT* has been superseded by the 1977 composite text. Dispute settlement has now been incorporated as Part XV: "Settlement of Disputes," Articles 279-297, pp. 142-150, of the composite text. Other reference to dispute settlement appears in section 6 of Part X, "Right of Access of Land-Locked States to and from the Sea and Freedom of Transit," Articles 187-192, pp. 104-106, of the composite text. Annex IV, "Conciliation," and Annex VII, "Special Arbitration Procedure," at pp. 177-179 and 196-198 respectively, are also relevant.

the 1977 composite text articles on dispute settlement appear to be a workable compromise. In any event, it can be utilized in our discussion of applicable suggestions for revising the 1958 conventional articles on piracy.[19]

As far as its relationship to this study is concerned, if a procedure were established for (compulsory) dispute settlement, it could possibly serve as a cornerstone for the resolution of jurisdictional issues arising under the suggested proposals in this study, just as the uniform procedure for dispute settlement can play a very important role in law of the sea disputes. In general, it may well be the method for resolving legal questions which could otherwise lead to war if the mechanism for dispute settlement were not universally recognized. As mentioned earlier in this chapter, the dispute settlement mechanism will interplay with all of the provisions contained in any revised conventional articles adopted by the Conference States.

OTHER TERMINOLOGY RELATED TO THIS STUDY

At the start of this chapter, it was stated that the reader should be made aware of the "traditional" terms and governing concepts (those being the 1958 conventional articles and draft articles in the 1977 composite text) regarding conventional law of the sea as applicable to this study. In addition, there are two other concepts related to this study which will be touched upon when dealing with the effort to resolve the problems related to the seizing of persons or property involved in piracy; the methods of seizure; the disposition of seized vessels and persons; the areas of seizure of persons and property; the effects of seizure; and the possible development of a revised definition of which elements are necessary in order to constitute acts of piracy. These two areas include the universality principle (and its characteristics) and the development of jurisdictional principles over states in international criminal law.[20] The universality principle will be discussed in connection with the jurisdictional problems regarding piracy (pp. 155-157). Since the publicists make use of the term, it is important to set forth its general

[19] Articles 279-297 of the *Informal Composite Negotiating Text* appear in Appendix 3 to this chapter.

[20] The universality principle and the jurisdictional principle are commonly evaluated by the authorities on international law in the context of the *delicta juris gentium*, that class of offenses which are crimes under international law. For a definitional statement of these principles see Bassiouni, *A Treatise on International Criminal Law* (Springfield, Ill.: Charles C. Thomas) 1973, vol. 2, pp. 32-34, 41. These sections have been reproduced in Appendix 4 to this chapter. See also Joyner, *op. cit.,* pp. 24-28.

meaning and characteristics at this stage of the study so that the reader can more fully comprehend the problem with regard to the creation of a special jurisdiction and with defining acts of piracy. The following excerpt is typical of the definitional references appearing in treatises on international law:

... from time to time claims are advanced to jurisdiction in situations arising outside a state's territory and where the persons responsible are not nationals of the state concerned. Thus, jurisdiction may also be (3) universal — only in the case of piracy is the universal principle, that any state may exercise jurisdiction over a crime committed abroad and whatever the nationality of the perpetrators, generally recognised, though some writers suggest that genocide, perhaps war crimes and slave trading, fall within the same category;[21]

Conference States are working toward the adoption of a form of dispute settlement mechanism which could serve as a necessary aid when considering expanding the definition of acts of piracy presently contained in the 1958 conventional articles, when determining the methods of seizure, and when considering expanding conventional jurisdictional concepts. For example, traditional taboos against pursuing a piratical vessel into the territorial waters of another nation may be overcome if a consensus is reached at a future law of the sea conference.

The importance of expanding jurisdictional concepts to include articles providing for uniform jurisdictional prescriptions presupposes the fact that none of the problems regarding piracy or of any other law of the sea matter, for example pollution, can be disposed of in a suitable manner unless an international body can be created to handle jurisdictional problems relating to law of the sea offenses committed by states and individuals. Therefore, as part of our chapter on appropriate terminology and general concepts, the reader should be aware of the prevailing wisdom on the topic of obtaining jurisdiction over states for crimes committed by states with a view toward applying this thinking to the possible approaches utilized in revising the 1958 conventional articles on piracy.[22] The discussion regarding state sovereignty will take on greater importance when considering new approaches which may be taken with regard to incidents labelled as acts of piracy that have been committed recently. For example, this study will be dealing with questions regarding the entry into a state's territorial waters by vessels in

---

[21] Greig, op. cit., p. 213.

[22] For an analysis of the terminology, doctrine, and limitations of the concept of an international criminal jurisdiction, as well as some discussion of major objections to the concept see Bassiouni, op. cit., pp. 86-93. Appropriate sections from this area have been reproduced in Appendix 5 to this chapter.

pursuit of alleged pirates as possibly one solution to the utilization of enforcement procedures prescribed by a dispute settlements mechanism. The creation of this mechanism is being discussed at the various law of the sea conferences.

Having set forth appropriate terminology and governing concepts with a view toward assisting the reader with terms which will be utilized throughout this study, we must now turn our attention to analyzing the history and development of the law of piracy as it has evolved over the centuries.

APPENDIX 1 TO CHAPTER II

Convention on the High Seas, opened for signature April 29, 1958, 13 U.S.T. 2312 (1962), T.I.A.S. No. 5200, 450 U.N.T.S. 82, Article 23

1. The hot pursuit of a foreign ship may be undertaken when the competent authorities of the coastal State have good reason to believe that the ship has violated the laws and regulations of that State. Such pursuit must be commenced when the foreign ship or one of its boats is within the internal waters or the territorial sea or the contiguous zone of the pursuing State, and may only be continued outside the territorial sea or the contiguous zone if the pursuit has not been interrupted. It is not necessary that, at the time when the foreign ship within the territorial sea or the contiguous zone receives the order to stop, the ship giving the order should likewise be within the territorial sea or the contiguous zone. If the foreign ship is within a contiguous zone, as defined in Article 24 of the Convention on the Territorial Sea and the Contiguous Zone, the pursuit may only be undertaken if there has been a violation of the rights for the protection of which the zone was established.

2. The right of hot pursuit ceases as soon as the ship pursued enters the territorial sea of its own country or of a third State.

3. Hot pursuit is not deemed to have begun unless the pursuing ship has satisfied itself by such practicable means as may be available that the ship pursued or one of its boats or other craft working as a team and using the ship pursued as a mother ship are within the limits of the territorial sea, or as the case may be within the contiguous zone. The pursuit may only be commenced after a visual or auditory signal to stop has been given at a distance which enables it to be seen or heard by the foreign ship.

4. The right of hot pursuit may be exercised only by warships or military aircraft, or other ships or aircraft on government service specially authorized to that effect.

5. Where hot pursuit is effected by an aircraft:

(a) The provisions of paragraphs 1 to 3 of this article shall apply mutatis mutandis;

(b) The aircraft giving the order to stop must itself actively pursue the ship until a ship or aircraft of the coastal State, summoned by the aircraft is itself able to arrest the ship. It does not suffice to justify an arrest on the high seas that the ship was merely sighted by the aircraft as an offender or suspected offender, if it was not both ordered to stop and pursued by the aircraft itself or other aircraft or ship which continue the pursuit without interrruption.

6. The release of a ship arrested within the jurisdiction of a State and escorted to a port of that State for the purpose of an inquiry before the competent authorities may not be claimed solely on the ground that the ship, in the course of its voyage, was escorted across a portion of the high seas, if the circumstances rendered this necessary.

7. Where a ship has been stopped or arrested on the high seas in circumstances which do not justify the exercise of the rights of hot pursuit, it shall be compensated for any loss or damage that may have been thereby sustained.

APPENDIX 2 TO CHAPTER II

Third United Nations Conference on the Law of the Sea: Informal Composite Negotiating Text, U.N. Doc. A/CONF.62/WP.10/CORR.1 (1977), Part V Exclusive Economic Zone

Article 55: Specific Legal Regime of the Exclusive Economic Zone
The exclusive economic zone is an area beyond and adjacent to the territorial sea, subject to the specific legal regime established in this Part, under which the rights and jurisdictions of the coastal State and the rights and freedoms of other States are governed by the relevant provisions of the present Convention.

Article 56: Rights, Jurisdiction and Duties of the Coastal State in the Exclusive Economic Zone
1. In the exclusive economic zone, the coastal State has:
(a) sovereign rights for the purpose of exploring and exploiting, conserving and managing the natural resources, whether living or non-living, of the sea-bed and subsoil and the superjacent waters, and with regard to other activities for the economic exploitation and exploration of the zone, such as the production of energy from the water, currents and winds;
(b) jurisdiction as provided for in the relevant provisions of the present Convention with regard to:
(i) the establishment and use of artificial islands, installations and structures;
(ii) the marine scientific research;
(iii) the preservation of the marine environment.
(c) other rights and duties provided for in the present Convention.
2. In exercising its rights and performing its duties under the present Convention in the exclusive economic zone, the coastal State shall have due regard to the rights and duties of other States and shall act in a manner compatible with the provisions of the present Convention.
3. The rights set out in this article with respect to the sea-bed and subsoil shall be exercised in accordance with Part VI.

Article 57: Breadth of the Exclusive Economic Zone
The exclusive economic zone shall not extend beyond 200 nautical miles from the baselines from which the breadth of the territorial sea is measured.

Article 58: Rights and Duties of Other States in the Exclusive Economic Zone

1. In the exclusive economic zone, all States, whether coastal or land-locked, enjoy, subject to the relevant provisions of the present Convention, the freedoms referred to in article 87 of navigation and overflight and of the laying of submarine cables and pipelines, and other internationally lawful uses of the sea related to these freedoms such as those associated with the operation of ships, aircraft and submarine cables and pipelines, and compatible with the other provisions of the present Convention.

2. Articles 88 to 115 and other pertinent rules of international law apply to the exclusive economic zone insofar as they are not incompatible with this Part.

3. In exercising their rights and performing their duties under the present Convention in the exclusive economic zone, States shall have due regard to the rights and duties of the coastal State and shall comply with the laws and regulations established by the coastal State in accordance with the provisions of this Convention and other rules of international law insofar as they are not incompatible with this Part.

Article 59: Basis for the Resolution of Conflicts Regarding the Attribution of Rights and Jurisdiction in the Exclusive Economic Zone

In cases where the present Convention does not attribute rights or jurisdiction to the coastal State or to other States within the exclusive economic zone, and a conflict arises between the interests of the coastal State and any other State or States, the conflict should be resolved on the basis of equity and in the light of all the relevant circumstances, taking into account the respective importance of the interests involved to the parties as well as to the international community as a whole.

Article 60: Artificial Islands, Installations and Structures in the Exclusive Economic Zone

1. In the exclusive economic zone, the coastal State shall have the exclusive right to construct and to authorize and regulate the construction, operation and use of:
(a) Artificial islands;
(b) Installations and structures for the purposes provided for in article 56 and other economic purposes;
(c) Installations and structures which may interfere with the exercise of the rights of the coastal State in the zone.

2. The coastal State shall have exclusive jurisdiction over such artificial islands, installations and structures, including jurisdiction with regard to customs, fiscal, health, safety and immigration regulations.

3. Due notice must be given of the construction of such artificial islands, installations or structures, and permanent means for giving warning of their presence must be maintained. Any installations or structures which are abandoned or disused must be entirely removed.

4. The coastal State may, where necessary, establish reasonable safety zones around such artificial islands, installations and structures.

5. The breadth of the safety zones shall be determined by the coastal State, taking into account applicable international standards. Such zones shall be

designed to ensure that they are reasonably related to the nature and function of the artificial islands, installations or structures, and shall not exceed a distance of 500 metres around them, measured from each point of their outer edge, except as authorized by generally accepted international standards or as recommended by the appropriate international organizations.

Article 73: Enforcement of Laws and Regulations of the Coastal State

1. The coastal State may, in the exercise of its sovereign rights to explore, exploit, conserve and manage the living resources in the exclusive economic zone, take such measures, including boarding, inspection, arrest and judicial proceedings, as may be necessary to ensure compliance with the laws and regulations enacted by it in conformity with the present Convention.

2. Arrested vessels and their crews shall be promptly released upon the posting of reasonable bond or other security.

3. Coastal State penalties for violations of fisheries regulations in the exclusive economic zone may not include imprisonment, in the absence of agreement to the contrary by the States concerned, or any other form of corporal punishment.

4. In cases of arrest or detention of foreign vessels the coastal State shall promptly notify, through appropriate channels, the flag State of the action taken and of any penalties subsequently imposed.

Article 74: Delimitation of the Exclusive Economic Zone Between Adjacent or Opposite States

1. The delimitation of the exclusive economic zone between adjacent or opposite States shall be effected by agreement in accordance with equitable principles, employing, where appropriate, the median or equidistance line, and taking account of all the relevant circumstances.

2. If no agreement can be reached within a reasonable period of time, the States concerned shall resort to the procedure provided for in Part XV.

3. Pending agreement or settlement, the States concerned shall make provisional arrangements, taking into account the provisions of paragraph 1.

4. For the purpose of the present Convention, "median or equidistance line" means the line every point of which is equidistant from the nearest points of the baselines from which the breadth of the territorial sea of each State is measured.

5. Where there is an agreement in force between the States concerned, questions relating to the delimitation of the exclusive economic zone shall be determined in accordance with the provisions of that agreement.

Article 75: Charts and Lists of Geographical Co-ordinates

1. Subject to this Part, the outer limit lines of the exclusive economic zone and the lines of delimitation drawn in accordance with article 74 shall be shown on charts of a scale or scales adequate for determining them. Where appropriate, lists of geographical co-ordinates of points, specifying the geodetic datum, may be substituted for such outer limit or lines of delimitation.

2. The coastal State shall give due publicity to such charts or lists of geographical co-ordinates and shall deposit a copy of each such chart or list with the Secretary-General of the United Nations.

APPENDIX 3 TO CHAPTER II

Third United Nations Conference on the Law of the Sea: Informal Composite Negotiating Text, U.N. Doc. A/CONF.62/WP.10/CORR.1 (1977), Part XV: Settlement of Disputes

SECTION 1

Article 279: Obligation to Settle Disputes by Peaceful Means
   The States Parties shall settle any dispute between them relating to the interpretation or application of the present Convention in accordance with paragraph 3 of article 2, and shall seek a solution through the peaceful means indicated in paragraph 1 of article 33, of the Charter of the United Nations.

Article 280: Settlement of Disputes by Means Chosen by the Parties
   Nothing in this Part shall impair the right of any States Parties to agree at any time to settle a dispute between them relating to the interpretation or application of the present Convention by any peaceful means of their own choice.

Article 281: Obligation to Exchange Views
   1. If a dispute arises between States Parties relating to the interpretation or application of the present Convention, the parties to the dispute shall proceed expeditiously to exchange views regarding settlement of the dispute through negotiations in good faith or other peaceful means.
   2. Similarly, the parties shall proceed to an exchange of views whenever a procedure for the settlement of a dispute has been terminated without a settlement of the dispute, or where a settlement has been reached and the circumstances require further consultation regarding the manner of its implementation.

Article 282: Obligations Under General, Regional or Special Agreements
   If States Parties which are parties to a dispute relating to the interpretation or application of the present Convention have accepted, through a general, regional or special agreement or some other instrument or instruments, an obligation to settle such dispute by resort to a final and binding procedure, such dispute shall, at the request of any party to the dispute, be referred to such procedure. In this case any other procedure provided in this Part shall not apply, unless the parties to the dispute otherwise agree.

Article 283: Procedure when Dispute is not Settled by Means Chosen by the Parties
   1. If States Parties which are parties to a dispute relating to the interpretation or application of the present Convention have agreed to seek a settlement of such dispute by a peaceful means of their own choice, the procedure specified in this Part shall apply only where no settlement has been reached, and the agreement between the parties does not preclude any further procedure.
   2. If the parties have also agreed on a time-limit for such a procedure, the provisions of paragraph 1 shall apply only upon the expiration of that time-limit.

Article 284: Conciliation

1. Any State Party which is party to a dispute relating to the interpretation or application of the present Convention may invite the other party or parties to the dispute to submit the dispute to conciliation in accordance with the procedure in annex IV or with some other procedure.

2. If the other party accepts this invitation and the parties agree upon the procedure, any party to the dispute may submit it to the agreed procedure.

3. If the other party does not accept the invitation or the parties do not agree upon the procedure, the conciliation proceedings shall be deemed to be terminated.

4. When a dispute has been submitted to conciliation, such conciliation proceedings may only be terminated in accordance with the provisions of annex IV or other agreed conciliation procedure, as the case may be.

Article 285: Application of this Section to Disputes Submitted Pursuant to Part XI

The provisions of this section shall apply to any dispute which pursuant to section 6 of Part XI is to be settled in accordance with procedures provided for in this Part. If an entity other than a State Party is a party to such a dispute, this section shall apply *mutatis mutandis.*

SECTION 2

Article 286: Application of Section 1 and Proceedings Under this Section

Subject to the provisions of articles 296 and 297, any dispute relating to the interpretation or application of the present Convention shall, where no settlement has been reached by recourse to the provisions of section 1, be submitted, at the request of any party to the dispute, to the court or tribunal having jurisdiction under the provisions of this section.

Article 287: Choice of Procedure

1. A State Party, when signing, ratifying or otherwise expressing its consent to be bound by the present Convention, or at any time thereafter, shall be free to choose, by means of a written declaration, one or more of the following means for the settlement of disputes relating to the interpretation or application of the present Convention:
(a) The Law of the Sea Tribunal constituted in accordance with annex V;
(b) The International Court of Justice;
(c) An arbitral tribunal constituted in accordance with annex VI;
(d) A special arbitral tribunal constituted in accordance with annex VII for one
   or more of the categories of disputes specified therein.

2. Any declaration made under paragraph 1 shall not affect or be affected by the obligation of a State Party to accept the jurisdiction of the Sea-Bed Disputes Chamber of the Law of the Sea Tribunal to the extent and in the manner provided for in section 6 of Part XI.

3. A State Party, which is a party to a dispute not covered by a declaration in force, shall be deemed to have accepted arbitration in accordance with annex VI.

4. If the parties to a dispute have accepted the same procedure for the settlement of such dispute, it may be submitted only to that procedure, unless the parties otherwise agree.

5. If the parties to a dispute have accepted the same procedure for the settlement of such dispute, it may be submitted only to arbitration in accordance with annex VI, unless the parties otherwise agree.

6. Any declaration made under this article shall remain in force until three months after notice of revocation has been deposited with the Secretary-General of the United Nations, who shall transmit copies thereof to the States Parties.

7. When a dispute has been submitted to a court or tribunal having jurisdiction under this article, a new declaration shall not affect in any way the proceedings so pending, unless the parties otherwise agree.

8. Declarations and notices referred to in this article shall be deposited with the Secretary-General of the United Nations, who shall transmit copies thereof to the States Parties.

Article 288: Competence

1. Any court or tribunal provided for in article 287 shall have jurisdiction in any dispute relating to the interpretation or application of the present Convention which is submitted to it in accordance with the provisions of this Part.

2. Any court or tribunal provided for in article 287 shall have jurisdiction in any dispute relating to the interpretation or application of an international agreement related to the purposes of the present Convention, which is submitted to it in accordance with the provisions of such agreement.

3. The Sea-Bed Disputes Chamber of the Law of the Sea Tribunal constituted in accordance with annex V, or an arbitral tribunal constituted in accordance with annex VI of this Part shall have jurisdiction in any matter provided for in section 6 of Part XI which is submitted to it in accordance with that Part.

4. Any disagreement as to whether a court or tribunal has jurisdiction, shall be settled by the decision of that court or tribunal.

Article 289: Expert Advice and Assistance

In any dispute involving scientific or technical matters, a court or tribunal exercising jurisdiction under this section may, at the request of a party to the dispute or on its own initiative, and in consultation with the parties, select not less than two scientific or technical experts from the appropriate list prepared in accordance with article 2 of annex VII, to sit with such court or tribunal but without the right to vote.

Article 290: Provisional Measures

1. If a dispute has been duly submitted to any court or tribunal which considers *prima facie* that it has jurisdiction under this Part, or section 6 of Part XI, such court or tribunal shall have the power to prescribe any provisional measures which it considers appropriate under the circumstances to preserve the respective rights of the parties to the dispute or to prevent serious harm to the marine environment, pending final adjudication.

2. Any provisional measures under this article may only be prescribed, modified or revoked upon the request of a party to the dispute and after giving the parties an opportunity to be heard. Notice of any provisional measures, or of their modification or revocation, shall be given forthwith by the court or tribunal to the parties to the dispute and to such other State Parties as it considers appropriate.

3. Pending the constitution of an arbitral or special arbitral tribunal to which a dispute has been submitted under this section, any court or tribunal

agreed upon by the parties or, failing such agreement within two weeks from the date of the request for provisional measures, the Law of the Sea Tribunal or, when appropriate, its Sea-Bed Disputes Chamber, shall have the power to prescribe provisional measures in conformity with paragraphs 1 and 2, if it considers *prima facie* that the tribunal to which the dispute has been submitted would have jurisdiction and that the urgency of the situation so requires. As soon as it has been constituted, the tribunal to which the dispute has been submitted may affirm, modify or revoke such provisional measures, acting in conformity with paragraphs 1 and 2.

4. As soon as the circumstances justifying the provisional measure have changed or ceased to exist, such provisional measures may be modified or revoked.

5. Any provisional measures prescribed or modified under this article shall be promptly complied with by the parties to the dispute.

Article 291: Access
1. All the dispute settlement procedures specified in this Part shall be open to States Parties.

2. The dispute settlement procedures specified in this Part shall be open to entities other than States Parties as provided for in section 6 of Part XI.

Article 292: Prompt Release of Vessels
1. Where the authorities of a State Party have detained a vessel flying the flag of another State Party and it is alleged that the coastal State has failed, neglected or refused to comply with the relevant provisions of the present Convention for the prompt release of the vessel or its crew upon the posting of a reasonable bond or other financial security, the question of release from detention may be brought before any court or tribunal agreed upon by the parties. Failing such agreement within 10 days from the time of detention, the question of release may be brought before any court or tribunal accepted by the detaining State under article 287 or before the Law of the Sea Tribunal, unless the Parties otherwise agree.

2. An application for such release may only be brought by or on behalf of the flag State of the vessel.

3. The question of release shall be dealt with promptly by such court or tribunal which shall deal only with the question of release, without prejudice to the merits of any case before the appropriate domestic forum against the vessel, its owner or its crew. The authorities of the detaining State shall remain competent to release the vessel or its crew at any time.

4. The decision of such court or tribunal as to the release of the vessel or its crew shall be promptly complied with by the authorities of the detaining State upon the posting of the bond or other financial security determined by the court or tribunal.

Article 293: Applicable law
1. The court or tribunal having jurisdiction under this section shall apply the present Convention and other rules of international law not incompatible with the present Convention.

2. If the parties to a dispute so agree, the court or tribunal having jurisdiction under this section shall make its decision *ex aequo et bono*.

Article 294: Exhaustion of local remedies
Deleted by Conference States.

Article 295: Finality and Binding Force of Decisions
1. Any decision rendered or measure prescribed by a court or tribunal having jurisdiction under this section shall be final and shall be complied with by all the parties to the dispute.
2. Any such decision or measure shall have no binding force except between the parties and in respect of that particular dispute.

Article 296: Limitations on Applicability of this Section
1. Without prejudice to the obligations arising under section 1, disputes relating to the exercise by a coastal State of sovereign rights or jurisdiction provided for in the present Convention shall only be subject to the procedures specified in the present Convention when the following conditions have been complied with:
(a) that in any dispute to which the provisions of this article apply the court or tribunal shall not call upon the other party or parties to respond until the party which has submitted the dispute has established *prima facie* that the claim is well founded;
(b) that such court or tribunal shall not entertain any application which in its opinion constitutes an abuse of legal process or is frivolous or vexatious; and
(c) that such court or tribunal shall immediately notify the other party to the dispute that the dispute has been submitted and such party shall be entitled, as it so desires, to present objections to the entertainment of the application.
2. Subject to the fulfilment of the conditions specified in paragraph 1, such court or tribunal shall have jurisdiction to deal with the following cases:
(a) When it is alleged that a coastal State has acted in contravention of the provisions of the present Convention in regard to the freedoms and rights of navigation or overflight or of the laying of submarine cables and pipelines and other internationally lawful uses of the sea specified in article 58; or
(b) When it is alleged that any State in exercising the aforementioned freedoms, rights or uses has acted in contravention of the provisions of the present Convention or of laws or regulations established by the coastal State in conformity with the present Convention and other rules of international law not incompatible with the present Convention; or
(c) When it is alleged that a coastal State has acted in contravention of specified international rules and standards for the protection and preservation of the marine environment which are applicable to the coastal State and which have been established by the present Convention or by a competent international organization or diplomatic conference acting in accordance with the present Convention.
3. No dispute relating to the interpretation or application of the provisions of the present Convention with regard to marine scientific research shall be brought before such court or tribunal unless the conditions specified in paragraph I have been fulfilled; provided that:
(a) when it is alleged that there has been a failure to comply with the provision of articles 247 and 254, in no case shall the exercise of a right or discretion in accordance with article 247, or a decision taken in accordance with article 254, be called in question; and
(b) the court or tribunal shall not substitute its discretion for that of the coastal State.

4. No dispute relating to the interpretation or application of the provisions of the present Convention with regard to the living resources of the sea shall be brought before such court or tribunal unless the conditions specified in paragraph 1 have been fulfilled; provided that:
(a) when it is alleged that there has been a failure to discharge obligations arising under articles 61, 62, 69 and 70, in no case shall the exercise of a discretion in accordance with articles 61 and 62 be called in question; and
(b) the court or tribunal shall not substitute its discretion for that of the coastal State; and
(c) in no case shall the sovereign rights of a coastal State be called in question.
5. Any dispute excluded by the previous paragraphs may be submitted to the procedures specified in section 2 only by agreement of the parties to such dispute.

Article 297: Optional Exceptions
1. Without prejudice to the obligations arising under section 1, a State Party when signing, ratifying or otherwise expressing its consent to be bound by the present Convention, or at any time thereafter, may declare that it does not accept any one or more of the procedures for the settlement of disputes specified in the present Convention with respect to one or more of the following categories of disputes:
(a) Disputes concerning sea boundary delimitations between adjacent or opposite States, or those involving historic bays or titles, provided that the State making such a declaration shall, when such dispute arises, indicate that for the settlement of such disputes it accepts a regional or other third party procedure entailing a binding decision, to which all parties to the dispute have access, and provided further that such procedure or decision shall exclude the determination of any claim to sovereignty or other rights with respect to continental or insular land territory;
(b) Disputes concerning military activities, including military activities by government vessels and aircraft engaged in non-commercial service and, subject to the exceptions referred to in Article 296, law enforcement activities in the exercise of sovereign rights or jurisdiction provided for in the present Convention;
(c) Disputes in respect of which the Security Council of the United Nations is exercising the functions assigned to it by the Charter of the United Nations, unless the Security Council decides to remove the matter from its agenda or calls upon the parties to settle it by the means provided for in the present Convention.
2. A State Party which has made a declaration under paragraph 1 may at any time withdraw it, or agree to submit a dispute excluded by such declaration to any procedure specified in the present Convention.
3. Any State Party which has made a declaration under paragraph 1 shall not be entitled to submit any dispute falling within the excepted category of disputes to any procedure in the present Convention as against any other State Party, without the consent of that party.
4. If one of the States Parties has made a declaration under subparagraph 1 (a), any other State Party may submit any dispute falling within an excepted category against the declarant party to the procedure specified in such declaration.
5. When a dispute has been submitted to any procedure in accordance with this article, a new declaration, or the withdrawal of a declaration shall not affect in any way the proceedings so pending, unless the parties otherwise agree.

6. Declarations and withdrawals under this article shall be deposited with the Secretary-General of the United Nations, who shall transmit copies thereof to the States Parties.

APPENDIX 4 TO CHAPTER II

Bassiouni, A Treatise on International Criminal Law (Springfield, Ill.: Charles C. Thomas) 1973, vol. 2, pp. 32-34

Sometimes the criminal law is applied by virtue of a principle which reflects the special quality of the class of offenses known as *delicta juris gentium,* crimes under international law. These crimes threaten to undermine the very foundations of the enlightened international community as a whole; and it is this quality that gives each one of the members of that community the right to extend the incidence of its criminal law to them, even though they are committed outside the state's boundaries and the offender has no special connection with the state. One essential prerequisite for the application of the municipal criminal law of a certain state in a particular case is that the offender be in its territory. The link between the offender and the *lex loci deprehensionis* is the injury which the offense causes to the foundations and security of the entire international community. This is what endows every state with the power to establish by law the incidence of its own municipal criminal law on *delicta juris gentium* if the offender is actually in custody in its territory. Hence, too, the name "universality principle."

Characteristics of the Universality Principle
   Ratione Materiae. This principle is of a *specific* nature, i.e., it relates to certain categories of offense and not to all the offenses known to the criminal law. In fact, from a substantive point of view the universality principle does generally relate to offenses defined in international conventions [the Convention on the High Seas of April 29, 1958 is one of the examples given by the author], offenses which every state that is a party to those conventions undertakes to punish no matter where they have been committed.
   Ratione Personae. In contrast, the universality principle must necessarily be of a general nature, i.e., the personal status of the offender cannot effect the incidence of the municipal criminal law by virtue of that principle. The offender may be the national of another state, he may be domiciled elsewhere, stateless or with no permanent domicile; nevertheless, in each of these cases he will fall within the scope of that law, provided that two basic conditions are satisfied, namely, he is within the territory of the state that seeks to apply its municipal law and the offense is one of those embraced by the universality principle.

Bassiouni, p. 41

The existence of the concept "international crimes," i.e., offenses which endanger the fundamental values of the international community as a whole, has given rise to the universality principle, whereby every state which is a member of that community has the power to retaliate against such offenses wherever they may have been committed. However, mankind has not yet proved mature enough to have set up an international criminal court competent to try those who commit them.

APPENDIX 5 TO CHAPTER II

Bassiouni, p. 86

The function of jurisdiction in international law is to determine the respective power of each nation in its relationship to other nations. . . . However, the primary focus here is on "crimes of state," such as "crimes against peace," "war crimes," and "crimes against humanity." They are typically committed by a state through its official authorities, or with its tacit acquiescence. . . . The idea of criminal jurisdiction over states for the "crimes of states" reaches far back in history and initially enjoyed great popularity. Since World War II, however, the shift has been toward exercising jurisdiction over individuals. The change was caused by the successful efforts of the victorious powers in Nuremberg and Tokyo and to prosecute individuals rather than states, even when those individuals had acted in the capacity of public officials. Since then, all international documents have reflected this shift.

Bassiouni, p. 90

EXISTING DOCTRINE. The vast majority of authors regard criminal jurisdiction over nonnatural persons, especially states, within the discipline of public international law. . . . Many authors, however, continue to be skeptical about the exercise of jurisdiction over states mainly on two grounds: (1) despite the evolving law of international organizations, punishment of states as yet is not provided for in substantive public international law, and (2) there are practical difficulties insofar as there is no enforcing authority. Doctrine therefore favors confining criminal responsibility to individuals for international crimes. The essential problem remains that of a lack of competent jurisdiction.

Bassiouni, p. 91

The Scope and Limitations of Jurisdiction over States for Crimes of State
    To develop an international criminal jurisdiction over states for the crime of state is not the exclusive means to attain peace, but one which hopefully will advance it. Major objections to this concept can be labeled as follows: (1) incompatibility with the principle of sovereignty, (2) incompatibility with the conventional concept of criminal responsibility, (3) inadequacy of conventional penal sanctions, and (4) inadequacy of the international institutional framework.

Incompatibility with the Principle of Sovereignty. This is by far the strongest objection; however, it is not a particularly persuasive one. Traditionally, the two principles, that of non-intervention and that of the prior consent of a state to confer jurisdiction over its actions, have been widely recognized. The concept of sovereignty has, however, undergone dramatic changes as of late, particularly with the recognition of individuals as proper subjects of international law and the wider acceptance of the common interest of the world community to take priority over the actions of a state. State sovereignty has lost its absolutist character. In some areas such as Human Rights, a state can

no longer invoke exclusive domestic jurisdiction to abridge individuals rights
for it has become a matter of international concern. Thus, the present concept
of state sovereignty does not preclude the exercise of criminal jurisdiction over
states.

CHAPTER III

THE HISTORY AND DEVELOPMENT OF
THE LAW OF INTERNATIONAL SEA PIRACY

INTRODUCTION TO THE DIFFICULTIES CONCERNING THE TWENTIETH-CENTURY EMBODIMENT OF "TRADITIONAL" ACTS OF PIRACY INTO A DRAFT CONVENTION

We come now to a discussion of the history and development of the law of international sea piracy as it developed over many centuries. The methodology employed in this chapter will be to examine the most significant work in the area[1] and to analyze and comment thereon. The comments will introduce some problems confronting the international community today with a view toward enlightening the reader as to possible approaches to these areas of concern, areas which will be more fully discussed in later chapters (pp. 160-165).

The purpose of analyzing thoroughly the work of the Harvard Research in International Law (hereinafter referred to as "the Group") in this chapter is to demonstrate that they discussed every possible aspect of sea and air piracy which could conceivably have been raised in 1932. In this regard, most legal publicists who have discussed the Group's work *since* 1932 usually gloss over the draft convention and comments with the statement that the main purpose of the Group's work was to create a common or special jurisdiction. However, as will be observed while reading this chapter, the Group included every possible thought and idea in existence at the time of its preparation. If the International Law Commission (created in 1949)[2] chose, for political reasons, to modify, bypass or exclude many ideas, it was because of the practicalities confronting

---

[1] Harvard Research in International Law, *Draft Convention on Piracy with Comments* (hereinafter referred to as the Harvard Draft Convention), 26 Am. J. of Int'l. L. 749 (1932). The draft articles have been reproduced in Appendix 1 of this chapter.

[2] The approach of the International Law Commission is reflected in the report of the International Law Commission covering the work of its eighth session, April 23-July 4, 1956. General Assembly, *Official Records*: 11th Sess., Suppl. 9 (A/3159); 2 Y.B. Int'l. L. Comm'n. (1956).

the commission when attempting to prepare draft articles which they thought would include "traditional" forms of piracy acceptable to the Conference States. Therefore, a separate chapter is devoted to their draft articles and to the discussions which led to their formulation. The Conference States (in 1958) later adopted articles on piracy (the 1958 conventional articles) after arguing and debating many of the points raised by the Group and the commission. In summary, we will compare and contrast the work of the Group (published in 1932) with the draft articles which were reported by the International Law Commission (prepared in the 1950's) and later adopted by the Conference States at the 1958 Law of the Sea Conference. These articles are embodied within the 1958 Convention on the High Seas.[3] The Conference States adopted some of the articles contained in the Harvard Draft Convention verbatim. The analysis and comments on the development of the law as contained in the Group's work will demonstrate which matters were taken into consideration in the preparation of their draft convention as well as why these matters deserved adoption. The reader must bear in mind that:

... International law was not crystallized in the 17th century, but is a living and expanding code. ... A careful examination of the subject shows a gradual widening of the earlier definition of piracy to bring it from time to time more in consonance with situations either not thought of or not in existence when the older jurisconsults were expressing their opinions.[4]

Before embarking on this analysis, it is interesting to read the jury charge given by the Judge of the Vice-Admiralty as it occurred in the Trials of Bonnet which took place in 1718.[5] This jury charge represents the English municipal law on the subject of piracy at the time of the trial. However, the main point, when attempting to define acts of piracy and other jurisdictional elements under international law, is that there are many diverse opinions as to what is the actual "traditional" wisdom on the subject.

___

[3] Convention on the High Seas, opened for signature April 29, 1958, 13 U.S.T. 2312 (1962), T.I.A.S. No. 5200, 450 U.N.T.S. 82. The appropriate articles of this convention relating to piracy have been reproduced at Appendix 1, Chapter I, and are discussed throughout this book.

[4] Excerpts from the jury charge delivered by Sir Viscount Sankey L.D., In Re Piracy Jure Gentium, [1934] A.C. 586, pp. 592, 600.

[5] The Trials of Major Stede Bonnet, and thirty-three others, at the Court of Vice-Admiralty, at Charles-Town, in South Carolina, for Piracy: 5 George I. A.D. 1718, pp. 1234-1237; 15 How St. Tr. 1231 (1718). This charge to the jury appears in Appendix 2 of this chapter.

The municipal legislation of nations regarding piracy varies,[6] and scholarly approaches to the subject are not uniform. There seems to be a tendency among contemporary nations to recognize acts of piracy only in the context of the past, as containing the necessary elements for ratification of a multilateral treaty,[7] a treaty which is ostensibly concerned with prohibitions against dated or "traditional" forms of piracy. The practical effect of this situation is that the word "piracy" is being used in certain treaties only because of its historical connotation, even though the context of the treaties demonstrates that the types of "piracy" included therein are usually nothing more than separate domestic crimes or terrorism (which knows no boundary demarcation) joined together under the word *piracy*.

The reader may find that the definition of acts of piracy which may be considered a crime or offense under the 1958 conventional articles is nothing more than one or more separate crimes grouped together under the one heading. If this is so, then there is really no uniform offense or crime of piracy.[8] Rather, the word *piracy* could constitute one or many different crimes and acts of terrorism according to the dictates of the state which is affected by the incident(s). When, then, did this situation develop?

In order to respond to this query, let us first explore thoroughly the draft convention (1932), comments and materials presented by the Harvard Research Group. In doing so, it will become apparent that there are many diverse opinions concerning the topic held by the legal publicists.

One of the principal objects of the Group was to show the diversity of opinion with respect to what should have been fundamental or "traditional" matters, such as a definition of piracy; the meaning and justification inherent in the view expressed by various legal publicists and municipal laws that piracy was an offense or a crime against the law of nations; and, whether there existed a jurisdiction that was common to all nations in the international community. As was mentioned earlier in this chapter, their draft convention was closely followed by the International Law Com-

---

[6] For a collection of municipal laws on the subject of piracy see the Harvard Draft Convention, pp. 889-1013. For a discussion of the distinctions between municipal law and the international law regarding sea piracy, see the materials cited at note 22, Chapter 1; and also Colombos, *International Law of the Sea,* 6th rev. ed., (New York: David McKay) 1967, pp. 447-448.

[7] Piracy is defined in the 1958 Convention on the High Seas, *op. cit.,* in Article 15. See Appendix 1 to Chapter I.

[8] A number of contemporary questions posed by the commentators concerning the nature of piracy appear on pp. 3-4 and at note 8, Chapter II.

mission and later by the Conference States.[9] These fundamental or "traditional" views led to conclusions which covered such subjects as the permissible areas, methods and effects of seizures of pirates. But where did this authorization originate?

Their first area of departure, therefore, is one involving the exploration of the divergence of opinion among the international community regarding the definition of acts of piracy. It will be observed that there are a great many opinions concerning the differences between piracy in the international law sense and piracy under municipal legislation. Under the municipal laws, nations define acts of piracy in order to meet their different needs with the result that the various municipal laws regarding piracy differ in definition and extent of coverage.[10] There is no uniformity of definition in the municipal legislation of different states. The municipal legislation will cover areas within which the particular state has the jurisdictional competence to legislate (for example its right to prescribe and enforce its domestic laws). Thus, the characteristics of the definitions of acts of piracy will vary.[11] It would appear that the international law of piracy must, under "traditional" thinking, apply outside the territorial waters and jurisdiction over which a sovereign state may legislate.[12] However, as will be discussed later, (pp. 120-122), this conclusion may not be correct.

THE CHARACTERISTICS OF PIRACY DIFFER UNDER MUNICIPAL LAW AND INTERNATIONAL LAW

The Group was desirous of drafting a convention which would include the creation of a special basis of common jurisdiction. It drew upon various source materials in order to discuss this fundamental problem of differing characteristics. In a Report of the Sub-

[9] See: Report of the International Law Commission, Comment to Article 13 (1956). 2 Y.B. Int'l L. Comm'n. 25, U.N. Doc. A/CONF.4/Ser.A/1955/add.1: "In its work on the articles concerning piracy, the Commission was greatly assisted by the research carried out at the Harvard Law School, which culminated in a draft convention of nineteen articles with commentary, prepared in 1932 under the direction of Professor Joseph Bingham. In general, the Commission was able to endorse the findings of that research."

[10] Harvard Draft Convention, pp. 889-1013.

[11] The extent of diversity in the municipal law of states regarding the subject of piracy becomes evident in comparing the statutes appended to the Harvard Draft Convention. For example Great Britain, a traditional naval power with a great national interest in maritime commerce, had passed a number of acts dealing exclusively with piracy. In contrast Norway, a state with less of a maritime tradition, relegated piracy to a subsection of the penal code statute on robbery and extortion. See: Harvard Draft Convention, Great Britain: pp. 909-950, Norway: p. 996.

[12] The emphasis on territorial jurisdiction becomes apparent on examination of the 1958 Convention on the High Seas, Articles 14, 15(1)(b), 19, 22 and 23(7), op. cit., note 4.

Committee of the League of Nations Committee of Experts for the Progressive Codification of International Law, it was stated, that, in their view:

... it would be preferable for the Committee to adopt a clear definition of piracy applicable to all States in virtue of international law in general.[13]

Professor Brierly stated that:

Any state may bring in pirates for trial by its own courts, on the ground that they are "hostes humani generis.". . . . There is no authoritative definition of international piracy, but it is of the essence of a piratical act to be an act of violence, committed at sea or at any rate closely connected with the sea, by persons not acting under proper authority.[14]

Blackstone, in his "Commentaries," states that:

By the ancient common law, piracy, if committed by a subject, was held to be a species of treason, being contrary to his natural allegiance; and by an alien, to be felony only, but now, since the statute of treason, 25 Edw. III, c.2, it is held to be only felony in a subject. . . . The offense of piracy, by common law, consists in committing those acts of robbery and depredation upon the high seas, which, if committed upon land, would have amounted to felony there. But, by statute, some other offenses are made piracy also.[15]

Having presented the opinions of numerous highly regarded jurists and publicists,[16] the Group then had to permit the reader to appreciate the fact that the *characteristics* of the crime of piracy under municipal law can vary and may be composed of different crimes, any one of which can lead to a conviction of the greater or lesser crime of piracy, depending on the wording of the legislation. On the other hand, it will be observed that since there are many different countries, which together constitute the world community (as opposed to one large governing body),[17] the municipal laws of each country can vary; and the remaining areas[18] are truly sovereign in

[13] Report of the Sub-Committee of the League of Nations Committee of Experts for the Progressive Codification of International Law (1926), C.196.M.70.1927.V, p. 119. This citation appears in the Harvard Draft Convention, at p. 749.

[14] Brierly, *The Law of Nations* (Oxford: Oxford University Press), 1928, p. 154; Harvard Draft Convention, pp. 749-750.

[15] As it appears in the Harvard Draft Convention, p. 750.

[16] The Group made reference to the following works: Dickinson, *Is the Crime of Piracy Obsolete*, 38 Harv. L. Rev. 334; Kennedy, L.J., in *Bolivia v. Indemnity Mutual Marine Assurance Co., Ltd.* (1909), 1 K.B. 875, p. 802; Bluntschli, *Le Droit international codifié*, Article 346; Calvo, *Le Droit international*, Section 488; Pradier-Fodère, *Droit international public*, vol. 5, p. 824.

[17] The conceptual significance of the idea of a world community as it applies to the international law of piracy is analyzed in a work by Sundberg: *Piracy: Air and Sea*, 20 De Paul L.R. 337 (Winter 1970), p. 390.

[18] It has long been recognized in international law that no state has sovereignty outside its territorial boundaries. See, for example, Article 2 of the 1958 Convention on the High Seas: "The High Seas being open to all nations, no state may validly purport to subject any part of them to its sovereignty."

the sense that they may be utilized by all nations but cannot be controlled exclusively by any one nation to the detriment of the world community. In this sense, there is municipal legislation affecting domestic crimes and offenses, but there is also the possibility of acts occurring in international zones not under any political subdivision or authority. Yet, violence, robbery, murder, plunder, and other acts that could and do constitute crimes under municipal laws, can occur in the international zones.

What has created confusion, therefore, are the attempts to apply a variety of municipal laws to create a uniform enactment which could apply in these international zones. The Group demonstrated that the "traditional" wisdom on the subject would therefore conclude that since these crimes or offenses under municipal laws can occur in international zones, such as the high seas, they cannot possibly be uniformly defined because of the diversity of opinions that exist among nations as to their scope, their geographical location, and because the "pirate" has been "traditionally" regarded as an enemy of the human race (*hostis humani generis*).[19] Following this line of reasoning to its inevitable conclusion, we find that: (a) all of these crimes that constitute "piracy" have occurred in areas outside the municipal jurisdictional competence of any nation; (b) the "pirate" is treated as an enemy of the human race; and (c) the "pirate" should be prosecuted under municipal law (assuming that said legislation covered the subject matter) after capture. Thus, if a state's vessel were attacked in an international zone, it could under its municipal legislation, prosecute the pirate. Since the pirate is considered an enemy of mankind, other nations have the duty and right to prosecute the pirate under their municipal legislations, as well. But, the *characteristics* of the crime of piracy can vary.

PIRACY AS A CRIME OR OFFENSE AGAINST THE LAW OF NATIONS

The Group set forth the variety of views expressed by legal publicists at the time of its study. The unorthodox views as expressed at that time state, in part,[20] (a) that there is no difference between

---

[19] Travers Twiss, *The Law of Nations*, 2nd ed., p. 26; cited in the Harvard Draft Convention, p. 752.

[20] The principal exponents of these views were Professors Pella and Matsuda during their tenure as members of the League of Nations Committee of Experts for the Progressive Codification of International Law. See Report of the League of Nations Committee of Experts for the Progressive Codification of International Law (1926),C.196.M.70.1927.V.

international and municipal laws except where there is no means of enforcement in international law; (b) that all of the international community are members of a "veritable" legal community and so all are subject to a definite legal order; (c) that there are international law crimes but no methods for punishing the offenders; and (d) that there should be some form of international tribunal which could try these offenders and therefore consider piracy a crime under international law.

Piracy *jure gentium* is regarded today as an offense of a special character because it is *"punishable wherever encountered."*[21]

Professor Pella of Rumania expressed the view that

if we can evolve with reference to the suppression of piracy, a new combination of the principles of penal law with those of international law, we shall be able to bring to light hitherto unsuspected aspects of this question which render an international convention indispensable.[22]

Yet, the prevailing "orthodox" view of the time was that said international law existed between states only; that said law placed limits upon each state's jurisdiction; that private persons are not legal persons under international law; that international law defines only duties, privileges and powers between states; and, that there is no legal universal society of private persons regulated by international law.[23]

In relating these two views to the law of piracy, the Group said that states act voluntarily to capture, prosecute and punish pirates because there is no "super-government" and *no "international tribunal"* to administer international civil or criminal justice against private individuals. Thus, there is no such crime or offense as piracy under the law of nations.

Having come to this conclusion, the question was posed as to what meaning could be given to the traditional view that piracy is a crime or offense against the law of nations? It was thought that piracy was, by the law of nations, a special or common basis of jurisdiction which went beyond the traditional grounds for asserting interests under a state's protection. As stated by Cicero: "pirata non est ex perduellium numero definitus, sed communis hostis omnium."[24] This statement is the source of "pirata est hostis

---

[21] Reply of Rumania, drafted by Pella, November 20, 1926 to Questionnaire 6, Report of the League of Nations Committee of Experts for the Progressive Codification of International Law (1926), C.196.M.70.1927.V, p. 202; as cited in the Harvard Draft Convention, p. 753. This document has been reproduced in Appendix 3 to this chapter.

[22] Harvard Draft Convention, p. 753.

[23] *Ibid.*, p. 754.

[24] As cited in Sundberg, *op. cit.*, note 17, p. 338.

generis humani,"[25] or, as Blackstone stated, ". . . a pirate being, according to Sir Edward Coke, 'hostis humani generis' is one that commits an offense against the universal law of society." Professor Moore went further in saying that ". . . piracy by law of nations, in its jurisdictional aspects, is *sui generis.* . . . it is an offense against the law of nations. . . ."

Based upon the various orthodox and unorthodox views expressed in its work, the Group concluded that piracy was not a legal crime or offense under international law:

> . . . International law piracy is only a special ground of state jurisdiction – of jurisdiction in every state. This jurisdiction may or may not be exercised by a certain state. It may be used in part only. How far it is used depends on the municipal law of the state, not on the law of nations. It justifies state action within limits and fixes those limits. It goes no further.[26]

Based upon this conclusion, the Group stated that the theory of its draft convention would be that piracy is not a crime under international law, but that it is merely the basis of some extraordinary jurisdiction in every state to seize, prosecute and to punish persons, and that the purpose of the convention was to "define this extraordinary jurisdiction in general outline."[27] Even if the draft convention were adopted universally, there still would not exist a legal crime of piracy;

> . . . The effect of the convention would be like the effect of the traditional law of nations – the draft convention defines only the jurisdiction (the powers and rights) and the duties of the several states *inter se,* leaving to each state the decision how and how far through its own law it will exercise its powers and rights.[28]

JURISDICTIONAL PROBLEMS RELATED TO THE RIGHTS OF STATES TO ENFORCE SANCTIONS AGAINST PIRATES

The Group next set forth the divergent views on the subject of the creation of a common jurisdiction among states to prosecute and punish pirates. It will be recalled that many nations do not have municipal laws concerning piracy. These nations could conceivably capture pirates and yet have no means of prosecuting them as pirates. One view presented by various legal publicists, as offered in the work of the Group, is that piracy is really not a special basis of

---

[25] Harvard Draft Convention, p. 758.
[26] *Ibid.,* p. 760.
[27] *Ibid.*
[28] *Ibid.*

jurisdiction under international law. To the contrary, one could argue that piracy is so significant under international law that there is some sort of special basis of authority that is common to all nations. But, what is the nature and extent of this special authority?

The Group and other legal publicists cite a monograph by Paul Stiel[29] to the effect that the special authority over piracy is a matter of sea-policing and that it consists in the permissibility and legal effect of state acts on the high seas with respect to foreign ships, property, and persons, which, were it not for the special authority over piracy, would be violations of international law. Stiel looks at "piracy" as a manner of life or undertaking which allows each state authority to suppress this manner of life rather than paying attention to single offenses. According to Stiel a state has a general authority, under the law of nations, to prosecute foreigners for foreign offenses.

In opposition to Stiel's opinion, under the Anglo-American, Latin American and certain European publicists' point of view, "piracy" is a special basis of jurisdiction first to prosecute and punish foreigners, even though the offense was committed in a place and under circumstances which did not subject it to the state's authority on any ordinary ground, and second to seize the pirate ship, its contents, its officers and crew, and all booty and property outside the territorial jurisdiction of other states.[30] Special jurisdiction is therefore judicial, executive, and legislative (in the sense that it gives a nation the right to prescribe and enforce penalties for offenses created under its municipal law). Based upon these divergent views, the Group believed the:

... draft convention should include the recognition of a special authority — or jurisdiction — to prosecute foreigners for piratical offences beyond the state's ordinary jurisdiction. Then Stiel's theme that piracy is important in the law of nations as a ground of state authority may be accepted with this modification which brings it into accordance with the traditional Anglo-American view. Piracy, however it is defined, is a special basis of jurisdiction, judicial, legislative, executive, and administrative.[31]

After all, "A pirate, under the law of nations, is an enemy of the human race; being the enemy of all, he is liable to be punished by all."[32]

[29] *Der Tatbestand der Piraterie* (Leipzig: Duncker und Humblot) 1905, pp. 15-23; cited in the Harvard Draft Convention, p. 761.
[30] Harvard Draft Convention, p. 762.
[31] *Ibid.*, p. 763.
[32] Appendix to *United States v. Smith,* 5 Wheat. (U.S.) 153 (1820), pp. 7-8. The complete quotation appears in the Harvard Draft Convention, p. 763.

Before setting forth the draft convention and comments made in connection therewith, the Group made some very pertinent observations in connection with the *scope* of the topic of piracy. These observations clearly state why the group proceeded with the categories which it drafted. The Group pointed out that there is no settled law of nations concerning the topic; in fact, *there is a great deal of learned controversy* which could lead to any of several varying conclusions serving as a basis of agreement:

The framework of the draft convention is designed to facilitate amendments in detail and any differing decisions which result from common counsel easily can be fitted into the general scheme.[33]

The Group pointed out that there is a paucity of pertinent cases and of evidence of modern state practice on most of the important aspects of the law of piracy. Most of the municipal law cases on piracy are of little value in resolving the international problems because that law covers different areas which are ". . . colored by the national legislation."[34] There is also a lack of official determinations which normally would help an ". . . investigator to cut a way through the jungle of expert opinion."[35] The reason for the lack of case precedent in the field of piracy is because

large scale piracy disappeared long ago . . . piracy of any sort on or over the high sea is sporadic . . . Piracy lost its great importance in the law of nations before the modern principles of finely discriminated state jurisdictions and of freedom of the seas became thoroughly established.[36]

Yet, the Group proceeded to set forth in its draft convention articles which they believed covered the *moot* area of piracy.[37] With the benefit of hindsight, the reader will observe that what is believed to be *moot,* however, are the *methods* for committing acts of piracy (that is, the swashbuckler type of situation), not the need for developing a draft convention or revising the 1958 conventional articles to make them applicable to the technological advances and terrorist activities of today.

The Group next set forth their draft articles and comments thereto. Their study is an exhaustive one and their comments were

[33] Harvard Draft Convention, p. 764.
[34] *Ibid.*
[35] *Ibid.*
[36] *Ibid.*
[37] The contemporary commentators have difficulty in reaching agreement as to what areas of the international law of sea piracy may be considered settled. For example, Professor Crockett addresses himself to an analysis of acts by political groups and by states in the context of piracy. See: Crockett, *Toward a Revision of the International Law of Piracy,* 26 De Paul L. 78 (1976).

set forth with references made to nearly all the writings and opinions given up to the time of their work. The methodology that they employed was to review the various legal publicists' viewpoints on the subject matter after which they drafted articles they believed would be "expedient" – in the sense that they wanted the draft convention, or a variation thereof, to serve as a basis for discussion which would eventually lead to its adoption in a multilateral treaty. They were taking into consideration the practical and political aspects which could be involved when attempting to have nations agree to a treaty concerning this subject. It should be emphasized once again that, although the Group believed that the question of piracy was really a "moot" one, the reader must bear in mind the period when this convention was drafted. The articles were not drafted by the Group to put an end to the matter once and for all; to the contrary, they were prepared with the hope that their draft articles would be updated and amended, if necessary, in order to assist in the development of international law. The reason why the draft convention and the study itself are so important is that the Group was able to compile nearly all the writings on the subject, to explain the reasons for the various viewpoints of legal publicists, jurists, and so on, and to select those opinions which they believed would be stable enough to become part of an international convention on the law of the sea.

THE DRAFT ARTICLES AND COMMENTS

The Group's study commences with a definition of various terms such as "jurisdiction," "territorial sea,"[38] and so on. The term "jurisdiction" refers to jurisdiction under international law, which is legal governmental power and right as limited by the law of nations.[39] The term "high sea" contained in the draft convention is simply defined as that part of the sea which is not included within the territorial waters of any state. It should be observed that at the time that these articles were drafted, the 1958 law of the sea conference had not transpired. Thus, most of the familiar law of the sea terms, applicable with regard to the piracy articles which were finally adopted in the 1958 Convention on the High Seas, are defined either in the same convention or in other conventions adopted at that conference.

---

[38] Harvard Draft Convention, p. 767, Article 1. See Appendix 1 to this chapter.
[39] Ibid., p. 767, Comment to Article 1.

Article 2 of the Group's draft convention gave each state juris-diction to prevent piracy, to seize and punish persons, and to seize and dispose of property obtained through acts of piracy. This jurisdiction is limited to the definition contained in Article 1. The comments on Article 2 point out that piracy falls under the juris-diction of each and every state; that it is a special basis of jurisdiction and; *"that the theme of this draft convention is the definition of this extraordinary basis of jurisdiction and the specification of the conditions and limitations pertaining to exercise of jurisdiction on this ground."*[40]

Article 3 goes on to state the acts which constitute piracy. The comments emphasize that there is a "chaos of expert opinion as to what the law of nations includes, or should include, in piracy. There is no authoritative definition."[41] The Group then sets forth various "rough descriptions" of what would be considered to be a "typical piracy." One such description:

Sir Leoline Jenkins, who was Judge of the Admiralty in the seventeenth cen-tury, thus defines piracy, in giving a charge to the grand jury at an Admiralty sessions: "The next sort of offences pointed out in the statute are robberies; and a robbery, when it is committed upon the sea, is what we call *piracy*. A robbery, when it is committed upon the land, does imply three things: (1) that there be a violent assault; (2) that a man's goods be actually taken from his person or possessions; (3) that he who is despoiled be put in fear thereby. When this is done upon the sea, when one or more persons enter on board a ship with force and arms, and those in the ship have their ship carried away by violence, or their goods taken away of their possession, and are put in fright by the assault, this is *piracy* and he that does so is a *pirate* or a *robber* within the statute. Nor does it differ the case though the party so assaulted and despoiled should be a foreigner, not born within the King's allegiance; if he be *de amicitia Regis* he is *eo nomine* under the King's protection, and to rob such a one upon the seas is piracy. Nor will it be any defence to a man, who takes away by force another's ship or goods at sea, that he hath a commission of war from some foreign prince, unless the person he takes from be a lawful enemy to that prince. ...." (Life of Sir Leoline Jenkins, i. 94, see also "A Charge at an Admiralty Sessions," with notes, by Sir Sherston Baker, Law Magazine and Review, No. 257, p. 412.)[42]

The Group went on to give various quotations all differing in respect as to what acts constituted a typical piracy. It was pointed out that the legal publicists offered arguments for and against inclusion of various piratical acts.

---

[40] *Ibid.*, p. 768.
[41] *Ibid.*, p. 769, Comment to Article 3.
[42] *Ibid.*, p. 770.

I. Acts on the high sea:
(1) Robbery committed by using a private ship (a pirate ship) to attack another ship. (This is the typical piracy of history and fiction.)
(2) Intentional, unjustifiable homicide, similarly committed for private ends.
(3) Unjustifiable violent attack on persons similarly accomplished for private ends.
(4) Any unjustifiable violent attack on persons similarly accomplished for private ends.
(5) Any unjustifiable depredation or malicious destruction of property similarly committed for private ends.
(6) Attempts to commit the foregoing offences.
(7) Cruising (in a pirate ship) with the purpose of committing any of the foregoing offences.
(8) Cruising as professional robbers in a ship devoted to the commission of such offences as the foregoing.[43]

According to a Report of the Sub-Committee of the League of Nations Committee of Experts for the Progressive Codification of International Law, under international law,

... piracy consists in sailing the seas for private ends without authorization from the Government of any State with the object of committing depredations upon property or acts of violence against persons.[44]

(9) Participation in sailing a ship (on the high sea) devoted to the purpose of making similar attacks in territorial waters or on land, by descent from the sea. (*This is another phase of familiar traditional piracy.*)[45]

It will be observed that the Group included in its acts of piracy the possibility of a ship preparing to make attacks in territorial waters or on land from the high seas. In support of this proposition, the Group referred to Hall, *International Law*, 8th ed., section 81, p. 313:

Usually piracy is spoken of as occurring only upon the high seas. If however a body of pirates land upon an island unappropriated by a civilized power, and rob and murder a trader who may be carrying on commerce there with the savage inhabitants, they are guilty of a crime possessing all the marks of commonplace professional piracy. In so far as any definitions of piracy exclude such acts, and others done by pirates elsewhere than on the ocean but of the kind which would be called piratical if done there, the omission may be assumed to be accidental. *Piracy no doubt cannot take place independently of the sea, under the conditions at least of modern civilization; but a pirate does not so lose his piratical character by landing within state territory that piratical acts done on shore cease to be piratical.*[46]

[43] *Ibid.*, p. 773. Compare the questions proposed by the contemporary commentators (*supra*, pp. 2-4) as to the elements of the definition of piracy.
[44] Report, *op. cit.*, note 13, pp. 116-117. For a discussion of the modern view of the "private ends" requirement see Johnson, *Piracy in Modern International Law*, 43 Trans. Grotius Soc. 63 (1957).
[45] Harvard Draft Convention, p. 775, emphasis added.
[46] *Ibid.*, p. 776, emphasis added.

Further acts on the high seas included:

(10) Sailing a ship not authorized by any state or recognized belligerent government while disclaiming allegiance to any state.

(11) Appropriation of a ship for unlawful private end by mutiny of its crew or passengers.

(12) *Using a ship to attack another for some political purpose* provided the attack is not made under the authority or protection of any state or recognized belligerent government.

(13) Attacks on commerce by illegitimate privateers during a war or revolution.

(14) Participation in privateering attacks of a foreign belligerent on commerce of a nation with which the offender's state of nationality is at peace.[47]

It will be observed that the Group first made reference to "political" as opposed to "private" acts.[48] Today, contrary to 1932, it is prevalent among those legal publicists who are calling for a change in the international law regarding sea piracy to say that because of incidents of terrorism and the proliferation of various liberation-type groups with political motivations, that "political" as well as "private" acts should be included in any revision of the piracy laws.

The Group quoted the views of various publicists concerning whether "political purpose" had been historically treated as a motivating case of piracy:

Halleck, International Law, (3rd ed.) Vol. II, p. 120 footnote: "it is an open question whether privateers, commissioned by a deposed sovereign, are pirates or not. . . ."

Dana in a note to Wheaton on International Law, Sec. 124, discusses at length the question whether insurgents are pirates and summarizes his views in part as follows: Wheaton, Int. Law (18th ed.) p. 200, footnote: The following propositions are offered, *not as statements of settled law* (for most of them are not covered by a settled usage of nations, by judicial decisions of present authority, or by the agreement of jurists), but as suggestions of principles:

III. If a foreigner knowingly cruises against the commerce of a State under a rebel commission, he takes the chance of being treated as a pirate *jure gentium*, or a belligerent. In point of law, his foreign allegiance or citizenship is immaterial. In this respect, it is immaterial whether the sovereign whose subject he is has recognized the rebel authorities as belligerent or not. It is not the custom for foreign nations to interfere to protect their citizens voluntarily aiding a rebellion against a friendly State, if that State makes no discriminations against them.

IV. If a foreigner cruises under a rebel commission, he takes the chance of being treated as a pirate or belligerent by his own nation and all other nations, as well as by that he is cruising against. If his own nation does not recognize the belligerency of the rebels, he is, by the law of his own country, a pirate. If

---

[47] *Ibid.*, pp. 776-777, emphasis added.

[48] The significance of a "political purpose" as the motivation for a piratical action has become increasingly important as a result of the proliferation of attacks by politically motivated terrorist groups. See: Crockett, *op. cit.*, note 37; and Green, The Santa Maria: *Rebels or Pirates?* 37 Brit. Y.B. Int'l L. 496 (1961).

it does, he is not. In this respect, each nation acts independently of others and for itself; and the courts of each nation are governed by the consideration whether their own political authorities have or have not, recognized the belligerency.[49]

As stated earlier in our study, whether a nation chooses to treat a vessel as insurgent or belligerent is usually a political choice, not a legal one. Examples of each will be discussed later in this manuscript in order to illustrate their interplay with recent incidents. However, the subjects of insurgency and belligerency should not be confused with the types of acts which legal publicists have recently called "piracy." Some of the questions being asked today are: Should terrorist activities, for example, constitute acts of piracy even when they are deemed to be "political" in nature? Has it become necessary to treat these occurrences as "piracy" in order to bring the 1958 conventional articles on piracy into a twentieth-century perspective?[50]

In the last two subparagraphs of the Group's summary of ". . . arguments for inclusion among piratical acts . . ." they again emphasized the "private ends" requirement:

(15) Causing a wreck of another's ship for private ends.
(16) Any unjustifiable act of violence or depredation committed for private ends on board a pirate ship or a ship which is not under the peculiar jurisdiction and protection of some state (its flag state or state of national character).[51]

II. Acts committed outside all territorial jurisdiction, *but not on the high sea.*[52]

It was observed that subparagraphs 1-16 listed by the Group concerned those acts committed on the "high seas" as a geographical area. Certain publicists believed that perhaps this location was the only geographical area where acts of piracy could be committed. To the contrary, as will be demonstrated, the Group was able to list acts of piracy which did not occur on the high seas and yet were supported as being such by the "traditional" wisdom of certain nations and publicists up to and including the present time.

(1) Acts of the several types catalogued under I, but committed in or from the air and involving air craft instead of only water craft.[53]

The draft convention prepared by the Group and the 1958 conventional articles on piracy provide that piratical acts can be com-

[49] Harvard Draft Convention, pp. 777-779.
[50] See Crockett, *op. cit.,* pp. 98-99.
[51] Harvard Draft Convention, pp. 779-780.
[52] *Ibid.,* p. 773, emphasis added.
[53] *Ibid.,* p. 780.

mitted by "air craft." This is so because certain members of the
International Law Commission believed that the 1958 conventional
articles should be applicable to types of piratical acts which could
conceivably occur in the future:

Nevertheless, the word "aircraft" might be added, especially as it is quite possible
that piracy may be practised in the future by means of hydroplanes. Though
confined at present to the high seas and unowned territory, the notion of
piracy by aircraft may find a new application in the future if certain regions
of the air above State territory are ultimately to be regarded as free.[54]

The aircraft provision was later inserted into the 1958 conventional articles on piracy. However, it is a virtually useless provision
when applied to aviation because (a) the definition calls for an act
committed by the crew or passengers of one vehicle against another
vehicle (something which defies the imagination unless one of the
aircraft is totally destroyed); (b) it is impossible to force a plane to
land without shooting it down unless the pilot agrees to do so; and
(c) the type of act referred to by the 1958 conventional articles
happens only where aircraft are used to capture vessels at sea.
However, it should again be noted that despite the absence of
incidents involving aircraft the Conference States did decide to
include the language in their 1958 conventional articles. If this is
so, publicists ask why not update the 1958 conventional articles to
include politically as well as privately motivated acts especially
where there are incidents which should be covered by revised piracy
articles.[55]

The Group's list of acts of piracy not committed on the high seas
continued:

(2) Robbery on land:
    (a) by professional robbers,
    (b) by other than professionals.
(3) Other unjustifiable acts of violence or depredation committed for private
    end on land:
    (a) by professional robbers,
    (b) by other than professional robbers.[56]

The Group supported the inclusion of the subject matter of subparagraphs 2 and 3:

[54] Reply of Rumania, *op. cit.*, note 21, p. 211; cited in the Harvard Draft Convention,
p. 780.
    [55] For a discussion of these issues see Sundberg, *op. cit.*, note 17, pp. 380-382; Green,
Piracy of Aircraft and the Law, 10 Alberta L.R. 72 (1971); or Joyner, *Aerial Hijacking as
an International Crime* (New York: Oceana) 1974, pp. 92-96.
    [56] Harvard Draft Convention, p. 781, taken from the Spanish Penal Code of September
8, 1928, Article 252).

It is quite untrue that the special legal notion of piracy is due to its maritime character. . . . Besides the high seas, there are also *unowned territories*, and though, of course, they are always becoming rarer, they still exist; and until some State acquires exclusive sovereignty over them, every State, in virtue of the principles described above, will naturally have a theoretical right of punitive jurisdiction over them. Supposing, for example, that a band of brigands in some unowned territory attacks and plunders a convoy or caravan and escapes capture by its victims, what is the difference from the legal point of view between piracy on the high seas and pillage in unowned territory? If the act was committed in unowned territory, it is universally punishable *in virtue of the same principles* as those which make piracy on the high seas universally punishable. It would therefore be most desirable to substitute for the term "high seas" the words "place not subject to the sovereignty of any State."

Hall, International Law (18th ed.), p. 314: "If the foregoing remarks are well founded, piracy may be said to consist in acts of violence done upon the ocean or unappropriated lands, *or within the territory of the state through descent from the sea, by a body of men acting independently of any politically organized society*"[57]

The Group stated that there were other elements in the various definitions of piracy which they believed could be considered although they were not of an essential character:[58] (1) an intention to acquire wealth; (2) an intention to attack indiscriminately the nationals and ships of all states (except insofar as motives of personal interest – e.g., safety – lead to discrimination); (3) an intention to disclaim all state allegiance and state authority; (4) a menace to the commerce or other interests of all states (or of all seafaring peoples). The Group pointed out that:

The central idea in recent times of the traditional concession of a common jurisdiction to all states over piracy has been that the offence occurs out of the territory of every state – generally on the high sea.[59]

The essential element, however, would seem to be any act that interferes with international commerce. Obviously this "interference" does not mean that someone who, as a passenger on board a ship, robs another passenger (or any such alternative possibility that is so limited) should be considered a pirate. The act required would seem to be one in which some sort of interference with the vessel occurs which could or does impede its transit.[60] At least, this has been the "traditional" thinking on the subject. The Group stated that:

---

[57] Reply of Rumania, *op. cit.*, p. 204; cited in the Harvard Draft Convention, p. 781, emphasis added.
[58] Harvard Draft Convention, p. 781.
[59] *Ibid.*
[60] See, for example, the case of the Santa Maria, discussed in Chapter V.

... piracy is important as a topic for international agreement mainly because it furnishes an extra-ordinary basis of common jurisdiction — a special basis consisting of the nature and locality of the offence — which cannot be enlarged by the separate action of a state on its own behalf.[61]

The Group emphasized the fact that the main purpose of their draft convention was "to define the common, special jurisdiction of the several States based on certain sorts of facts which it calls piracy";[62] and that if the draft convention were adopted, the signatory states would be required to conform their laws in accordance with the provisions, thereby creating some measure of uniformity in municipal law. Most publicists agree that this was the main purpose of the Group's painstaking work. However, as will be seen later, the Group thought it necessary to modify part of the "traditional" jurisdiction because of what it termed "modern conditions."

This study is also concerned with "modern conditions," but the main reason for emphasizing the Group's research is to emphasize the problems confronting them regarding the creation of this special jurisdiction and to determine what elements they thought should constitute acts of piracy. They drew upon all available writings and opinions in preparing their draft convention. However, it was never envisaged that their work would be the last word on the subject. Indeed, the works drawn upon in preparing their draft convention disclose that there was no consensus among the experts as to what elements would be best utilized in creating this common jurisdiction. Rather, the Group selected what it thought would be the most common denominator or expedient provisions for Conference States to ratify. As seen in the Group's work, it was a matter of selecting the most orthodox views existing at the time they drew up the convention. The controversial incidents occurred after their work and after the 1958 conference. These views may not have represented the best possible solutions, but since they were fairly representative in scope, the Conference States were free to accept any or all of the proposed draft convention. The differing views, again, could be attributed to the various municipal laws which developed over the centuries. As with any other type of domestic legislation, the enactments were prejudiced to the needs of the particular country. The Group thought that:

---

[61] Harvard Draft Convention, p. 782. Note that the effect of defining piracy within the convention was not to exclude other elements and other definitions from still being utilized. The convention did not supersede all definitions of piracy as it applied only to states which ratified it.

[62] *Ibid.*, p. 785.

A most important phase of the common jurisdiction is the right to seize pirate ships outside all territorial jurisdiction although they are owned and manned by foreigners and fly a foreign flag. The expediency of conceding this common police jurisdiction will lead to the inclusion of certain types of cases in the definition of piracy which perhaps would not be included if only the juris-diction to prosecute before a court (judicial jurisdiction) were in question.[63]

Many of the legal publicists who discuss updating the law of piracy observe that perhaps it is time to include political as well as private acts in order to cover situations which have occurred in this century. They point out that the Group was concerned with the creation of this common jurisdiction but that a revision of the acts and definition is necessary today. Many of these writers are con-cerned with "air piracy" and their discussions of sea piracy are used only as a justification for their thoughts regarding the creation of an international crime of air piracy.[64] However, in fairness to the Group's strong effort, and with deference to the goals which they were desirous of accomplishing, it is fair to state that their in-depth research is by far the most extensive and thorough work on the subject of sea piracy. As was stated earlier in this chapter, their proposals and comments are too often ignored by legal publicists who simply assert that most of the recommendations contained in the draft convention were adopted without change by the 1958 Conference States. The Group's draft articles and comments are invaluable because their effort represents the first time that such thorough research was undertaken in connection with the law relating to sea piracy.

Before setting forth the acts that constituted piracy, the Group emphasized the consideration which they took into account:

While the scope of the draft convention is controlled by the international law of piracy, it is expedient to modify in part the traditional jurisdiction because of *modern conditions*. The modification may work in both directions. It may be thought advisable to exclude from the common jurisdiction certain doubtful phases of traditional piracy which can now be left satisfactorily to the ordinary jurisdiction of a state, or of two or three states, stimulated to action on occasion by diplomatic pressure; and it may be *expedient* to concede com-mon jurisdiction over certain sorts of events which are not beyond dispute piracy by tradition, but bear enough analogy to cases of undoubted piracy to justify assimilation under the caption. Therefore the draft convention excludes from its definition of piracy all cases of wrongful attacks on persons or property

---

[63] *Ibid.*, pp. 785-786.

[64] Many of the commentators, concerned with the increasing frequency of air hijack-ings by political terrorist groups, drew analogies to sea piracy as a basis for a universal criminal jurisdiction. See Horlick, *The Developing Law of Air Hijacking*, 12 Harv. Int'l. L. J. 33 (1972); and Jacobsen, *From Piracy on the High Seas to Piracy in the High Skies: A Study of Aircraft Hijacking*, 5 Cornell Int'l. L. J. 161 (1972).

for *political* ends, whether they are made on behalf of states, or of unrecognized belligerent organizations, or of unrecognized revolutionary bands.[65]

In connection with this statement and, as will be discussed more fully later in this study, it is obvious that at the time the Group was engaged in their research, the various political incidents, which took place *after* their studies were completed (and which have led publicists to raise questions concerning the possibility of updating and revising the 1958 conventional articles on piracy), were, and could be, so significant that perhaps an updating is called for. Just a quick glimpse of acts constituting terrorism, for example (1) a serious offense involving an attack against the life, physical integrity or liberty of internationally protected persons, including diplomatic agents; (2) an offense involving kidnapping, the taking of a hostage or serious unlawful detention; (3) an offense involving the use of a bomb, grenade, rocket, automatic firearm or letter or parcel bomb if this use endangers persons; (4) an attempt to commit any of the foregoing offenses or participation as an accomplice of a person who commits or attempts to commit such an offense,[66] discloses that these acts of terrorism are really a recent and updated version of "traditional" acts of piracy. In any event, even in 1932, the Group went on to state that:

... Under *present* conditions there seems no good reason why jurisdiction over genuine cases of this type should not be confined to the injured state, the state or recognized government on whose behalf the forces were acting, and the states of nationality and domicile of the offender. Most of these cases would not fall indisputably under the common jurisdiction by traditional law, and this is an additional reason for disposing of them as the draft convention does. Contrariwise, the draft convention's definition of piracy covers some types of cases which have not been placed under the common jurisdiction by definite precedents or uniform professional opinion. If depredations occur in or from the air outside all territorial jurisdiction which are similar to piratical attacks on the high seas, why should not these depredations be treated as piracies? Acts done with other purposes than robbery also are put under the common jurisdiction, although the typical piracy is usually defined as robbery on the high seas; for there is no good reason why one who does an act with intent to kill, wound, rape, enslave, or imprison, or to steal or maliciously destroy property, which would be piracy if done to rob, should not be subjected to more probable retribution through the common jurisdiction of all states, instead of to a lesser chance of apprehension and punishment by a single state (or one of two or three states) which may not have the present force, or opportunity or interest to serve the cause of security and order in the locality.

[65] Harvard Draft Convention, p. 786, emphasis added.
[66] See: Council of Europe: European Convention on the Suppression of Terrorism, opened for signature January 27, 1977. 15 (6) International Legal Materials 1272 (November 1976), Article 1; Paust, *A Survey of the Possible Legal Responses to International Terrorism: Prevention, Punishment, and Cooperative Action*, 5 Ga. J. Int'l. and Comp. L. 431 (1975).

Whichever motive or intent inspires the act, it is a menace to travel and commerce beyond territorial jurisdiction.[67]

Yet the Group recognized that:

... It is *expediency* that should be the chief guide in the formulation of a convention. *The use of traditional ideas of the nature of piracy and the scope of the common jurisdiction should be tempered and controlled by realization of the great changes that have occurred through the centuries in the conditions of commerce and travel and in offences affecting them outside territorial jurisdiction,* in the actual relations of states, and in fundamental postulates of the law of nations pertaining to our topic... The facts that piracy has had a distinct place in law and that the foreign private pirate has been treated with universal public enmity continuously from ancient times, should not mislead us into assuming that the law of piracy in its basic principles, or in its definition of the offence, or in the details of state authority to act in the interest of suppressing it always has been the same. Especially, in view of the greatly changed conditions of international intercourse today, *we could expect that the scope of the modern offence cannot be limited satisfactorily by a controlling reference to the old conditions of robbery on the sea by outlaw communities.*[68]

Thus, the need for change was visualized in a world community where events dictate changes in "traditional" wisdom. At the time that they prepared their draft convention and comments they set forth what they considered to be an appropriate convention for their day. As was stated earlier in this chapter, they even included a provision concerning acts of piracy committed by "air craft" though they had no real basis, understanding, or precedent concerning how such an act of piracy could be effectuated. They were guided by the "traditional" wisdom in drafting their convention and indeed their research later served as the backbone for the 1958 conventional articles. Does this then mean that the matter is permanently settled? Based upon their comments, it would hardly seem likely that the Group did not want the subject to be reconsidered at a future time. This certainly was not their intention.[69]

The Group then set forth their definition of piracy.

Piracy is any of the following acts, committed in a place not within the territorial jurisdiction of any state: ...[70]

They pointed out that this clause would include acts of violence or depredation only and that said acts of piracy are "committed in a

---

[67] Harvard Draft Convention, at p. 786, emphasis added.

[68] *Ibid.*, p. 787, emphasis added.

[69] "The framework of the draft convention is designed to facilitate amendments in detail and differing decisions which result from common counsel can easily be fitted into the general scheme" Harvard Draft Convention, p. 764.

[70] *Ibid.*, Article 3, p. 788.

place not within the territorial jurisdiction of any state." The Group referred, *inter alia,* to Oppenheim, International Law (4th ed.), section 277, which states that:

Piracy as an "international crime" can be committed on the open sea only. Piracy in territorial coast waters has as little to do with International Law as other robberies within the territory of a State. Some writers maintain that piracy need not necessarily be committed on the open sea, but that it suffices that the respective acts of violence are committed by descent *from* the open sea. They maintain, therefore, that if "a body of pirates land on an island unappropriated by a civilized Power, and rob and murder a trader, who may be carrying on commerce there with the savage inhabitants, they are guilty of a crime possessing all the marks of commonplace professional piracy." With this opinion I cannot agree. Piracy is, and always has been, a crime against the safety of traffic on the open sea, and therefore it cannot be committed anywhere else than on the open sea.[71]

The Group commented that ". . . exclusion from the common jurisdiction does not exclude the possibility of prosecution. . ."[72] Of course, under modern conditions, it is unlikely that land areas exist which do not come within the jurisdiction of a nation.[73] Later, when formulating possible suggestions concerning the updating of the 1958 conventional articles on piracy, this study will discuss the possibility of altering the "traditional" concept of piracy in order to bring the acts within the context of current-day incidents and possible occurrences. It will become apparent that in order to aid in the progressive development of international law, it may be necessary to set aside the so-called "traditional" terminology and governing concepts embodied in the 1958 conventional articles.

The first piratical act enumerated in the draft convention is one in which the Group again recognized that the "traditional" wisdom was rather divergent:

1. Any act of violence or of depredation committed with intent to rob, rape, wound, enslave, imprison, or kill a person or with intent to steal or destroy property.[74]

---

[71] Cited in the Harvard Draft Convention, p. 789.

[72] *Ibid.*

[73] It should be noted, at this point, that those areas of the sea subject to the common jurisdiction have significantly decreased in recent years as a result of such factors as the proliferation of island states and a new emphasis on the economic zone. See note 17, Chapter II. The universal adoption of a 200-mile territorial sea, as advocated by many states, would put the Mediterranean, the North Sea, the South China Sea, and the Caribbean within national jurisdictions. See: Janis, *Dispute Settlement in the Law of the Sea Convention: The Military Activities Exception,* 4 Ocean Development and Int'l. Law 51 (1977), p. 60.

[74] Harvard Draft Convention, Article 3, p. 790.

The Group pointed out that force and depredation have always colored our mental pictures of piratical enterprises. The typical pirate has been a robber for whom, some publicists insisted, the purpose of private gain is essential. Other publicists argued that the motive may vary and that even vengeance or bare malice may be the inspiration of piratical attacks. The Group, however, did not deem it necessary to delve into the various viewpoints, except in passing, and stated that the function of their draft articles was to define a common jurisdiction of all states over certain types of major offenses committed beyond the territorial jurisdiction of every state. This purpose would be accomplished only by allowing the common jurisdiction to encompass *all* serious offenses even though the *motive* of the "traditional" pirate may vary. The Report of the Sub-Committee of the League of Nations stated in this regard that:

Certain authors take the view that desire for gain is necessarily one of the characteristics of piracy. But the motive of the acts of violence might be not the prospect of gain but hatred or a desire for vengeance. In my opinion it is preferable not to adopt the criterion of desire for gain, since it is both too restrictive and contained in the larger qualification "for private ends." It is better, in laying down a general principle, to be content with the external character of the facts without entering too far into the often delicate question of motives. Nevertheless, when the acts in question are committed from purely political motives, it is hardly possible to regard them as acts of piracy involving all the important consequences which follow upon the commission of that crime. Such a rule does not assure any absolute impunity for the political acts in question, since they remain subject to the ordinary rule of international law.[75]

When reflecting on modern conditions and incidents, of course, the main problem is that traditional piracy (that is, the swashbuckler) no longer exists (and did not exist even when the Group prepared its draft convention). It may prove to be totally unrealistic to ignore political motivation and still arrive at a suitable definition of acts of piracy.

Nearly all publicists today are asking this question with regard to political motivation — Why should it be a stumbling-block when attempting to revitalize the acts of piracy?[76] Why can we not still define acts of piracy in an updated form in order to include the type of terrorist activity which would occur today without the necessity for excluding these acts as politically motivated simply because

[75] *Ibid.,* p. 791.
[76] The issue of political motivation is dealt with extensively in Johnson, *op. cit.,* note 44, p. 68; Crockett, *op. cit.,* note 37, p. 99; Green, *op. cit.,* note 48, and Joyner, *op. cit.,* note 55, pp. 41-50.

they may be covered elsewhere in international law? Certainly robbery or murder done for political reasons is still robbery or murder.
Why let other areas of international law deal with this situation
because of expediency? Most of the problem in connection with
developing international law concerns the lack of any enforcement
mechanism and the reluctance of certain nations, because they are
unable or unwilling, to take appropriate action in a given situation.
However, where piracy is concerned, why not utilize a dispute
settlement mechanism to enforce international prescriptions? It
would seem to be in the self-interest of all nations to have an act
considered "piracy" rather than "war"; to be able to turn to a dispute settlement mechanism in order to work out appropriate
uniform penalties for states refusing to enforce international prescriptions; to utilize a dispute settlement mechanism in order to
stamp out acts of piracy or terrorism whether committed for private
or political motivation, whether committed on the high seas or in
territorial waters. These are the considerations which must be
effectuated in order to have a viable international law. Shall it
always be sufficient for states to claim their sovereignty in order to
avoid their international responsibility? Certainly this was not so
when preparing the Genocide Convention.

The Group referred, *inter alia,* to Oppenheim, International Law
(4th ed.), vol. 1, section 275, pp. 503-504, when discussing the
traditional divergence of opinion on this subject:

The object of piracy is any public or private vessel, or the persons or the goods
thereon, whilst on the open sea. In the regular case of piracy the pirate wants
to make booty; it is the cargo of the attacked vessel which is the centre of his
interest, and he might free the vessel and the crew after having appropriated
the cargo. But he remains a pirate, whether he does so or whether he kills the
crew and appropriates the ship, or sinks her. On the other hand, the cargo need
not be the object of his act of violence. If he stops a vessel and takes a rich
passenger off with the intention of keeping him for the purpose of a high ransom, his act is piracy; it is likewise piracy if he stops a vessel merely to kill a
certain person on board, although he may afterwards free vessel, crew, and
cargo.

Wheaton, International Law, (8th ed.,), Sec. 124, footnote by Dana: ". . . It
has sometimes been said, that the act must be done *lucri causa,* and the English
common-law definition of *animus furandi* has been treated as a requisite; but
the motive may be gratuitous malice, or the purpose may be to destroy, in
private revenge for real or supposed injuries done *by persons, or classes of
persons, or by a particular national authority.*"[77]

The Group then raised the following questions in connection
with justifying the utilization of such a wide definition:

[77] Cited in the Harvard Draft Convention, p. 792.

Suppose that a band of lawless men set sail with the purpose of committing such violence or depredations on the high seas as chance and their views of advantage might determine. If, on occurrence of an opportunity;

(a) they attacked a foreign merchant ship to kill a man who had incurred their vengeance,

(b) they attacked a foreign merchant ship to wound a man who had incurred their vengeance,

(c) they attacked a foreign merchant ship to rape,

(d) they attacked a foreign merchant ship to capture and enslave the persons on board (compare the acts of Moorish pirates in former centuries),

(e) they attacked a foreign merchant ship to capture and hold for ransom the persons on board (compare the acts of Moorish pirates),

(f) or even if they attacked only to maliciously destroy property, or found property unprotected on the high seas and maliciously destroyed it, would the law of nations in any of these cases prohibit any state from treating the perpetrators as pirates (quite without regard to any purpose of robbery)? Certainly such a band would be as much a menace to international commerce as a band of sea-robbers of like force and readiness for mischief.

If these questions all receive answers in favor of the common jurisdiction, then as far as the motivation of the act of violence or depredation is concerned, the draft convention has met the test except as to the case of "intent to steal."[78]

The Group qualified this statement by pointing out that the common jurisdiction would not attach unless other elements also were present in the case:

If the attack or attempt takes place from on shipboard there must be involved a pirate ship or one without national character, and in any event the act must be done beyond all territorial jurisdiction.[79]

Wheaton, International Law (8th ed.), section 124, footnote by Dana:

... Some writers, and even judges, seem to have treated the phrase *hostis humani generis* as if it were a definition of piracy. ... "It is neither a definition nor as much as a description of a pirate, but a rhetorical invective." ... The criminal may have committed but one crime, and intended but one, and that against a vessel of a particular nation; yet, if done on the high seas, under certain circumstances hereafter to be referred to, he may be seized and tried by any nation.[80]

Notwithstanding the variety of references on the subject, the Group thought that committing a single piratical act is not really what threatens the commerce of international community,

[78] *Ibid.*, p. 794.
[79] *Ibid.*
[80] As cited in the Harvard Draft Convention, p. 796.

but piratical attacks and attempts on the high sea or elsewhere beyond territorial jurisdiction are of a sort which justifies suppression by all states to prevent the growth of a menace to international commerce and transportation.[81]

If there is any doubt that the Group did not want "States" included as parties capable of committing piratical acts, the example they gave to ". . . distinguish . . . the case of a casual attack by persons on board a ship of State X against a ship of State Y on the high seas . . ."[82] clarifies the situation because the Group believed that ". . . Unless the ship of State X has been devoted to a piratical enterprise by those in dominant control of it, it is not a pirate ship and therefore the attack would not fall under the common jurisdiction. . ."[83]

The Group then went on to discuss one of the highlights of the draft convention. "Highlights" in the sense that the ". . . *for private ends*. . ."[84] delimitation is perhaps the most controversial part of the draft convention and the 1958 conventional articles which were later adopted by the Conference States. The legal publicists who have written about the subject of piracy have always raised the question of whether the "private ends" limitation should be done away with altogether. There is no question that it is a very limiting feature of the 1958 conventional articles on piracy.[85] The Group explained:

Although states at times have claimed the right to treat as pirates unrecognized insurgents against a foreign government who have pretended to exercise belligerent rights on the sea against neutral commerce, or privateers whose commissions violated the announced policy of the captor, and although there is authority for subjecting some cases of these types to the common jurisdiction of all states, it seems best to confine the common jurisdiction to offenders for private ends only.[86]

The Group discussed the possibility of a mutiny on board a state vessel which vessel was later used to commit piracy on the high seas. In this connection, the Group stated that still ". . . The acts would be committed for private ends, not for public ends, and there would be no question of the *immunity* which pertains to state or governmental acts."[87]

---

[81] *Ibid.*, p. 797.
[82] *Ibid.*
[83] *Ibid.*, pp. 797-798.
[84] *Ibid.*, p. 798.
[85] See note 43, and also Johnson, *op. cit.*, note 44, p. 68.
[86] Harvard Draft Convention, p. 798.
[87] *Ibid.*, emphasis added. See Article 105 of the Composite Text (Articles 100-107 have been reproduced at Appendix 4 to this chapter). See also the discussion of sovereign immunity at Appendix 5 to Chapter II.

Thus, one method of avoiding "touchy" political questions of immunity (as well as extradition, political asylum, insurgency and belligerency) was to provide for the "private ends" limitation in the draft convention. The problem is that many publicists are calling for the end to the limitation because of modern political terrorism, many acts of which could constitute piracy and could be covered by the 1958 conventional articles on piracy or amended conventional articles on piracy if the sole reliance on the private ends limitation were not present. There is no question that acts of terrorism under modern conditions would constitute piracy under traditional and conventional law if the limitation were not present. The question of whether the limitation is still necessary today, or will be required in the future, is one that will be discussed in later chapters.

Some of the material referred to by the Group is rather interesting and aids to emphasize the divergent views on the "traditional" wisdom of the subject of "private ends":

Halleck, International Law, Vol. I, p. 450: "Sir Leoline Jenkins, who was Judge of the Admiralty in the seventeenth century, thus defines piracy, in giving a charge to the grand jury at an Admiralty sessions: 'The next sort of offences pointed out in the statute are robberies; and a robbery, when it is committed upon the sea, is what we call *piracy*... Nor does it differ the case though the party so assaulted and despoiled should be a foreigner, not born within the King's allegiance; if he be *de amicitia Regis* he is *eo nomine* under the King's protection, and to rob such a one upon the seas is piracy. Nor will it be any defence to a man, who takes away by force another's ship or goods at sea, that he hath a commission of war from some foreign prince, unless the person he takes from be a lawful enemy to that prince. . .'. (life of Sir Leoline Jenkins i. 94; see also "A Charge at an Admiralty Sessions,' with notes, by Sir Sherston Baker, Law Magazine and Review, No. 257, p. 412.)"[88]

Halleck, International Law (3rd ed.), Vol. II, p. 120, footnote: "It is an open question whether privateers, commissioned by a deposed sovereign, are pirates or not. For arguments on the subject see, An Essay Concerning the Law of Nations and the Rights of Sovereigns, by Matthew Tindal, LL.D., London, 1734. This work is quoted at some length by Sir R. Phillmore (Int. Law, I, 362,) who inclines to the opinion that such ships are pirates. . . .[89]

Hall, International Law, 8th ed., p. 317, footnote: "In the French Instructions issued to the officers of the Navy on the application of International Law in war (Jan. 30, 1916) it is stated that 'the captain, officers, and crew of every privateer commissioned by a Government signatory of the Declaration of Paris, 1856, being liable to the punishments provided for the crime of piracy, must not be considered as prisoners of war but must be sent to the nearest French authority to be proceeded against according to the laws of the Republic'

[88] Cited in the Harvard Draft Convention, p. 798.
[89] *Ibid.*, p. 799.

(Art. 117) The Washington Treaty relating to the use of submarines and noxious gases in warfare, of the 6 Feb., 1922, also provides that any person violating the rules therein adopted, even if such violation was by order of their government 'shall be liable to trial and punishment as if for an act of piracy, and may be brought to trial before the civil or military authorities of any Power within the jurisdiction of which he may be found' (Art. 3). In both these cases there is imported into the term of piracy a meaning different from that which it is generally recognized as having, though in the case of the *Magellan Pirates* (1853, 1 Spinks 81), Dr. Lushington said, 'I am aware that it has been said that a state cannot be piratical, but I am not disposed to assent to such a dictum as a universal proposition.'"[90]

To the contrary, the Committee of Experts for the Progressive Codification of International Law stated that:

. . . It is better, in laying down a general principle, to be content with the external character of the facts without entering too far into the often delicate question of motives. Nevertheless, when the acts in question are committed from purely political motives, it is hardly possible to regard them as acts of piracy involving all the important consequences which follow upon the commission of that crime. Such a rule does not assure any absolute impunity for the political acts in question, since they remain subject to the ordinary rules of international law. . . .[91]

To the various views presented by the Group, they commented that ". . . It is true that some of the most famous pirates have become on occasion privateers with commissions open or secret from a great power or a revolutionary government to prey on the commerce of its enemies or competitors . . ." however,

. . . there is encouraging evidence that the old barbarous discordant competition is to be replaced by constantly spreading efforts at cooperation and adjustment based on a recognition of economic interdependence. It is not likely that the conditions of the sixteenth and seventeenth centuries will soon revive or be tolerated by members of the family of nations.[92]

The Group stated that ". . . international manners have improved greatly in these particulars, and it is customary to assume that international morals have improved similarly. . ."[93] Needless to say, many publicists would possibly argue that although the swashbuckler type of piracy has disappeared, perhaps other forms of piracy or terrorism have taken its place. Is it not possible for the pirates of the skies in the twentieth-century to take to the seas and use updated methods of committing piratical acts? The Group went on to state:

[90] *Ibid.*, pp. 800-801.
[91] *Ibid.*, p. 802, from League of Nations, *op. cit.*, note 13, p. 117.
[92] *Ibid.*, p. 803.
[93] *Ibid.*

... The idea *that a pirate* preys on the world at large has been stressed by some writers in later years, partly on the ground that all states have not a common interest in preventing attacks which purposely are confined to the commerce of a single state or to the commerce of one or two firms or individuals; and partly because of the often repeated statement that a pirate is *"hostis humani generis."*
... It is an ancient verbal condemnation of the conduct of a pirate and a figurative epitome of the common war against him. Its origin was not an attempt to delimit his offence. Furthermore, although it is true that the typical pirate of fiction and tradition was an indiscriminative plunderer, *expediency and not traditional epithets or the fancy of traditional concepts should direct the definition of the common jurisdiction over piracy.* ... that the jurisdiction to seize and to punish a robber or a killer for private ends should not depend on whether the offender has by acts or words displayed an intent to plunder or slay only once or oftener, or on whether he intended to attack only the citizens of certain states and their ships and other property, or to prey on the people and commerce of all nations indiscriminately. Such matters of collateral intent of an offender (often uncertain and indistinct) and of his transactions other than those involved in the case at hand, are very unsatisfactory as elements in a basis of state jurisdiction.[94]

It should be noted that the argument presented by the Group is quite applicable today.[95] If conventional articles (calling for political acts as well as private acts to be considered piratical) are adopted by the Conference States there would be created an international crime based upon the new definition. Thus, if a piratical act is committed for political reasons, then states have the opportunity, upon capture, to prosecute under their municipal legislation, if any, for the acts of piracy committed under this international convention. However, if a state, for example, refuses to prosecute or otherwise take action against a pirate who has come within its jurisdiction, is that state not aiding and abetting an alleged pirate, an international outlaw? This is where a main problem comes into focus. How can the immunity of an offending state (be it the direct perpetrator of the act by use of one of its vessels or one that aided and abetted the piratical act by not prosecuting the villain) be pierced by the international community? Every other member of the international community is fully aware that, although it is not the target this time, it could be the target the next time around. The reader should therefore be thinking of possible approaches to the problem (for instance allowing states to engage in hot pursuit within the territorial waters of another state; the possibility of an international zone being created around the fugitive; the possibility of an international jail to hold the prisoner until a newly created dispute

[94] *Ibid.*, emphasis added.
[95] This is the same argument advanced by the contemporary commentators who advocate this position. See note 76.

settlement mechanism could be triggered under the law of the sea convention; whether this type of approach is better than having the terrorist activity considered an act of war; whether insurgency, belligerency, political asylum, and extradition problems could be avoided by utilizing a dispute settlement mechanism).

Returning to the Group's comments and citations, the Group cited Dr. Lushington, *The Magellan Pirates* (High Court of Admiralty, 1853), 18 Jur. 18, 1 Spinks Ecc. and Adm. R. 81, p. 83; 164 Eng. R. 47, p. 48:

... I do not believe that, even where human life was at stake our Courts of Common Law ever thought it necessary to extend their inquiries further, if it was clearly proved against the accused that they had committed robbery and murder upon the high seas. In that case they were adjudged to be pirates, and suffered accordingly. Whatever may have been the definition in some books, and I have been referred by Her Majesty's advocate to an American case (*The United States v. Smith*, 5 Wheaton, 153, post p. 90) where, I believe all the authorities bearing on this subject are collected, it was never, so far as I am able to find, deemed necessary to inquire whether parties so convicted of these crimes had intended to rob on the high seas, or to murder on the high seas indiscriminately. . . .[96]

Davis, J., in *Dole v. Merchants' Insurance Co.*, 51 Me. 465, 468: ". . . If an act of piracy is proved, it surely would not be a good defence for the pirates, that their purpose was to seize vessels belonging to citizens of one nation only; or even that the piratical enterprise was designed for the taking of only a single ship.[97]

Wheaton, International Law, Sec. 124, note by Dana: "It must be admitted, *that the attempted definitions of piracy are unsatisfactory;* some being too wide, and some too narrow. The Author's description, rather than definition, is perhaps the most adequate. Some writers, and even judges, seem to have treated the phrase *hostis humani generis* as if it were a definition of piracy. . . . 'It is neither a definition nor as much as a description of a pirate, but a rhetorical invective.' . . . . that it is committed where all have a common, and no nation an exclusive, jurisdiction, i.e., upon the high seas; and, if on board ship, and by her own crew, then the ship must be one in which no national authority reigns. . ."[98]

The Group stated that:

... each state is jealous of any encroachment on its exclusive jurisdiction; but the definition of piracy in this article confines it to offences committed in places outside the territorial jurisdiction of every state. . . . *Indeed a clever plunderer might diminish greatly his risks of punishment under such a limitation of jurisdiction, strictly and impartially applied, by attacking the commerce*

[96] As cited in the Harvard Draft Convention, p. 805. An extensive discussion of *The Magellan Pirates* and related cases will be set forth before discussing the Santa Maria incident.

[97] *Ibid.*, p. 806.

[98] *Ibid.*, pp. 806-807.

*only the weaker and distant states or by conceding immunity to the commerce
of one or two great states whose police forces were uncomfortably potent. . . .*
(Emphasis added.)

Nevertheless, the opposition to bringing under the common jurisdiction
offences against the interests of a single state, and the insistence on some international factual element in the definition of piracy, are strong enough to make
it *expedient* to exclude from the definition of piracy offences which involve
only ships and territory under the ordinary jurisdiction of one state and which
are not incidents of an enterprise with purposes of wider scope.[99]

without bona fide purpose of asserting a claim of right . . .[100]

This particular phrase was inserted into the draft convention by
the Group because it was believed that the alternative element of
intent to slay, wound, imprison, or enslave was permitted by the
definition; thus the exclusionary phrase was necessary in connection
with cases of violence committed in asserting a claim of right because
these could not be assimilated by the common consent of all states.
Examples which would fall into this category were arguments
between fishermen of different nationalities.[101] An obvious comment regarding this phrase is that it must be remembered that the
Group was attempting to dispose of matters in an "expedient"
manner, or one which could be agreed upon eventually by consensus
of the Conference States. Having this purpose in mind, the handicaps
presented by this desire to create a common jurisdiction are self-
evident and possibly self-defeating. Nevertheless, if the Group
believed that their draft convention would be subject to developing
circumstances, which would occur in the future; and if they were
utilizing the draft convention as a first step in achieving some framework within which to operate for the creation of a common consensus among the states, then, viewed in that light, their purpose is
valid. *Their comments indicated that their work would not be the
last word on the subject but rather a solid guide for future amendment should the necessity for revision present itself.*

. . . provided that the act is connected with an attack on or from the sea or in
or from the air.[102]

This provision is extremely important because it demonstrates
how and why the Group would react to an entirely new situation.
Remembering the shortcomings discussed earlier in this chapter

---

[99] *Ibid.*, p. 807.
[100] *Ibid.*, Article 3(1), p. 808.
[101] See: *Law of the Sea: The Scope of the Third Party, Compulsory Procedures for
Settlement of Disputes,* 71 Am. J. of Int'l. L. 305 (1977).
[102] Harvard Draft Convention, Article 3(1), p. 809.

with regard to attacks upon aircraft and so on, it will be observed that this provision was inserted by the Group despite "traditional" diverse notions on sea piracy:

The pirate of tradition attacked on or from the sea. Certainly today, however, one should not deem the possibility of similar attacks in or from the air as too slight or too remote for consideration in drafting a convention on jurisdiction over piratical acts. With rapid advance in the arts of flying and air-sailing, it may not be long before bands of malefactors, who now confine their efforts to land, will find it profitable to engage in depredations in or from the air beyond territorial jurisdiction. Indeed there even may occur thus a recrudescence of large scale piracy. *A codification of the jurisdiction of states under the law of nations should not be drafted to fit only cases raised by present conditions of business, the arts, and criminal operations. Continual amendment should be obviated by foresight as far as possible.*[103]

The only supporting "traditional" wisdom on this subject was a Mexican Penal Code of August 13, 1931, Article 146,[104] together with a reference to a Spanish Penal Code of September 8, 1928, Article 252.[105]

It will be observed by the reader that the Group took a rather advanced step forward by including reference to a matter about which they knew little (although flight over territorial waters was included later in other 1958 conventional articles of the 1958 conference). They did not indicate how these attacks could take place since they assumed that technology could be advanced to the stage where, one day in the future, piratical acts might come from the air. It should be noted that the 1958 conventional articles on piracy also included this provision. If the Group, The International Law Commission and the Conference States were willing to adopt such a superfluous provision regarding aircraft, cannot the 1958 conventional articles be amended today to cover incidents which can take place, or have already taken place, on the seas with *known* methods and techniques and for *known* political reasons? Certainly there is enough precedent in cases of air piracy to warrant including such acts of terrorism within the scope of the international law of

---

[103] *Ibid.*, p. 809, emphasis added.

[104] *Ibid.*, p. 809: "The following shall be considered pirates:

III. Those privateers who, in case of war between two or more nations, cruise without letters of marque or commission from any one of them, or with a commission from two or more (opposed) belligerents, or who, with a commission from one of them, practice depredations against vessels of the [Mexican] Republic or of another nation against which they were not authorized to commit acts of aggression. These provisions shall likewise be enforced, when applicable, *in the case of aircraft*" (translation, emphasis added).

[105] *Ibid.*, p. 1009: "The provisions contained in the preceding articles shall likewise be applicable when, in the commission of the Crimes to which they refer, *aircraft are used as the means thereof or the crimes are committed against aircraft*" (emphasis added).

piracy.[106] In fact, the various legal publicists who advocate an international crime of air piracy have traditionally relied on either comparing or distinguishing (or both) ordinary sea piracy, as defined under the 1958 conventional articles (and the work of the Group and the International Law Commission), in support of their argument to create the crime of air piracy. Here is an opportunity to utilize their descriptions and arguments for the creation of a common jurisdiction for the suppression of air piracy in order to update the 1958 conventional law of sea piracy (which they consider, as did the Group and the International Law Commission, to be a settled question).[107]

The reader should be aware of the fact that the dated 1958 conventional articles regarding piracy may be considered as moot when applied to the conditions of today. Aside from the few legal publicists who discuss the possibility of updating the articles, most international jurists and states consider the matter of "traditional" piracy a dead issue. The only reason that it is a dead issue is because nothing is being done to update the 1958 conventional articles to apply to incidents of alleged terrorism on the seas. Possibly, there is a fear that an international consensus among the Conference States would be impossible to achieve. As will be discussed in the chapter concerning possible suggestions, revisions can be made which would pierce the sovereignty of states found to be guilty of acts of piracy, or of aiding and abetting alleged pirates, by utilizing some sort of dispute settlement mechanism. It is suggested to the reader that here is a tremendous opportunity to take a rather "settled" area of international law and update it, demonstrating that there is a mechanism, on an international level, which can resolve international disputes. Instead of having acts of war, we can have piratical acts committed by states or individuals acting on behalf of states or for politically motivated reasons. Appropriate uniform penalties and sanctions could be created and applied to correspond to the degree of seriousness of the incident.

[106] It cannot be disputed that air piracy has become a problem of major proportions in recent years. Between 1967 and 1972 there were 146 attempts to take over American aircraft alone. The frequency of these attempts and the fact that they are often accompanied by the death of innocent hostages has forced the adoption of a worldwide "get tough" policy. A spectacular demonstration of this policy was West Germany's rescue of 86 hostages from a hijacked Lufthansa airliner on October 18, 1977, during which four terrorists were killed (*Is the Tide Turning Against Terrorists?*, U.S. New and World Report, October 31, 1977, pp. 23-24).

[107] Substantial progress has been made toward the creation of a common jurisdiction over acts of air piracy. See: Convention on Offences and Certain Other Acts Committed on Board Aircraft (Tokyo Convention) of September 14, 1963, 20 U.S.T. 2941, 704 U.N.T.S. 10106 (1969); and Convention for Suppression of Unlawful Acts Against the Safety of Civil Aviation (Montreal Convention) of September 23, 1971, T.I.A.S. No. 7570.

If the act is connected with an attack which starts from on board ship, either that ship or another ship which is involved must be a pirate ship or a ship without national character.[108]

The Group included this provision in order to "... exclude offences committed in a place subject to the ordinary jurisdiction of a state."[109] As stated by the Committee of Experts for the Progressive Codification of International Law:

A ship may clearly be a pirate ship even if it was not fitted out for that purpose or if it began its voyage without criminal intention. If a mutiny breaks out on board and the mutineers seize the vessel and use it to commit acts of piracy, the vessel *ipso facto* loses the original protection of its flag.[110]

The Group also referred, *inter alia,* to the case of *United States v. The Pirates:*

... that when embarked on a piratical cruise, every individual becomes equally punishable, under the law of 1790, whatever may be his national character, or whatever may have been that of the vessel in which he sailed, or of the vessel attacked.... But we have decided, that in becoming a pirate, the *Mary* of Mobile, from which the prisoner committed this offence, lost her national character. Could she then be denominated an American vessel? We are of opinion that the question is immaterial; for, whether as an American, or a pirate ship, the offence committed from her was equally punishable, and the words of the act extend to her in both characters. But if it were necessary to decide the question, we should find no difficulty in maintaining that no man shall, by crime, put off an incident to his situation, which subjects him to punishment. A claim to protection may be forfeited, by the loss of national character, where no rights are acquired, or immunity produced by that cause.[111]

Article 3(2)
    2. Any act of voluntary participation in the operation of a ship with knowledge of facts which make it a pirate ship.[112]

The Group stated that this provision covered the phase of piratical roving prior to an attack. In this context, the provision could be utilized to permit international police intervention before attacks on the grounds of jurisdiction to prosecute for a form of conspiracy to commit the crime of piracy. The Group commented:

In connection with Article 4, it also places among piracies, sailing a ship on the high sea in order to commit such violence or depredation in foreign territorial

---

    [108] Harvard Draft Convention, Article 3(1), p. 809.
    [109] *Ibid.,* p. 809.
    [110] *Ibid.,* p. 810, from League of Nations, *op. cit.,* note 13, p. 117.
    [111] *Ibid.,* p. 811, from *United States v. The Pirates,* 5 Wheat. (U.S.) 184 (1820), pp. 192-196. The Group made reference to the works of a number of the commentators at this point. See Appendix 5 to this chapter.
    [112] *Ibid.,* p. 820.

waters or on a foreign coast as would be piracy if committed beyond territorial jurisdiction. Thus are included such ravaging expeditions as the Moorish pirates used to make against American settlements, *and as are made today against the coasts of the Philippines and other far eastern countries.* [113]

It was thought that such a provision was important because it granted the authority to seize an offending foreign ship on the high seas before the threatened attack was made, or after the attack, when there had been no hot pursuit. In addition, the Group demonstrated the confusion that occurred when discussing the two distinctive matters of:

(1) The range of state jurisdiction on the ground of piracy;
(2) The range of the traditional municipal law crime of piracy. [114]

They referred to examples of this confusion by utilizing Stephen's *Digest of the Criminal Law* in which there is stated at the end of the definition of "Piracy by the law of nations," a sentence: "It is doubtful whether persons cruising in armed vessels with intent to commit piracies, are pirates or not." [115] The footnote that followed this sentence commented:

The doubt expressed at the end of the Article is founded on the absence of any express authority for the affirmative of the proposition, and on the absurdity of the negative. If a Queen's ship were to fall in with an armed vessel belonging to no state, and obviously cruising for piratical purposes, would the commanding officer hesitate to seize that vessel because it had not actually taken a prize? It seems equally difficult to suppose that the vessel would be permitted to escape, or that it could lawfully be arrested if the crew were not pirates. The language of several of the statutes given in Articles 112, 113, and 114, seems to imply that a pirate is the name of a known class of persons, like a soldier or sailor, and that a man may be a pirate though he has never actually robbed, as he may be a soldier though he has not actually fought.... [116]

In connection therewith, the Group raised the question:

Should not the doubt expressed by Stephen and by Oppenheim . . . be confined to the English traditional municipal law crime of piracy? [117]

And answered that:

. . . although the traditional nonstatutory crime of piracy in English law corresponded to international law piracy, there is not sufficient authority to justify the assertion that it was coextensive. Few if any states punish criminally the perpetrators of all acts which are piratical by the law of nations. [118]

---

[113] *Ibid.,* p. 820, emphasis added.
[114] *Ibid.,* p. 821.
[115] *Ibid.,* p. 820, from Stephen, *Digest of the Criminal Law* (5th ed.), p. 79.
[116] *Ibid.,* from Stephen, *op. cit.,* p. 78, footnote.
[117] *Ibid.,* p. 821.
[118] *Ibid.* At this point the Group refers to Steil, *op. cit.,* note 29, pp. 15-17; and Schlikker, *Die Völkerrechtliche Lehre von der Piraterie,* pp. 13, 24-27.

The Group demonstrated the contrasting views of Hall and Oppenheim regarding the location of the piratical act (see pp. 49 and
50).[119] Doubtless, the diverse opinions expressed by these two
leading experts in the field of international jurisprudence can be
succinctly defined by referring to the two distinctive matters set
forth by the Group. However, it is noteworthy, at this juncture,
to mention that Hall's position would tend to conform with
the thought of certain legal publicists of today who are interested
in revising the 1958 conventional articles regarding international
sea piracy. The possible extension of the doctrine of hot pursuit;
the possibility of piercing a state's sovereign immunity for aiding
and abetting an alleged pirate in refusing to take action (as opposed
to the actual granting of political asylum); and the possibility of
creating an international zone around the pirate, in order to neu-
tralize any rights accruing to him as an individual, will be matters
discussed later in this study. The main item to notice at this juncture
is the apparent lack of agreement and confusion amongst the
publicists concerning one of the most important areas; namely,
whether the piratical act is exclusively restricted to the geographic
area of high seas.[120] It would seem that there are few presumptions
or premises to work from in this study when dealing with recommendations. Valid arguments, pro and con, can be made for each
of the recommendations based upon the many different opinions
on the subject matter and the ultimate goals being sought. This
diversity of opinion is useful because it allows for a certain degree
of creativity in developing terms and concepts. The adaptability
of current incidents is not usually available to the publicist interested
in discussing a reexamination of the concepts necessary to update
what was presumed to be a settled area of international jurisprudence. Yet, it is a task which must be accomplished in order to add
vitality to international law. One cannot ignore the questions
raised by the legal publicists even if one disagrees with their views.

Article 3(3)
   3. Any act of instigation or of intentional facilitation of an act described in
paragraph 1 or paragraph 2 of this article.[121]

The Group intended, by this clause, to include "instigations
and facilitations of piratical acts . . ."[122] within the coverage of the

[119] *Ibid.*, pp. 821-822.
[120] For an analysis of the issue see Johnson, *op. cit.*, note 44, p. 68.
[121] Harvard Draft Convention, p. 822.
[122] *Ibid.*

definition of piracy with the provision that the "instigation or facilitation" is not subject to the common jurisdiction unless it takes place outside territorial jurisdiction.

Article 4

1. A ship is a pirate ship when it is devoted by the persons in dominant control to the purpose of committing an act described in the first sentence of paragraph 1 of Article 3, or to the purpose of committing any similar act within the territory of a state by descent from the high sea, provided in either case that the purposes of the persons in dominant control are not definitely limited to committing such acts against ships or territory subject to the jurisdiction of the state to which the ship belongs.

2. A ship does not cease to be a pirate ship after the commission of an act described in paragraph 1 of Article 3, or after the commission of any similar act within the territory of a state by descent from the high sea, as long as it continues under the same control.[123]

The Group stated that the purpose of this draft article was to exclude from the category of pirate ships those in control of persons whose purposes of violence or depredation are definitely limited to attacks against only ships and territory of the state to which the offending ship belongs. The reason for the inclusion of this article was that

... writers say that ships in the possession of crews with piratical intent are out of the protection of all laws and privileges, and sometimes the explanation is given that the offenders in control have thrown off their allegiance and are acting in defiance of law.[124]

An illustrative example given by the Group was set forth in the following question and their response thereto:

Should a band with criminal tendencies escape the jurisdiction of a state seizing their ship on the high sea because they could establish that they intended only a single definite offence or only offences against the ships of one or two foreign states? It is undesirable to permit the collateral motives or purposes of an offender to control the matter of state jurisdiction... However, the opposition to conceding a common jurisdiction over acts which definitely are directed only against the interest of the state of nationality of the offending ship, is strong enough to make it expedient to require an international element in at least the purposes of the offenders.[125]

The Group believed that crafts other than ships (for example small boats and aircraft) should be categorized with ships in this draft article as well as in Articles 1 and 5 of the draft convention.

[123] *Ibid.*
[124] *Ibid.*, p. 823.
[125] *Ibid.*

Therefore, where the criteria for the Article 4 definition are met, all these vessels are called pirate ships for convenience.[126]

Article 5
A ship may retain its national character although it has become a pirate ship. The retention or loss of national character is determined by the law of the state from which it was derived.[127]

The Group discussed the divergent positions concerning this article by stating that some publicists assert the view that a private vessel is "denationalized" because of its acts of piracy; whereas other publicists would contend that the pirates are "denationalized" as well as the vessel. However, the Group stated that:

... The legal consequences to which these assertions refer, ... include only the common jurisdiction (1) to seize the pirate ship and its officers, crew and contents and other piratical property and booty outside foreign territorial jurisdiction, (2) to direct the consequences of such a seizure, and (3) to prosecute and punish pirates under the law of the prosecuting state.[128]

Thus, the Group believed that the ordinary jurisdiction which existed because of the piracy no longer excluded the common jurisdiction on the high seas but would still exist and be otherwise unaffected.

In connection with this article, there were noted certain important differences between earlier and present wisdom. The Group commented:

Sea-robbery has not been dishonorable in all ages. Indeed at times, pirates of a sort have been regarded as local heroes, and political communities of considerable power have authorized and commended piratical enterprises. Nevertheless in all times of generally developed international trade, the private foreign pirate has been treated as an enemy of law and civilization by sea-faring mercantile communities... *Hostilities waged by and against him were not war...* Today, however, the international law of piracy does not simply cover a field of public armed conflict distinct from that of war. The present legal importance of piracy lies in the fact that it is a special basis of state jurisdiction, constituting a qualification of the modern doctrine and law of the freedom of the seas. ... This change in international relations has induced a finer discrimination and a wider range in the modern legal conception of piratical acts... *In the law of nations, properly speaking, a pirate is not a criminal, but his factual offence is the basis of a special jurisdiction in all states.*[129]

[126] *Ibid.*, p. 824. Article 1(5) defines ship as "any water craft or *air craft* of whatever size" (emphasis added).
[127] *Ibid.*, p. 825.
[128] *Ibid.*
[129] *Ibid.*, pp. 825-826, emphasis added.

If we can digress for a moment, what the Group stated may be correct, but, the legal publicists of today are actually calling for the piracy articles to mandate an "international crime" by requesting that the 1958 conventional articles on piracy be expanded to cover, *inter alia,* political as well as private acts. However, in order to constitute an international crime, there should be some form of uniform punishment and/or sanction prescribed rather than leaving this coverage to varying municipal laws. What would be necessary, therefore, would be to remove the "punishment" from the jurisdictional competence of the various states and to utilize a form of dispute settlement mechanism which would have a uniform scheme of prescriptions regarding penalties and punishment. If this does not become possible, perhaps the law of international sea piracy should be extended to cover situations regarding the utilization of the dispute settlement mechanism with relation to the capture and trial of the individual with forms of *advisory* penalties and punishments which could be requested by the offended state.[130] A state could be a defendant in such a trial and appropriate sanctions could be imposed if it were found that the state in any way assisted or encouraged the piracy which took place. In other words, why not extend this concept of a common or special jurisdiction to include punishment? Why should prosecution and punishment be left to states which do not have uniform municipal laws, if any laws at all? If there is a uniform conventional definition of acts of piracy, why not create a uniform conventional enforcement mechanism also?

Returning to the comments of the Group, they cited many different publicists with regard to material in connection with draft article 5:

... when the law of nations exercises criminal jurisdiction directly, it deals with persons whom it claims as its own citizens. When it punishes pirates, it does not punish the citizens of the State to which the pirates belonged, but cosmopolitan criminals, whom it regards as having ceased to be State citizens altogether in consequence of their having broken the laws of humanity as a whole, and become enemies of the human race. Citizen criminals, on the other hand, it simply hands over to the States whose laws they have broken.[131]

... The Pirate has no National character, and to whatever country he may have originally belonged, he is *justiciable* everywhere, being reputed out of the protection of all laws and privileges whatever.[132]

---

[130] For a discussion of "present" law, see Smith, *The Probable Necessity of an International Prison in Solving Hijacking,* 5 Int. Lawyer 269 (1971); and Paust, *op. cit.,* note 66.

[131] Harvard Draft Convention, p. 828, from Lorimer, *Institutes of the Law of Nations,* vol. II, p. 132.

[132] *Ibid.,* from Twiss, *op. cit.,* note 19, pp. 290-291, section 177.

A pirate ship may have a nationality and keep it even after it has committed acts of piracy, but this nationality would make no difference, and would not affect the exercise of measures of suppression.[133]

Article 6
   In a place not within the territorial jurisdiction of another state, a state may seize a pirate ship or a ship taken by piracy and possessed by pirates, and things or persons on board.[134]

The Group inserted this article (in contrast to Article 7) in order to allow the seizure of pirate ships and ships taken by piracy in any location outside the territorial jurisdiction of another state. However, notwithstanding this draft article, the Group included a much broader jurisdictional provision in Article 7.

Article 7
   1. In a place within the territorial jurisdiction of another state, a state may not pursue or seize a pirate ship or a ship taken by piracy and possessed by pirates; *except that if pursuit of such a ship is commenced by a state within its own territorial jurisdiction or in a place not within the territorial jurisdiction of any state, the pursuit may be continued into or over the territorial sea of another state and seizure may be made there,* unless prohibited by the other state.
   2. *If a seizure is made within the territorial jurisdiction of another state* in accordance with the provisions of paragraph 1 of this article, *the state making the seizure shall give prompt notice to the other state,* and shall tender possession of the ship and other things seized and the custody of persons seized.
   3. If the tender provided for in paragraph 2 of this article is not accepted, the state making the seizure may proceed as if the seizure had been made on the high sea.[135]

The Group commented that *prevention* was the purpose of this article. Those pirates attempting to avoid capture of pursuers by going into the territorial waters of another state would therefore be apprehended. What the article is permitting is the

... *continuance of pursuit of a pirate ship,* rightfully commenced, into or over marginal seas foreign to the pursuing state, unless the privilege has been withdrawn by the littoral state...[136]

The Group also commented that any damage caused by the pursuing state would be fully compensated for by virtue of the proposed draft Article 8 as well as by

   [133] *Ibid.,* p. 830, from Reply of Rumania, *op. cit.,* note 21, p. 210.
   [134] *Ibid.,* p. 832. Compare Article 105 of the *Informal Composite Negotiating Text* as it appears in Appendix 3 to this chapter.
   [135] *Ibid.,* emphasis added. Compare Article 111 of the *Informal Composite Negotiating Text* as it appears in Appendix 3.
   [136] *Ibid.*

... the paramount right of the littoral state to the disposition of the captured persons and property.[137]

As with nearly every other draft article that had heretofore been discussed by the Group, it was pointed out that there was diverse opinion among legal publicists on this subject. There were publicists who would state that international law allowed this form of hot pursuit into the territorial waters of another state at least if the

... littoral state has not a force at hand to make the capture and does not prohibit the pursuit. . .[138]

Other writers argued that the right of hot pursuit existed regardless of the protests of the littoral state. The main point of interest, aside from the very existence of this article, itself, is that

... there is no determining precedent on the matter. It is believed that the article satisfies at once the argument for emergency rights of pursuit into foreign territorial waters and the argument for protection of the littoral state's sovereignty against abusive invasions.[139]

Various authorities were offered on the subject.[140] The reader will observe that this article was *not* eventually adopted by the Conference States at the 1958 conference; however, the article, or a modified version of it, could prove useful if the piracy laws were expanded and revised to correct current problems arising from recent incidents. Obviously, the article was considered too controversial to be included in any international conference occurring in the 1950's. At that time states were concerned with the abuses which might arise due to any extension of the hot pursuit doctrine to permit pursuit into the territorial waters of another state.[141] These states could still be concerned but they may consider that the recent incidents which have occurred present an overriding necessity for revision of the 1958 conventional articles. With the advent of a

---

[137] *Ibid.*, p. 833.

[138] *Ibid.*

[139] *Ibid.* See Poulantzas, *The Right of Hot Pursuit in International Law* (Leiden: A. W. Sijthoff), 1969.

[140] The Group made reference to the following works (as appears in the Harvard Draft Convention): "Wheaton, *International Law* (8th ed.) Sec. 428, Dana's note 207 on the case of the *Chesapeake; The Magellan Pirates* (1853), 1 Spinks Ecclesiastical and Admiralty Reports 81, 164 Eng. R. 47; J. De Louter, *Le droit international public passif*, Vol. 1, p. 412; Report of the Sub-Committee of the League of Nations Committee of Experts for the Progressive Codification of International Law, *Draft Treaty on Piracy*, Article 5; Pradier-Fodéré, *Droit international public*, Vol. 5, pp. 803-804, Sec. 2495."

[141] What was in fact incorporated in the 1958 Convention on the High Seas regarding hot pursuit was Article 23 (see Appendix 1 to Chapter II). Paragraph 2 of this article states that "The right of hot pursuit *ceases as soon as the ship pursued enters the territorial sea of its own country or of a third State*" (emphasis added).

possible dispute settlement mechanism, this abuse or danger of abuse may be less of a problem. Further discussion of this topic, however, will appear in later chapters (pp. 161-163). For the time being it is important to observe that even though "expediency" was a priority concern, the Group thought that such a provision would be a workable one and that it should be included in their draft convention on piracy.

Article 8
    If a pursuit is continued or a seizure is made within the territorial jurisdiction of another state in accordance with the provisions of paragraph 1 of Article 7, the state continuing the pursuit or making the seizure is liable to the other state for any damage done by the pursuing ship, other than damage done to the pirate ship or the ship possessed by pirates, or to persons and things on board.[142]

The Group believed that this draft article should be included to complement Article 7. If the littoral state gave an implied license to allow pursuit into its territorial waters pursuant to this article, then the pursuing state should be responsible for any damage done to the interest of the littoral state. The Group believed that without this provision, the international community would not agree to hot pursuit.[143]
    As will be discussed more fully in later chapters,[144] this damage provision or a similar one could be utilized by any dispute settlement mechanism should the necessity arise. The main problem is not the littoral state's fear of not receiving payment for damages, but that its sovereign right over its territorial waters will, in some manner, be infringed upon by allowing the entry of foreign vessels which are allegedly in hot pursuit. To the contrary, one can argue that the doctrine of hot pursuit could be negated by a sympathetic littoral state just by granting the alleged pirate political asylum, thereby ending the matter without allowing the hot pursuit to continue further into its territorial waters. Perhaps this is feasible under the current 1958 conventional articles. However, should the 1958 conventional articles be changed, the granting or denying of political asylum should be taken out of the hands of the littoral state and placed within the purview of the dispute settlement mechanism in order to avoid the explosion of an alleged piratical

---

[142] Harvard Draft Convention, p. 834.
[143] Compare the cases of the *Chesapeake* (1863) and the *Florida* (1864), Wharton, *International Law Digest*, section 27; Wheaton, *International Law* (8th ed.), section 428, note by Dana, p. 207. These materials are discussed by the Group in the Harvard Draft Convention, pp. 835-838.
[144] Appendix 7 to Chapter IV.

act into a major upheaval. The prisoner could be placed in an international prison[145] in order to avoid sanctions brought by terrorist groups against the states involved. In any event, it is certainly a consideration worthy of exploring if, after reviewing the recent incidents, it is conceded that piracy laws need revision.

Article 9
If a seizure because of piracy is made by a state in violation of the jurisdiction of another state, the state making the seizure shall, upon the demand of the other state surrender or release the ship, things and persons seized, and shall make appropriate reparation.[146]

The Group included this provision as a corollary to draft Article 8. It was thought that there should be coverage for reparation in connection with wrongful seizures other than those occurring in the context of Article 8 – for example where the license of Article 7(1) or some other license does not apply – and, for seizures on board a foreign ship (not a pirate ship), on the high seas. The Group included certain citations which represented the "traditional" wisdom on the subject in connection with this type of situation.[147] but this authority appears to be rather dated – procedurally, at least.

Article 10
If a ship seized on suspicion of piracy outside the territorial jurisdiction of the state making the seizure, is neither a pirate ship nor a ship taken by piracy and possessed by pirates, and if the ship is not subject to seizure on other grounds, the state making the seizure shall be liable to the state to which the ship belongs for any damage caused by the seizure.[148]

Article 11
1. In a place not within the territorial jurisdiction of any state, a foreign ship may be approached and on reasonable suspicion that it is a pirate ship or a ship taken by piracy and possessed by pirates, it may be stopped and questioned to ascertain its character.
2. If the ship is neither a pirate ship nor a ship taken by piracy and possessed by pirates, and if it is not subject to such interference on other grounds, the state making the interference shall be liable to the state to which the ship belongs for any damage caused by the interference.[149]

---

[145] Smith, *op. cit.*, note 130, p. 274, recommends the development of an international prison for hijackers at Spandau (the West German prison where war criminals from World War II were held) or, in the alternative, the construction of a prison in a country without an airline, such as Liechtenstein.
[146] Harvard Draft Convention, p. 834.
[147] The various types of situations in which the Group felt reparations might be appropriate as well as the methods of determining the measure of reparation are dealt with extensively by the Group.
[148] Harvard Draft Convention, p. 834. Compare Article 106 of the *Informal Composite Negotiating Text* as it appears in Appendix 3.
[149] *Ibid.*, p. 838.

One problem confronting the Group when it prepared these two draft articles concerned the fact that, although there was authority for warships to stop, search, and seize a ship on the high seas on mere suspicion of piracy, without incurring any liability, this practice would not now be tolerated especially since this right no longer appeared to be necessary because

... For nearly a hundred years large scale piracy has been almost unknown, the right to search as a police measure is no longer of pressing importance, the demand for freedom of the seas has attained overwhelming force, and a state would repel any proposal which might entail foreign officious police supervision of its commerce on the high sea with the same obstinate determination that met attempts to police the seas against the detested and internationally condemned slave trade during the nineteenth century.[150]

Extensive authorities were cited by the Group on this subject but in its own comments the Group stated that

... in circumstances of common danger, properly managed police supervision would meet with hearty co-operation instead of objection from other states.[151]

As a practical matter, if there were adequate grounds for suspicion, the state would more than likely order the seizure and assume the responsibility.

Article 12
A seizure because of piracy may be made only on behalf of a state, and only by a person who has been authorized to act on its behalf.[152]

One view on this subject is that private ships should be permitted to seize pirate vessels, with or without state authority, especially if the piratical vessel had attacked the private ship. Another is maintained that only warships or other vessels carrying the authority of the flag state should be permitted to attack the pirate vessel. The Group believed that it was better to adopt a position

... that only states should exercise the special authority under international law to seize for piracy, so that clear state responsibility will accompany each exercise of this special authority.[153]

Thus, while warships may have been the traditional vessel used for capture, other means, such as police boats, could be utilized today.

---

[150] *Ibid.*, p. 839.
[151] *Ibid.* See Appendix 6 to this chapter.
[152] *Ibid.*, p. 846. Compare Article 107 of the Composite Text as it appears in Appendix 3.
[153] *Ibid.*, p. 847.

Article 13
1. A state, in accordance with its law, may dispose of ships and other property lawfully seized because of piracy.
2. The law of the state must conform to the following principles:
(a) The interests of innocent persons are not affected by the piratical possession or use of property, nor by seizure because of such possession or use.
(b) Claimants of any interest in the property are entitled to a reasonable opportunity to prove their claims.
(c) A claimant who establishes the validity of his claim is entitled to receive the property or compensation therefor, subject to a charge for salvage and expenses of administration.[154]

The Group pointed out that one of the views emanating from Roman times and sometimes adopted by states in their municipal laws regarding the treatment of goods taken by pirates was "pirata dominium non mutat."[155] Therefore, the purpose of drafting Article 13 was to eliminate all differences in principles concerning the treatment of claims of innocent parties to a pirate ship and its equipment, and claims to other property seized as piratical or from the possession of pirates. Thus, all property would be covered by a uniform rule of international law. This draft article permitted the state to decide what property, acquired by piratical acts, it would seize within its jurisdiction but also required the state to recognize the interest of innocent owners and lienors.

The Group pointed out that at the time of preparing its study, only the ship and other property actually devoted or destined for use in a piratical enterprise were subject to prize condemnation or to confiscation in criminal proceedings against the property claims of innocent third parties. Other property seized from the possession of pirates generally was subject to reclamation by robbed or defrauded owners or lienors, upon proof of their claims within a certain period and upon payment of charges, which sometimes included a reward to the captors.[156]

Article 14
1. A state which has lawful custody of a person suspected of piracy may prosecute and punish that person.
2. Subject to the provisions of this convention, the law of the state which exercises such jurisdiction defines the crime, governs the procedure and prescribes the penalty.

---

[154] *Ibid.*, pp. 847-848.
[155] *Ibid.*, p. 848.
[156] Compare Article 105 of the Composite Text: ".. . The courts of the State which carried out the seizure may . . . determine the action to be taken with regard to the ships, aircraft, or property [seized], subject to the rights of third parties acting in good faith." See also Appendix 7 to this chapter.

3. The law of the state must, however, assure protection to accused aliens as follows:
(a) The accused persons must be given a fair trial before an impartial tribunal without unreasonable delay.
(b) The accused person must be given humane treatment during his confinement pending trial.
(c) No cruel and unusual punishment may be inflicted.
(d) No discrimination may be made against the nationals of any state.
    4. A state may intercede diplomatically to assure this protection to one of its nationals who is accused in another state.[157]

The Group included this draft article in its draft convention in order to give the capturing state jurisdiction to prosecute the alleged pirate, provided that the state seized the pirate "lawfully." This "lawfulness" would depend upon international law and could be enlarged, as the Group envisaged the matter, by treaty or other forms of agreements between states. It was also thought that to "define in detail the power to seize" would not be wise because the "principles are familiar" and any rare occurrence which was not covered by these familiar principles would probably not be "peculiar to the law of piracy."[158] The Group was primarily concerned with the possibility that the alleged pirate would be summarily tried and executed without a fair trial:

> Obviously general adoption of a uniform procedural code for cases of piracy is not possible at present, even if it were clearly desirable. Also it would be difficult to obtain agreement on uniform penalties. Therefore, the law of the prosecuting state in general should control these matters. However, it is feasible and desirable to stipulate for reasonable procedure, a fair trial, and humane treatment and punishment.[159]

It is apparent that the Group was concerned with the expediency and practicality of the situation. They proposed draft articles which they thought would meet with a general consensus among Conference States and that a resulting convention would thereby create the special basis of jurisdiction which they were striving to achieve. Of course, it is also apparent that the various municipal laws of states would not even contain provisions relating to piracy. Therefore, these states would have to prosecute the alleged pirate for murder or some other crime prescribed in their penal codes.[160] In any event, up until the *Revised Single Negotiating Text* (1976),[161]

---

[157] Harvard Draft Convention, p. 852.
[158] *Ibid.*
[159] *Ibid.*, at p. 853, emphasis added.
[160] Most modern states do not, in fact, have any statutes directed specifically at the crime of piracy, as becomes evident on examining the statutes collected in the Harvard Draft Convention, pp. 891-1011.
[161] U.N. Doc. A/CONF.62/WP.8/Rev.1 and A/CONF.62/WP.9/Rev.1 (1976).

draft articles concerning a dispute settlement mechanism had not been included in the draft conventions prepared as a basis for discussion by the law of the sea conferences. With the advent of states being willing to review draft articles concerning this mechanism and the possibility, therefore, of creating some type of authority to control disputes,[162] perhaps it is desirable for states to discuss the adoption of a uniform procedural code for cases of alleged piracy. It is envisaged that the authority, pursuant to conventional dictates, be permitted to prescribe a penalty or sanction from a list of possible alternatives which have been prepared in conjunction with this uniform code. Perhaps the authority could detain the prisoners (assuming them to be individuals) in an international prison[163] until that authority could hear the case. The authority could decide the merits of the case and take into consideration any pleas in mitigation or for political asylum.[164] the capturing state or the state harboring the pirate could argue that it would consider granting political asylum and the authority could decide if it should grant relief in a given situation. (The authority could also prescribe penalties if it found that states were guilty of aiding and abetting alleged pirates or acts of piracy.) In other words, one suggestion could be to take the competence to prescribe and enforce laws regarding acts of piracy completely out of the hands of state municipal laws (assuming they have said laws) and place the entire jurisdictional area, whether "political" or not, within the framework of revised 1958 conventional articles. One of the problems faced today by nations with regard to acts of terrorism is the fact that some states may agree with the terrorists' political goals and may not wish to allow extradition either because of their own sympathetic views or because they simply do not have any mechanism permitting extradition. Some nations may be afraid of antagonizing the terrorists or are fearful of retribution. While there is no method of guaranteeing that revengeful acts will not take place, at least a mechanism could be created to have the alleged pirate

[162] For specific information on the type of dispute settlement mechanism proposed see notes 21 and 22 of Chapter I, and also Janis, *op. cit.*, note 73; and *Law of the Sea, op. cit.*, note 101.

[163] For an analysis of possible international responses to terrorism see note 130.

[164] The issue of "political asylum" presents a difficult question to a state which must attempt to balance the personal safety of air travelers and an orderly international air transport against its political and ideological values. Many commentators believe that air hijacking can only be deterred by an international convention which accords a right of extradition to the state whose aircraft was hijacked. To this extent, for a number of reasons, many states are unwilling to go. See Green, *op. cit.*, note 55; and Joyner, *op. cit.*, note 55, pp. 116-165.

presented to the authority for what would hopefully be an impartial judgement.[165]

Article 15
A state may not prosecute an alien for an act of piracy for which he has been charged and convicted or acquitted in a prosecution in another state.[166]

Here, the obvious intent of the Group was to protect the alleged pirates from double jeopardy and double punishment. However, the Group, realizing that the draft article did not represent a consensus or principle of international law, stated that

... There is authority for the view that a similar principle should be applied in municipal law as a logical consequence of the tenet that general piracy is an offence against all states.[167]

The quotation from the *United States v. The Pirates* (*supra*, p. 70)[168] was presented by the Group without comment. Obviously, it is self-evident why states should not be left to enforce their municipal laws regarding piracy. If nations are truly interested in the progressive development of international law, all conventional articles should be reviewed regularly in order to see if revision and change are in order. What is needed is uniformity and codification of international law with constant revision and updating of convention articles in order to maintain the integrity of the agreed-upon consensus of the Conference States.

Article 16
The provisions of this convention do not diminish a state's right under international law to take measures for the protection of its nationals, its ships and its commerce against interference on or over the high sea, when such measures are not based upon jurisdiction over piracy.[169]

This rather innocuous draft article was apparently inserted by the Group in order to offset the "private ends" requirement. Before discussing its implications, reasons for insertion, and the various diverse viewpoints regarding political motivations, it is important to recall once again that the purpose of the Group's work was to create a special and common basis for jurisdiction regarding the "traditional" norms relating to piracy as existed at that time. The Group, throughout its work, was looking to all

[165] See Green, *op. cit.*, note 55, pp. 87-88.
[166] Harvard Draft Convention, p. 856.
[167] *Ibid.*
[168] 5 Wheat (U.S.) 184. The reader is encouraged, at this point, to reread the part of this opinion already presented. See Appendix 8 of this chapter for another part of the opinion relevant at this point.
[169] Harvard Draft Convention, p. 857.

precedents on the subject of piracy.[170] However, nearly all of the publicists, cases and conventions cited occurred during a period when piracy flourished on the high seas. And, it has also been observed that even though various traditional acts of piracy on the high seas (as opposed to territorial waters) had been diminishing for at least 100 years prior to their research, the Group still had difficulty in attempting to translate the diverse opinions into "norms" which could be embodied into a draft convention which could later serve, for the sake of expediency and practical considerations, as a "consensus" for nations to agree upon. The problem, of course, is that although traditional methods of piracy have long since died on the high seas (as opposed to territorial waters), new methods and reasons for committing piratical and terrorist activities have taken the place of the old. Today, some legal publicists believe that an international crime of piracy should include modern, political forms of terrorism. If this argument is extended one step further, perhaps this international crime could be created to include uniform penalties, as well as a special jurisdiction before a new type of authority or other dispute settlement mechanism, for acts committed regardless of geographical location.

Returning to the Group's work, the draft article was inserted to cover

... *inter alia* the troublesome matter of illegal forcible acts of political ends against foreign commerce, committed on the high sea by unrecognized organizations.[171]

The Group's example:

For instance a revolutionary organization uses an armed ship to establish a blockage against foreign commerce, or to stop and search foreign ships for contraband, or to seize necessary supplies from foreign ships. These acts are illegal under international law, at least if the revolutionary organization has not been recognized as a belligerent by the offended state, and in some cases the offended state has proceeded to capture or destroy the offending ship.[172]

[170] See Article 38, Statute of the International Court of Justice, 59 Stat. 1055, T.S. No. 993, p. 25, 1970 Y.B. of the U.N. 1310, as follows:
"1. The Court, whose function is to decide in accordance with international law such disputes as are submitted to it, shall apply:
a. international conventions, whether general or particular, establishing rules expressly recognized by the contesting states;
b. international custom, as evidence of a general practice accepted as law;
c. the general principles of law recognized by civilized nations;
d. subject to the provisions of Article 59, judicial decisions and the teachings of the most highly qualified publicists of the various nations, as subsidiary means for the determination of rules of law.
2. This provision shall not prejudice the power of the Court to decide a case ex aequo et bono, if the parties agree thereto."
[171] Harvard Draft Convention, p. 857.
[172] *Ibid.*

Again, as occurred in connection with every draft article discussed in this chapter, there really was no consensus among nations in connection with this problem. The Group pointed out that some legal publicists would hold that

... such illegal attacks on foreign commerce by unrecognized revolutionaries are piracies in the international law sense; and there is even judicial authority to this effect . . .[173]

The Group, however, thought it better that these types of cases do not fall within the common jurisdiction, thereby letting the offended state deal with the matter as it saw fit. The Group did not offer any reason why this would be the better view but probably, if they were being consistent in thought, they believed it would be "expedient" and more readily acceptable by the international community. One could argue whether these are justifiable reasons for accepting one view in lieu of another. However, the Group stated that:

These cases often involve serious political considerations which may direct the course of action of the offended State. The Article does not dictate any course of action; it merely preserves such criminal and police jurisdiction as is given by traditional law.[174]

In addition, the Group stated that if insurgents attacked vessels with ". . . a motive of private plunder . . .", it could constitute piracy under its draft convention.[175] In connection with this draft article, the diverse opinions which existed among the legal publicists and jurists can be highlighted by referring to just a few of the authorities utilized by the Group.[176]

It is not surprising that there existed such diverse opinions when one considers that municipal laws of different states relating to the topic of piracy, as in other topics covered by domestic legislation, can vary greatly. Also, the reader is confronted with treatments in treatises which pronounce the "better" views on the subject. When the draft articles prepared by the International Law Commission were eventually presented to the Conference States, the rationale behind all of these diverse opinions had to be molded into various

---

[173] *Ibid.*

[174] *Ibid.*

[175] *Ibid.*

[176] The Group made reference to a number of authorities at this point. See: Report of the Sub-Committee for the Progressive Codification of International Law, *op. cit.*, note 13; *Hyde, International Law* (Boston: Little, Brown), 1945, section 233; Brown, in *The Ambrose Light*, 25 Fed. 408, pp. 412-413; Steil, *op. cit.*, note 29, pp. 94-96; Hall, *A Treatise on International Law* (Oxford: Oxford University Press), 8th ed., pp. 314-315; Wheaton, *Elements of International Law* (Oxford: Oxford University Press), 8th ed., p. 200. See Appendix 9 of this chapter for a reproduction of some of the most significant parts of this authority.

political considerations so that it could be determined if a consensus
of opinion could be reached among the Conference States as to the
ultimate adoption of a conventional definition for acts of piracy. It
must have been obvious to these states that perhaps the only
traditional "norm" lay in the dated methods of committing piracy.
These methods of committing piracy were considered as a settled
matter save for the possibility of "aircraft" committing said acts.[177]
In other words, the Conference States felt comfortable about
selecting a suitable definition for acts of piracy when they were
referring to traditional norms and governing concepts. There were
many diverse views on the subject of piracy because of the varying
municipal laws; however, the states could select the opinions which
they thought were most satisfactory for the creation of this common
jurisdiction at a time when traditional forms of piracy and piratical
acts were considered moot or, at least, dated.

Article 17
1. The provisions of this convention shall supersede any inconsistent provisions relating to piracy in treaties in force among parties to this convention,
except that such inconsistent provisions shall not be superseded in so far as
they affect only the interests of the parties to such treaties *inter se.*
2. The provisions of this convention shall not prevent a party from entering
into an agreement concerning piracy containing provisions inconsistent with
this convention which affect only the interests of the parties to that agreement
inter se.[178]

The Group pointed out that one of the "defects" of multilateral
conventions which are supposed to express "international law" is
that changes and modifications cannot take place without the common consent of all parties:

... Probably some modification of this traditional thesis will be forced by
events in time, but at present the difficulty it raises is a matter of importance.
Especially in connection with conventions which define the jurisdiction of
states the difficulty needs attention; for these at least are similar in purpose
and effect to a federal constitution. Therefore, it is worth considering whether
it would not be wise to provide early in the process of codifying international
law, *some amending device,* other than unanimous consent, against such
annoying impediments to needed changes.[179]

It is obvious that this draft article permitted nations to enter into
other arguments which would either extend or restrict the provisions
of the draft convention. Nevertheless, said agreements would affect

---

[177] Note that Article 1(5) of the Harvard Draft Convention defines ship as any ". . .
water craft or air craft of whatever size," thus including air craft within the purview of
the convention.
[178] Harvard Draft Convention, p. 866.
[179] *Ibid.,* emphasis added.

only ". . . relations between the parties to the new agreements."[180] The purpose of this device would be to allow for greater flexibility rather than to attempt to achieve a consensus among the states.

Article 18
   The parties to this convention agree to make every expedient use of their powers to prevent piracy, separately and in co-operation.[181]

This article was inserted to respond to the subject of Questionnaire No. 6 propounded by the League of Nations Committee of Experts:

Whether, and to what extent, it would be possible to establish, by an international convention, appropriate provisions to secure the suppression of piracy.[182]

The feeling of the Group with respect to this matter was that:

States probably would not be willing to assume a more definite general duty to seize or to prosecute all pirates, for this would involve liabilities for nonperformance which might in some cases prove burdensome.[183]

However, the Group believed that piracy could be suppressed further by supplementary agreements between states which would define policing, prosecution and extradition. Relating this position concerning implementation of the draft convention to our study, if certain suggestions become feasible, the 1958 conventional articles on piracy and related 1958 conventional articles concerning hot pursuit[184] could be revised in order to coincide with a dispute settlement procedure adopted by the Conference States. For example, the international authority charged with the duty of settling disputes could have a uniform scheme which would provide for, *inter alia,* policing, prosecution and extradition procedures. As far as seizing pirates, certain regulations could be established to provide for the offended nation or an international police to capture the alleged pirate where a coastal or other state is either unable or unwilling to act.

Article 19
   1. If there should arise between the High Contracting Parties a dispute of any kind relating to the interpretation or application of the present convention, and if such dispute cannot be satisfactorily settled by diplomacy, it shall be settled in accordance with any applicable agreements in force between the parties to the dispute providing for the settlement of international disputes.

   [180] *Ibid.*
   [181] *Ibid.*, p. 867.
   [182] *Ibid.* Note the reply of France to Questionnaire 6, reproduced in Appendix 10 to this chapter.
   [183] *Ibid.*
   [184] Article 23 of the 1958 Convention on the High Seas deals with the subject of hot pursuit. It is reproduced in Appendix 1 to Chapter II.

2. In case there is no such agreement in force between the parties to the dispute, the dispute shall be referred to arbitration or judicial settlement. In the absence of agreement on the choice of another tribunal, the dispute shall, at the request of any one of the parties to the dispute, be referred to the Permanent Court of International Justice, if all the parties to the dispute are parties to the protocol of December 16, 1920, relating to the Statute of the Court; and if any of the parties to the dispute is not a party to the Protocol of December 16, 1920, to an arbitral tribunal constituted in accordance with the provisions of the Convention for the Pacific Settlement of International Disputes, signed at The Hague, October 18, 1907.[185]

The Group pointed out that this draft article was included in the draft conventions on Diplomatic Privileges and Immunities, Piracy, Legal Position and Function of Consuls, and Competence of Courts with regard to Foreign States. The fact that

... Many states are bound by treaties, conventions, and agreements, to follow a carefully outlined procedure for the settlement of disputes with other states ...[186]

was the reason for inserting the expression "applicable agreements in force between the parties to the dispute" which was likewise thought to take into account the extensions of the law of pacific settlement in the recent years leading up to the research conducted by the Group, as well as to consider any possible future extensions.

Naturally, with the advent of the United Nations and the International Court of Justice, some of the comments made by the Group would not be applicable today. However, today the Conference States are currently considering revisions in 1958 law of the sea conventions. They are also discussing the possibility of creating a dispute settlement mechanism which could, if new conventional articles were drafted with this intent, cover disputes arising from the 1958 conventional articles on piracy.

Before discussing the development of the 1958 conventional articles on piracy, however, it is important to review the work of the International Law Commission (the Commission) which commenced in 1949, some seventeen years after the publication of the draft convention prepared by the Group. This is the next step in the examination of the development of the international law on sea piracy. The Commission had before it the draft convention and comments of the Group. The Commission was also concerned with drafting articles which would be suitable to the Conference States. Its attitudes and reflections will be set forth in order to permit the reader to obtain some insight into the "practicalities" of presenting

[185] Harvard Draft Convention, p. 867.
[186] Ibid. p. 870.

recommendations for adoption at an international conference on law of the sea.

APPENDIX 1 TO CHAPTER III

Harvard Research in International Law, Draft Convention on Piracy with Comments, 26 Am. J. of Int'l L. 749 (1932)

Article 1
As the terms are used in this convention:

1. The term "jurisdiction" means the jurisdiction of a state under international law as distinguished from municipal law.

2. The term "territorial jurisdiction" means the jurisdiction of a state under international law over its land, its territorial waters and the air above its land and territorial waters. The term does not include the jurisdiction of a state over its ships outside its territory.

3. The term "territorial sea" means that part of the sea which is included in the territorial waters of a state.

4. The term "high sea" means that part of the sea which is not included in the territorial waters of any state.

5. The term "ship" means any water craft or air craft of whatever size.

Article 2
Every state has jurisdiction to prevent piracy and to seize and punish persons and to seize and dispose of property because of piracy. This jurisdiction is defined and limited by this convention.

Article 3
Piracy is any of the following acts, committed in a place not within the territorial jurisdiction of any state: ·

1. Any act of violence or of depredation committed with intent to rob, rape, wound, enslave, imprison or kill a person or with intent to steal or destroy property, for private ends without bona fide purpose of asserting a claim of right, provided that the act is connected with an attack on or from the sea or in or from the air. If the act is connected with an attack which starts from on board ship, either that ship or another ship which is involved must be a pirate ship or a ship without national character.

2. Any act of voluntary participation in the operation of a ship with knowledge of facts which make it a pirate ship.

3. Any act of instigation or of intentional facilitation of an act described in paragraph 1 or paragraph 2 of this article.

Article 4
1. A ship is a pirate ship when it is devoted by the persons in dominant control to the purpose of committing an act described in the first sentence of paragraph 1 of Article 3, or to the purpose of committing any similar act within the territory of a state by descent from the high sea, provided in either case that the purposes of the persons in dominant control are not definitely limited to committing such acts against ships or territory subject to the jurisdiction of the state to which the ship belongs.

2. A ship does not cease to be a pirate ship after the commission of an act described in paragraph 1 of Article 3, or after the commission of any similar

act within the territory of a state by descent from the high sea, as long as it continues under the same control.

Article 5
A ship may retain its national character although it has become a pirate ship. The retention or loss of national character is determined by the law of the state from which it was derived.

Article 6
In a place not within the territorial jurisdiction of another state, a state may seize a pirate ship taken by piracy and possessed by pirates, and things or persons on board.

Article 7
1. In a place within the territorial jurisdiction of another state, a state may not pursue or seize a pirate ship or a ship taken by piracy and possessed by pirates; except that if pursuit of such a ship is commenced by a state within its own territorial jurisdiction or in a place not within the territorial jurisdiction of any state, the pursuit may be continued into or over the territorial sea of another state and seizure may be made there, unless prohibited by the other state.
2. If a seizure is made within the territorial jurisdiction of another state in accordance with the provisions of paragraph 1 of this article, the state making the seizure shall give prompt notice to the other state, and shall tender possession of the ship and other things seized and the custody of persons seized.
3. If the tender provided for in paragraph 2 of this article is not accepted, the state making the seizure may proceed as if the seizure had been made on the high sea.

Article 8
If a pursuit is continued or a seizure is made within the territorial jurisdiction of another state in accordance with the provisions of paragraph 1 of Article 7, the state continuing the pursuit or making the seizure is liable to the other state for any damage done by the pursuing ship, other than damage done to the pirate ship or the ship possessed by pirates, or to persons and things on board.

Article 9
If a seizure because of piracy is made by a state in violation of the jurisdiction of another state, the state making the seizure shall, upon the demand of the other state, surrender or release the ship, things and persons seized, and shall make appropriate reparation.

Article 10
If a ship seized on suspicion of piracy outside the territorial jurisdiction of the state making the seizure, is neither a pirate ship nor a ship taken by piracy and possessed by pirates, and if the ship is not subject to seizure on other grounds, the state making the seizure shall be liable to the state to which the ship belongs for any damage caused by the seizure.

Article 11
1. In a place not within the territorial jurisdiction of any state, a foreign ship may be approached and on reasonable suspicion that it is a pirate ship or a ship taken by piracy and possessed by pirates, it may be stopped and questioned to ascertain its character.
2. If the ship is neither a pirate ship nor a ship taken by piracy and possessed by pirates, and if it is not subject to such interference on other grounds, the state making the interference shall be liable to the state to which the ship belongs for any damage caused by the interference.

Article 12
A seizure because of piracy may be made only on behalf of a state, and only by a person who has been authorized to act on its behalf.

Article 13
1. A state, in accordance with its law, may dispose of ships and other property lawfully seized because of piracy.
2. The law of the state must conform to the following principles:
(a) The interests of innocent persons are not affected by the piratical possession or use of property, nor by seizure because of such possession or use.
(b) Claimants of any interest in the property are entitled to receive the property or compensation therefor, subject to a fair charge for salvage and expenses of administration.

Article 14
1. A state which has lawful custody of a person suspected of piracy may prosecute and punish that person.
2. Subject to the provisions of this convention, the law of the state which exercises such jurisdiction defines the crime, governs the procedure and prescribes the penalty.
3. The law of the state must, however, assure protection to accused aliens as follows:
(a) The accused person must be given a fair trial before an impartial tribunal without unreasonable delay.
(b) The accused person must be given humane treatment during his confinement pending trial.
(c) No cruel and unusual punishment may be inflicted.
(d) No discrimination may be made against the nationals of any state.
4. A state may intercede diplomatically to assure this protection to one of its nationals who is accused in another state.

Article 15
A state may not prosecute an alien for an act of piracy for which he has been charged and convicted or acquitted in a prosecution in another state.

Article 16
The provisions of this convention do not diminish a state's right under international law to take measures for the protection of its nationals, its ships and its commerce against interference on or over the high sea, when such measures are not based upon jurisdiction over piracy.

Article 17

1. The provisions of this convention shall supersede any inconsistent provisions relating to piracy in treaties in force among parties to this convention, except that such inconsistent provisions shall not be superseded in so far as they affect only the interests of the parties to such treaties *inter se.*

2. The provisions of this convention shall not prevent a party from entering into an agreement concerning piracy containing provisions inconsistent with this convention which affect only the interests of the parties to that agreement *inter se.*

Article 18

The parties to this convention agree to make every expedient use of their powers to prevent piracy, separately and in co-operation.

Article 19

1. If there should arise between the High Contracting Parties a dispute of any kind relating to the interpretation or application of the present convention, and if such dispute cannot be satisfactorily settled by diplomacy, it shall be settled in accordance with any applicable agreements in force between the parties to the dispute providing for the settlement of international disputes.

2. In case there is no such agreement in force between the parties to the dispute, the dispute shall be referred to arbitration or judicial settlement. In the absence of agreement on the choice of another tribunal, the dispute shall, at the request of any one of the parties to the dispute, be referred to the Permanent Court of International Justice, if all the parties to the dispute are parties to the Protocol of December 16, 1920, relating to the Statute of the Court; and if any of the parties to the dispute is not a party to the Protocol of December 16, 1920, to an arbitral tribunal constituted in accordance with the provisions of the Convention for the Pacific Settlement of International Disputes, signed at The Hague, October 18, 1907.

APPENDIX 2 TO CHAPTER III

The Trials of Major Stede Bonnet, and thirty-three others, at the Court of Vice-Admiralty, at Charles-Town, in South Carolina, for Piracy: 5 George I. A.D. 1718, pp. 1234-1237; 15 How, St. Tr. 1231 (1718): Charge to the jury. [Original Greek references and footnotes have been omitted.]

How as to the nature of the offence: piracy is a robbery committed upon the sea, and a pirate is a sea thief. Indeed, the word "pirata" as it derived from...[187] "transire, a transeundo mare," was anciently taken in a good and honourable sense, and signified a maritime knight, and an admiral or commander at sea; as appears by the several testimonies and records cited to that purpose, by that learned antiquary Sir Henry Spelman in his Glossarium. And out of him the same sense of the word is remarked by Dr. Cowel, in his Interpreter; and by

[187] Greek derivations are omitted.

Blount in his Law Dictionary. But afterwards the word was taken in an ill sense, and signified a sea rover or robber; either from . . ., deceptio, dolus, deceipt, or from . . ., transire, of their wandering up and down, and resting in no place, but coasting hither and thither to do mischief: and from this sense, . . . seamale-factors were called . . ., pirates.

Therefore a pirate is thus defined by my Lord Coke: "This word 'pirate,'" saith he, in Latin "pirata," is derived from the Greek . . ., which again is fetched from . . . a transeundo mare,' of roving upon the sea; and therefore in English a pirate is called a rover and robber upon the sea."

Thus the nature of the offense is sufficiently set forth in the definition of it.

As to the heinousness or wickedness of the offense, it needs no aggravation, it being evident to the reason of all men. Therefore a pirate is called 'hostis humani generis,' with whom neither faith nor oath is to be kept. And in our law they are termed 'brutes,' and 'beasts of prey' and that it is lawful for any one that takes them, if they cannot with safety to themselves bring them under some government to be tried, to put them to death.

And by the civil law any one may take from them their ships or vessels: so that excellent civilian Dr. Zouch, in his book De Jure Nautico, saith, "In detestation of piracy, besides other punishments, it is enacted, that it may be lawful for any one to take their ships."

And yet by the same civil laws, goods taken by piracy gain not any property against the owners. Thus in the Roman Digests, or Pandects of Justinian, it is said, "Persons taken by pirates or thieves, are nevertheless to be esteemed as free."

And then it follows, "He that is taken by thieves, is not therefore a servant of the thieves, neither is postliminy necessary for him."

And the learned Grotius, in his book De Jure Belli ac Pacis, saith, "Those things which pirates and thieves have taken from us, have no need of postliminy, because the law of nations never granted to them a power to change the right of property; therefore things taken by them, wheresoever they are found, may be claimed."

And agreeable to the civil law are the laws of England, which will not allow that taking goods by piracy doth divest the owners of their property, though sold at land, unless sold in market overt.

Before the statute of the 25 E. 3, piracy was holden to be petit treason, and the offense said to be done "contra ligeantiae suae debitum," for which the offenders were to be drawn and hanged; but since that statute the offenders received judgment as felons.

And by the said statute of 28 H. 8, the offenders are ousted by the clergy.

But still it remains a felony by the civil law; and therefore though the afore-said statute of 28 H. 8, gives a trail by the course of the common law, yet it alters not the nature of the offense; and the indictment must mention the same to be done 'super altum mare,' upon the high sea, and must have both the work "felonice" and "piratice" and therefore a pardon of all felonies doth not extend to this offense, but the same ought to be specially named.

Thus having explained to you the nature of the offense, and the wickedness thereof, as being destructive of trade and commerce; I suppose I need not use any arguments to you, to persuade you to a faithful discharge of your duty, in the bringing such offenders to punishment.

APPENDIX 3 TO CHAPTER III

Reply of Rumania, drafted by Pella, November 20, 1926, to Questionnaire 6 propounded by the League of Nations Committee of Experts for the Progressive Codification of International Law. League of Nations Document C.196.M.70.1927.V. p. 202

Absolute piracy (piracy jure gentium) is regarded today as an offence of a special character, because it is punishable wherever encountered. We already see here in embryo the principle – which, in future social relations will become the practice – of penalising throughout the world violations of laws which are common to every country. How ought we to treat the problem of piracy today in the light of the possibility of an international agreement for its suppression? Ought we simply to give conventional form to international usage in the matter, omitting any reference to theoretical controversies? Or ought we, within reasonable limits, to combine the principles of penal and international law and so prepare a draft showing the specific characteristics of piracy and, at the same time, by the strict application of universally accepted principles, settling all controversies hitherto regarded as insoluble? If we can evolve with reference to the suppression of piracy, a new combination of the principles of penal law with those of international law, we shall be able to bring to light hitherto unsuspected aspects of this question which render an international convention indispensable. In order, however, to avoid departing from the subject of the present report – which relates to the draft provisions for the suppression of piracy, as drawn up by M. Matsuda and M. Wang Chung-Hui and modified by the Committee of Experts – we shall reveal these new aspects of the question by analyzing each of the provisions of the draft in turn and suggesting texts which will bring out the specific characteristic of this offence.

APPENDIX 4 TO CHAPTER III

Third United Nations Conference on the Law of the Sea: Informal Composite Negotiating Text, U.N. Doc A/CONF.62/WP.10/CORR.1 (1977)

Article 100: Duty to co-operate in the repression of piracy
   All States shall co-operate to the fullest possible extent in the repression of piracy on the high seas or in any other place outside the jurisdiction of any States.

Article 101: Definition of piracy
   Piracy consists of any of the following acts:
(a) Any illegal acts of violence, detention or any act of depredation, committed for private ends by the crew or the passengers of a private ship or a private aircraft, and directed:
   (i) On the high seas, against another ship or aircraft, or against persons or property on board such ship or aircraft;

     (ii) Against a ship, persons or property in a place outside the jurisdiction of any State;

(b) Any act of voluntary participation in the operation of a ship or of an aircraft with knowledge of facts making it a pirate ship or aircraft;

(c) Any act of inciting or of intentionally facilitating an act described in paragraphs (a) and (b).

Article 102: Piracy by a warship, government ship, or government aircraft whose crew has mutinied

The acts of piracy, as defined in article 101, committed by a warship, government ship or government aircraft whose crew has mutinied and taken control of the ship or aircraft are assimilated to acts committed by a private ship.

Article 103: Definition of a pirate ship or aircraft

A ship or aircraft is considered a pirate ship or aircraft if it is intended by the persons in dominant control to be used for the purpose of committing one of the acts referred to in article 101. The same applies if the ship or aircraft has been used to commit any such act, so long as it remains under the control of the persons guilty of that act.

Article 104: Retention or loss of the nationality of a pirate ship or aircraft

A ship or aircraft may retain its nationality although it has become a pirate ship or aircraft. The retention or loss of nationality is determined by the law of the State from which such nationality was derived.

Article 105: Seizure of a pirate ship or aircraft

On the high seas, or in any other place outside the jurisdiction of any State, every State may seize a pirate ship or aircraft, or a ship taken by piracy and under the control of pirates, and arrest the persons and seize the property on board. The courts of the State which carried out the seizure may decide upon the penalties to be imposed, and may also determine the action to be taken with regard to the ships, aircraft or property, subject to the rights of third parties acting in good faith.

Article 106: Liability for seizure without adequate grounds

Where the seizure of a ship or aircraft on suspicion of piracy has been effected without adequate grounds, the State making the seizure shall be liable to the State the nationality of which is possessed by the ship or aircraft, for any loss or damage caused by the seizure.

Article 107: Ships and aircraft which are entitled to seize on account of piracy

A seizure on account of piracy may only be carried out by warships or military aircraft, or other ships or aircraft clearly marked and identifiable as being on government service and authorized to that effect.

APPENDIX 5 TO CHAPTER III

Harvard Research in International Law, Draft Convention on Piracy with Comments, 26 Am. J. of Int'l. L. 749 (1932), pp. 815-819 (excerpts)

Oppenheim, International Law (4th ed.), section 274

If the crew, or passengers, revolt on the open sea, and convert the vessel and her goods to their own use, they commit piracy, whether the vessel is private or public. But a simple act of violence on the part of crew or passengers does not constitute in itself the crime of piracy, not at least as far as International Law is concerned. If, for instance, the crew were to murder the master on account of his cruelty, and afterwards carried on the voyage, they would be murderers, but not pirates. *They are pirates only when the revolt is directed, not merely against the master, but also against the vessel, for the purpose of converting her and her goods to their own use.* (emphasis added).

Hall, International Law (8th ed.), section 81, pp. 310-311

Piracy includes acts differing much from each other in kind and in moral values; but one thing they all have in common; *they are done under conditions which render it impossible or unfair to hold any state responsible for their commission.* A pirate either belongs to no state or organized political society, or by the nature of his act he has shown his intention and his power to reject the authority of that to which he is properly subject. . . . If a commissioned vessel of war indulges in illegal acts, recourse can be had to its government for redress; if a sailor commits a murder on board a vessel the authority of the state to which it belongs is not displaced, and its laws are able to assert themselves; but if a body of men of uncertain origin seize upon a vessel and scour the ocean for plunder, no one nation has more right of control over them, or more responsibility for their doings, than another, and if the crew of a ship takes possession of it after confining or murdering the captain, legitimate authority has disappeared for the moment, and it is uncertain for how long it may be kept out. Hence every nation may seize and punish a pirate, and hence, in the strong language of judges and writers whose minds have dwelt mainly upon piracy of a particular sort, *he is reputed to be the enemy of the whole race* (emphasis added).

Wheaton, International Law (8th ed.), note by Dana to section 124

It is true, that a pirate *jure gentium* can be seized and tried by any nation, irrespective of his national character, or of that of the vessel on board which, against which, or from which, the act was done. The reason for this must be, that the act is one over which all nations have equal jurisdiction. This can result only from the fact, that it is committed *where all have a common, and no nation an exclusive, jurisdiction,* i.e., upon the high seas; and, if on board ship, and by her own crew, then the ship must be one in which no national authority reigns. The criminal may have committed but one crime, and intended but one, and that against a vessel of a particular nation; yet, if done on the high seas, under certain circumstances hereafter to be referred to, he may be seized and tried by any nation. In such a case, it cannot be necessary to satisfy the court affirmatively, as a fact, that he had a purpose to plunder vessels of all nations, or vessels irrespective of nationality; nor would the court be driven to an artificial presumption of law, contrary to the facts in the case, that such hostile purpose existed. . . . The following suggestions are offered as to the elements of piracy *jure gentium*:

I. It is not necessary that a purpose to depredate on property, beyond such as belongs to one nation or one class of persons or one individual, should be proved or artificially presumed.

II. The motive need not be *lucri causa*, nor need the acts and intent square themselves to the English common-law definitions of *animus furandi*, or malice. It is enough if the *corpus delicti* exists; and the *animus* be one which the law of nations regards as criminal, and hostile to the rights of persons and property on the high seas, . . .

III. Although the act and intent may be sufficient to constitute piracy, all nations have not jurisdiction to try it, unless it was committed beyond the exclusive jurisdiction of any nation. To put it in such predicament, the act must have been committed not only on the high seas, but beyond that kind of jurisdiction which all nations concede to each nation over vessels sailing the seas under at once its *de facto* and *de jure* authority and responsibility, and in the peace of all nations. Crimes, therefore, of whatever character, committed on board by inmates of such vessel pass into the control of the robbers or murderers on board, and the lawful authority is in fact displaced, and she becomes an outlaw, any nation may seize the vessel and try the criminals. . . . (emphasis added).

APPENDIX 6 TO CHAPTER III

Report of the Sub-Committee of the League of Nations Committee of Experts for the Progressive Codification of International Law, League of Nations Document C.196.M.70.1927.V, Draft of Treaty on Piracy, Article 6, comment, p. 117; cited in the Harvard Draft Convention, p. 839. Cf. Appendix 1, Article 6, p. 119

II. Before taking action against pirates, it must first be ascertained that they really are pirates. The mere fact of hoisting a flag does not prove the right to fly it; and, accordingly, if a vessel is suspected of piracy, other means have to be used to establish its nationality.

The two following principles are recognized both by law and in practice:
(1) Any warship has the right upon the high seas to stop and seize any vessel, under whatever flag it may be sailing, which has undoubtedly committed an act of piracy.
(2) If the vessel is only under suspicion, the warship is authorized to verify its true character. It must, however, use this right judiciously and with caution. The commander of the warship is responsible for any action taken. If, after inspection of the suspected vessel, the suspicion proves to have been unfounded, the captain of the suspected vessel is entitled to reparation or compensation, according to circumstances.

APPENDIX 7 TO CHAPTER III

Report of the Sub-Committee of the League of Nations Committee of Experts for the Progressive Codification of International Law, League of Nations Document C.196.M.70.1927.V., p. 118, comment; cited in the Harvard Draft Convention, p. 849

The effects of the capture, the consequences of the validity of the seizure, the right of recovery by the lawful owners and the reward to be given to the captors are questions which are governed by the law of the State having jurisdiction. Accordingly they are solved in a different manner by each State, either in its domestic legislation or in its special conventions. The following four conditions must as a rule be fulfilled in the exercise of the right of recovery and restitution of the goods stolen:
(1) The owner must lodge his claim within a year after sentence of capture has been passed;
(2) The claimant must vindicate his claim of ownership before the competent tribunals;
(3) The costs of recovery are fixed by such tribunals;
(4) The costs must be borne by the owner.

APPENDIX 8 TO CHAPTER III

Johnson, J., in United States v. The Pirates, 5 Wheat, (U.S.), 184 (1820) pp. 196-197

It is obvious that the penman who drafted the section under consideration, acted from an indistinct view of the divisions of his subject. He has blended all crimes punishable under the admiralty jurisdiction, in the general term of piracy. But there exist well-known distinctions between the crimes of piracy and murder, both as to constituents and incidents. Robbery on the seas is considered as an offense within the criminal jurisdiction of all nations. It is against all, and punished by all; and there can be no doubt that the plea of *autrefois acquit* would be good, in any civilized state, though resting on a prosecution instituted in the courts of any other civilized state. Not so, with the crime of murder. It is an offense too abhorrent to the feelings of man, to have made it necessary that it also should have been brought within this universal jurisdiction. And hence, punishing it when committed within the jurisdiction, or (what is the same thing) in the vessel of another nation, has not been acknowledged as a right, much less an obligation. It is punishable under the laws of each state, and I am inclined to think, that an acquittal in this case would not have been a good plea, in a court of Great Britain....

APPENDIX 9 TO CHAPTER III

Harvard Research in International Law, Draft Convention on Piracy with Comments, 26 Am. J. of Int'l L. 749 (1932), pp. 859-861 (excerpts)

Hyde, International Law, section 233
At the present time there remains the inquiry as to the extent to which the particular operations of unrecognized insurgents are to be fairly regarded as both internationally illegal and possessed of a piratical character. The body of maritime States is not necessarily affected by the operations of insurgents

directed solely against vessels of the State whose government it is sought to overthrow. For that reason, there has been at times a disposition on the part of such states to pay a certain degree of respect to the authority conferred upon insurgent vessels and their occupants, before formally according recognition to the insurgent movement. . . .

It is not believed that the acts of insurgents when duly authorized by those in control of the insurgent movement, if committed in furtherance thereof, and directed solely against the vessels of the government sought to be overthrown, should be regarded as piratical.

Whether the acts of unrecognized insurgents, directed against the ships of foreign States, are to be deemed piratical should, on principle, depend upon the magnitude of the movement and also upon the relation of the acts to the struggle for the reins of government. If the acts are incidental to the contest, and consist merely in the attempt to prevent an outside State or its nationals from rendering aid to the *de jure* government opposed, and in a struggle of such magnitude as would justify the recognition of the insurgents as such by a foreign power, it is not believed that they should be treated as piratical.

The contrary view of Brown, J., in The Ambrose Light (1885), 25 Fed. 408, pp. 412-413

From these principles it necessarily follows that in the absence of recognition by any government of their belligerent rights, insurgents that send out vessels of war are, in legal contemplation, merely combinations of private persons engaged in unlawful depredations on the high seas; that they are civilly and criminally responsible in the tribunals for all their acts of violence; that in blockading ports which all nations are entitled to enter, they attack the rights of all mankind, and menace with destruction the lives and property of all who resist their unlawful acts; that such acts are therefore piratical, and entitle the ships and tribunals of every nation whose interests are attacked or menaced, to suppress, at their discretion, such unauthorized warfare by the seizure and confiscation of the vessels engaged in it. The right of seizure by other nations arises in such cases, *ex necessitate*, from the very nature of the case. . . .

The most interesting comment that was presented by Judge Brown directly follows. The reader should at once observe the rationale that he is employing and refer to it when reviewing the suggestions that are set forth later in this study. Particularly, that portion of the suggestions relating to other available alternatives in international law rather than that of piracy:

. . . . There is no other remedy except open war; and nations are not required to declare war against individual rebels whom they are unwilling and are not required to recognize as a belligerent power. Nor are other nations required, for their own security, in such a case, to make any alliance with the parent state. By the right of self-defense, they may simply seize such law-breakers as come in their way and menace them with injury. Without this right, insurgents, though recognition were rightly refused them, and however insignificant their cause or unworthy their conduct, might violate the rights of all other nations, harass their commerce, and capture or sink their ships with impunity. The whole significance and importance of the doctrine of belligerency would be gone, since the absence of recognition could be safely disregarded, the distinction between lawful and unlawful war would be practically abolished; and the most unworthy revolt would have the same immunities for acts of violence on the high seas, without any recognition of belligerent rights, as the most justifiable revolt would have with it. The right to treat unlawful and unauthorized warfare as piratical, seems to me, therefore, clearly imbedded in the very roots of international law.

Hall, International Law (8th ed.), pp. 314-315
The various acts which are recognized or alleged to be piratical may be classed as follows:

1. Robbery or attempt at robbery of a vessel, by force or intimidation, either by way of attack from without, or by way of revolt of the crew and conversion of the vessel and cargo to their own use.

2. Depredation upon two belligerents at war with one another under commissions granted by each of them.

3. *Depredations committed at sea upon the public or private vessels of a state, or descents upon its territory from the sea by persons not acting under the authority of any politically organized community, notwithstanding that the objects of the persons so acting may be professedly political. Strictly all acts which can be thus described must be regarded as in a sense piratical.* In the most respectable instances *they are acts of war* which, being done in places where international law alone rules, or from such places as a base, and being therefore capable of juristification only through international law, are nevertheless done by persons who do not even satisfy the conditions precedent of an attempt to become subjects of law, and who cannot consequently claim like unrecognized political societies to be endeavoring to establish their position as such. Often however the true character of the acts in question is far from corresponding with their legal aspect. Sometimes they are wholly political in their objects and are directed solely against a particular state, with careful avoidance of depredation or attack upon the persons or property of the subject of *other* states. In such cases, though the acts done are piratical with reference to the state attacked, they are for practical purposes not piratical with reference to other states, because they neither interfere with nor menace the safety of those states nor the general good order of the seas. It will be seen presently that the difference between piracy of this kind and piracy in its coarser forms has a bearing upon usage with respect to the exercise of jurisdiction (emphasis added).

Wheaton, International Law, (8th ed.), p. 200, footnote
The following propositions are offered, *not as statements of settled law (for most of them are not covered by a settled usage of nations, by judicial decisions of present authority, or by the agreement of jurists)*, but as *suggestions* of principles:

I. The courts of a State must treat rebellion against the State as a crime, and the persons engaged in it as criminals. If the acts are depredations on commerce protected by the State, they may be adjudged piracy, *jure gentium* by the courts of the State. It is a political and not a legal question, whether the right so to treat them shall be exercised.

II. The fact that the State has actually treated its prisoners as prisoners of war, exchanged prisoners, respected flags of truce, and, or has claimed and exercised the powers and privileges of war as against the neutrals, does not change the abstract rule of law, in the Court. If the State presents such persons to the court for trial, the court must adjudge them criminals. The question whether they shall be so presented is one, not of law, but of policy, which the political department of the State must hold in its hand, and *which may be varied from time to time*, according to circumstances. (emphasis added).

APPENDIX 10 TO CHAPTER III

Reply of France, November 15, 1926, to Questionnaire 6 propounded by the League of Nations Committee of Experts for the Progressive Codification of International Law, League of Nations Document C.196.M.70.1927.V, p. 165; cited in the Harvard Draft Convention, p. 867

Finally, Piracy dealt with in document No. 6, would seem at first sight to be a matter on which a general agreement would be desirable and practicable. But if the question is examined from the practical and political point of view, it will be found that the condition of establishing a general regulation on such a matter would be that every contracting State should possess a police organization and powers of supervision and jurisdiction over its own flag which could be recognized by the other States. No general regulation seems desirable until this condition is everywhere fulfilled.

CHAPTER IV

THE BASIC FRAMEWORK ESTABLISHED BY THE INTERNATIONAL COMMUNITY

Having reviewed the appropriate terminology and governing concepts as utilized in this study in Chapter II, and the history and development of the law of sea piracy as reflected in the draft articles and comments of the Group (1932) in Chapter III, we will now focus our attention on the accomplishments of the international community in connection with the creation of a standard regarding international sea piracy. It will be recalled that one of the reasons for setting forth the draft articles and comments of the Group was to observe the tremendous effort and painstaking analysis necessary to draw together all of the diverse opinions regarding the subject matter.[1] Prior to the work of the Group, very little had been written on the subject of creating a common or special jurisdiction with respect to the establishment of a uniform international approach to sea piracy. Although the Group's draft convention did not lead directly to the adoption of a multilateral treaty, it did refer to all of the relevant materials regarding piracy by utilizing past international conventions, international custom, general principles of law recognized by civilized nations, judicial decisions, and the teachings of most of the highly qualified publicists, as a method of analyzing the topic. For the purpose of this study, the Group's work was extremely important because it demonstrated both the theoretical and practical problems which would confront the international community if it was desirous of creating a convention on the subject of sea piracy. It showed us many different municipal views and the inadequacy of attempting to utilize domestic legislation as a

---

[1] It should be noted at this point that, although the Group published its draft convention of piracy in 1932, no effort was made to incorporate the convention in an international agreement until 1958. The Conference States attending the 1958 Law of the Sea Conference adopted only those parts of the draft convention recommended by the International Law Commission. Compare the Harvard Draft Convention (Chapter III, Appendix 1), with the articles on piracy in the 1958 Convention on the High Seas (Chapter I, Appendix 1) and the articles on piracy which appear in the *Informal Composite Negotiating Text* (Chapter III, Appendix 3).

substitute for the creation of an international crime or common basis for jurisdiction.[2]

Despite the excellent work accomplished by the Group, the next set of draft articles and comments on the international law of piracy took a more practical (or political) approach to the problem. The Group's work was a very important theoretical study on the subject of sea piracy (although they constantly made the reader aware of the fact that their draft articles were prepared for the purpose of *expediency*; that is, with a view toward having their draft convention adopted by a rather fickle group of nations comprising the international community).[3] The purpose of this chapter, therefore, is to set forth and discuss the draft articles and comments prepared by the International Law Commission (the Commission). The reader will have to refer to the draft convention of the Group as a discussion of the work of the Commission takes place.[4]

It will soon be observed that the "practical forces" within the Commission adopted provisions which they thought would be acceptable to the international community even though they had to ignore or set aside some of the draft articles prepared by the Group.[5] The importance of this chapter, therefore, lies in the reader's being able to understand *why* certain matters were taken into consideration when preparing the draft articles set forth by the Commission. These practical considerations will be especially significant when suggestions for revision of the 1958 conventional articles are set forth later in this study.

THE WORK OF THE INTERNATIONAL LAW COMMISSION

The International Law Commission was established pursuant to General Assembly Resolution 174(II) dated November 21, 1947.[6] The Commission held its first session in 1949. At that time, they

[2] See the discussion of these issues on pp. 40-44.
[3] Harvard Research in International Law, *Draft Convention on Piracy with Comments*, 26 Am. J. of Int'l. L. 749 (1932), p. 760. "... The draft convention defines only the jurisdiction (the powers and rights) and the duties of the states *inter se*, leaving to each state the decision how and how far through its own law it will exercise its powers and rights."
[4] The Harvard Draft Convention has been reproduced at Appendix 1, Chapter III.
[5] Compare the nineteen articles of the Harvard Draft Convention (Appendix 1, Chapter III) with the eight articles that were incorporated in the 1958 Convention on the High Seas (Appendix 1, Chapter I).
[6] The function of the International Law Commission was described in Article 15 of its statute, which was promulgated as part of General Assembly Resolution 174 (II), and reads in relevant part as follows: "In the following articles the expression 'progressive development of international law' is used for convenience as meaning the preparation of draft conventions on subjects which have not yet been regulated by international law or in

prepared a provisional list of topics which they considered to be necessary and feasible for adoption at any subsequent law of the sea conference. One of the topics under consideration that was relevant to this study was the possible creation of a regime of the high seas. Professor J.P.A. François was appointed as special rapporteur for this topic (and was later appointed as special rapporteur for the initiation of work on the territorial sea as well). However, it was not until its seventh session, in 1955, that the Commission adopted, on the basis of the special rapporteur's sixth report,[7] a provisional draft on the regime on the high seas,[8] with commentaries, which was thereafter submitted to the international community for observation and comments.

Thereafter, at its eighth session, in 1956, the Commission examined the replies which it received from 25 states[9] and from the International Commission for the Northwest Atlantic Fisheries,[10] together with a new report prepared by the special rapporteur.[11] After reviewing the replies of the various states, the Commission prepared a final report[12] in which it incorporated some of the points made. The final report on the subject was submitted pursuant to General Assembly Resolution 899 (IX) of December 14, 1954.[13] In its report, the Commission grouped together, in the form of articles, all of the rules it adopted concerning the high seas; the territorial sea; the continental shelf; the contiguous zone; and the conservation of the living resources of the sea. The final report was divided into two parts, the first part dealing with the territorial sea and the second part with the high seas. The portion of the final report which concerns the high seas was broken into three sections: (1) general

regard to which the law has not yet been sufficiently developed in the practice of States. Similarly, the expression "codification of international law" is used for convenience as meaning the more precise formulation and systematization of rules of international law in fields where there already has been extensive state practice, precedent and doctrine."

[7] Report of the International Law Commission, 7th Session (1955), A/CN.4/79; 1 Y.B. Int'l L. Comm'n 69 (1955).

[8] Official Records of the General Assembly, 10th Session, Supplement No. 9 (A/2934), Chapter II, cited at 2 Y.B. Int'l L. Comm'n 254 (1956).

[9] Report of the International Law Commission, 8th Session (1956), A/CN.4/99 and Add. 1 to 9; 2 Y.B. Int'l L. Comm'n 37-101 (1956).

[10] Report of the International Commission for the Northwest Atlantic Fisheries, A/CN.4/100; 2 Y.B. Int'l L. Comm'n 102 (1956).

[11] Report of the International Law Commission, 8th Session (1956), A/CN.4/97 and Add. 1 and 3; 2 Y.B. Int'l L. Comm'n 1-13 (1956).

[12] Report of the International Law Commission to the General Assembly, A/3159 (Report of the International Law Commission covering the work of its eighth session, 23 April-4 July 1956); 2 Y.B. Int'l L. Comm'n 253-303 (1956).

[13] 512th plenary meeting. This reads, in relevant part, as follows: "2. Decides to include the final report of the International Law Commission on these topics in the provisional agenda for the eleventh session of the General Assembly."

regime of the high seas; (2) contiguous zone; and (3) continental shelf.[14] Each article in the report was accompanied by a commentary which explained why the provision had been inserted. The Commission prefaced the text of the articles adopted by a statement:[15]

24. The Commission wishes to preface the text of the articles adopted, by certain observations as to the way in which it considers that practical effect should be given to these rules.

25. When the International Law Commission was set up, it was thought that the Commission's work might have two different aspects: on the one hand the "codification of international law" or, in the words of article 15 of the Commission's statute, "the more precise formulation and systematization of rules of international law in fields where there already has been extensive State practice, precedent and doctrine"; and on the other hand, the "progressive development of international law" or "the preparation of draft conventions on subjects which have not yet been regulated by international law or in regard to which the law has not yet been sufficiently developed in the practice of States".

26. In preparing its rules on the law of the sea, the Commission has become convinced that, in this domain at any rate, the distinction established in the statute between these two activities can hardly be maintained. Not only may there be wide differences of opinion as to whether a subject is already "sufficiently developed in practice," but also several of the provisions adopted by the Commission, based on a "recognized principle of international law," have been framed in such a way as to place them in the "progressive development" category. Although it tried at first to specify which articles fell into one and which into the other category, the Commission has had to abandon the attempt, as several do not wholly belong to either.

27. In these circumstances, in order to give effect to the project as a whole, it will be necessary to have recourse to conventional means.

28. The Commission therefore recommends, in conformity with article 23, paragraph 1(d) of its statute, that the General Assembly should summon an international conference of plenipotentiaries to examine the law of the sea, taking account not only of the legal but also of the technical, biological, economic and political aspects of the problem, and to embody the results of its work in one or more international conventions or such other instruments as it may deem appropriate.

29. The Commission is of the opinion that the conference should deal with the various parts of the law of the sea covered by the present report. Judging from its own experience, the Commission considers — and the comments of Governments have confirmed this view — that the various sections of the law of the sea hold together, and are so closely interdependent that it would be extremely difficult to deal with only one part and leave the others aside.

30. The Commission considers that such a conference has been adequately prepared for by the work the Commission has done. The fact that there have been fairly substantial differences of opinion on certain points should not be regarded as a reason for putting off such a conference. There has been widespread regret at the attitude of Governments after The Hague Codification

[14] The final report is organized pursuant to the provisions of part (c) (23), 2 Y.B. Int'l L. Comm'n 255 (1956).
[15] 2 Y.B. Int'l L. Comm'n 255-256 (1956).

Conference of 1930 in allowing the disagreement over the breadth of the territorial sea to dissuade them from any attempt at concluding a convention on the points on which agreement has been reached. The Commission expresses the hope that this mistake will not be repeated.

31. In recommending confirmation of the proposed rules as indicated in paragraph 28, the Commission has not had to concern itself with the question of the relationship between the proposed rules and existing conventions. The answer to that question must be found in the general rules of international law and the provisions drawn up by the proposed international conference.

32. The Commission also wishes to make two other observations, which apply to the whole draft:
1. The draft regulates the law of the sea in time of peace only.
2. The term "mile" means nautical mile (1,852 metres) reckoned at sixty to one degree of latitude.

33. The text of the articles concerning the law of the sea, as adopted by the Commission, and the Commission's commentary to the articles are reproduced below.[15]

Thus, as observed in the preface to the text of the articles, it is apparent that the Commission was confronted with a monumental task in preparing its draft articles and thereafter reporting them to the General Assembly. When reviewing the work of the Commission, the reader should bear two items in mind: (1) that they were not dealing solely with the subject of piracy but were also preparing articles which had to mesh with the development of other ideas and concepts contained in the proposed articles on the high seas (for instance the doctrine of hot pursuit); and (2), while they were confronted with current and historical problems regarding the law of piracy, they had to take into consideration the *practical* substantive content contained in the draft articles.

Concerning *political* considerations which could arise during the course of the Commission's study and later at the various law of the sea conferences, it is noteworthy to mention that, in accordance with the General Assembly Resolution 821 (IX) of December 17, 1954,[16] the Commission also studied the reports of the meetings of the Ad hoc Political Committee. One of the topics considered in

---

[15] 2 Y.B. Int'l L. Comm'n 255-256 (1956).

[16] 514th plenary meeting. The resolution (complaint of violation of the freedom of navigation in the area of the China seas) reads as follows: "Recalling its resolution 899 (IX) of 14 December 1954 which, inter alia, requested the International Law Commission to complete its final report concerning the regime of the high seas, the regime of territorial waters and related problems in time for the General Assembly to consider these matters at its eleventh session,

1. Decides to transmit to the International Law Commission the records and documents, including the draft resolution of Syria contained in document A/AC.76/L.25, of the meetings of the Ad Hoc Political Committee at which item 71 of the agenda of the ninth session of the General Assembly was considered;

2. Invites the Governments of Member States to transmit to the International Law Commission their views concerning the principle of freedom of navigation on the high seas.

those reports was a complaint of violations of the freedom of navigation in the China seas. In addition, the Commission had before it a memorandum concerning freedom of navigation on the high seas, submitted on behalf of the government of the People's Republic of Poland by Mr. Jan Balicki, an official Polish observer at the seventh session of the Commission.[17] Nevertheless, after discussing this matter, the Commission decided that it was incompetent to examine the charge. The memorandum is significant to this study only insofar as it illustrates the various stances nations could take with regard to acts committed on the high seas that were allegedly piratical in nature. (Other examples include the *Santa Maria*[18] and the *Mayaguez*[19] incidents which occurred after the 1958 Law of the Sea Conference.) Thus, when looking at the possible alternatives concerning revising the 1958 conventional articles on piracy, one must consider the political considerations involved when dealing with terrorist activities[20] as well as the degree to which states might submit to a compulsory dispute settlement mechanism.[21]

Let us now examine, in chronological order, that part of the report of the Commission dealing with its articles and comments on piracy which are contained in the provisional articles concerning the regime of the high seas. When setting forth these articles and comments, it will also be appropriate to disclose discussions, as applicable, which took place in connection with their preparation. These discussions are contained in the summary records of the seventh session.[22] The summary records, in general, provide a

---

[17] 2 Y.B. Int'l L. Comm'n 1 (1955), Document A/CN.4/L.53: Observations of the Government of Poland, concerning freedom of navigation on the high seas, transmitted by Mr. Jan Balicki, observer of Poland to the 7th session of the International Law Commission – 6 May 1955. The complete version of this document appears in Appendix 1 of this chapter. Mr. Balicki was concerned about freedom of navigation in the area of the South China Sea as the following excerpt indicates: ". . . For some time, however, we have been witnessing the most brutal violation of age-old principles by those who direct hostile activities against vessels of many states. In the China seas the stopping of merchantmen, the seizure of their cargoes, the detention of the crews are organized on a wide scale. According to statements by Lloyds, 70 vessels under various flags were subject to these illegal acts between 23 August 1949 and 16 December 1953. This figure is not complete as other vessels were detained at a later time, inter alia, the Soviet tanker *Tuapse*. Among the seized vessels there were two Polish merchant ships; *Praca* detained and captured in October 1953, and *Prezydent Gottwald* in May 1954."

[18] See Green, The Santa Maria: *Rebels or Pirates?*, 37 Brit. Y.B. Int'l. L. 496 (1961).

[19] See 18 I.C.L.Q. 961 (1969).

[20] See notes 48 and 64 of Chapter III and the discussion in the text on pp. 50-54 and 83-86.

[21] See notes 21 and 22 of Chapter I; and Glickman, *Enforcement Mechanism of the Law of the Sea Treaty*, 1 Suff. Transnat'l L. J. 1 (1976-77).

[22] Summary Records of the Seventh Session, 2 May-July 8 1955, A/CN.4/SER.A/61955; 1 Y.B. Int'l L. Comm'n (1955).

useful source of material for setting forth some of the discussion that took place when the articles and comments were prepared. By reviewing these records, we can see the problems faced by members of the Commission.[23]

The Seventh Session (1955)

Article 13
All States shall co-operate to the fullest possible extent in the repression of piracy on the high seas.

Comment
In its work on the articles concerning piracy, *the Commission was greatly assisted by the research carried out at the Harvard Law School, which culminated in a draft convention of nineteen articles with commentary*, prepared in 1932 under the direction of Professor Joseph Bingham. *In general – the Commission was able to endorse the findings of that research.*

Article 13 lays down a sound principle. Any State having an opportunity of taking measures against piracy and neglecting to do so *would be failing in a duty laid upon it by international law. Obviously, the State must be allowed a certain latitude as to the measures it should take to this end in any individual instance* (emphasis added).[24]

In preparing the Comment to Article 13, the only problem presented was that concerning the first sentence of the second paragraph which originally read "Article 13 lays down a principle which cannot be challenged." An observation of the discussion concerning this article discloses that while the Commission upheld the view that piracy was an international crime, there was a divergence of opinion as to whether the failure of a state to suppress piracy was also to be considered a violation of international law. However, the members of the Commission compromised their disagreements and, after certain objections, the comment was changed to "Article 13 lays down a sound principle." It should be remembered that, although the discussion in the summary records is not a verbatim transcription of the actual debate, it is useful to see why the views of some of the members of the Commission differed from the conclusions reached by the Group.[25] In addition the reader, at this point, should be making other observations. It must be remembered

---

[23] The problems faced by the members of the Commission in writing Article 13 became evident upon examining the records of the 327th meeting (July 5, 1955); 1 Y.B. Int'l L. Comm'n 266 (1955). This discussion appears in Appendix 2.

[24] 2 Y.B. Int'l L. Comm'n 25 (1955).

[25] 1 Y.B. Int'l L. Comm'n 266 (1955). See Appendix 2. For example, apparently Sir Gerald Fitzmaurice assumed the position taken by the Harvard Research Group in Article 18, i.e. ". . . the parties . . . agree to make every expedient use of their powers to prevent piracy". See the discussion of this article in the Harvard Draft Convention, *op. cit.*, p. 867.

that the Commission relied greatly on the Group's draft conventions, comments and research regarding piracy. Therefore, they would have had to have seen the diverse opinions set forth by the various publicists, jurists and municipal laws, in general. It is rather interesting to read the various summary discussions in order to see the range of views of members of the Commission regarding whether piracy was an international crime or not, whether failure to suppress piracy was a violation of international law or not, where the duty to suppress piracy originated from, and what degree of latitude would be allowed in connection with the measures that a state should take in order to fulfill this duty to suppress piracy in international law. After reading the discussion that took place among the members of the Commission, it is apparent that Article 13 is no more than a *statement of intent* that states should cooperate to repress piracy on the high seas. Before including this type of conventional clause in any revision at future law of the sea conferences, the Conference States first have to consider whether the *modern political* incidents of piracy or terrorism should constitute an international crime and the extent to which states would be amenable to binding themselves to its suppression.[26] Without this sense of urgency or despondency, it is doubtful whether any revised conventional articles could be agreed upon. In addition, another problem at future conferences would be whether to include uniform penalties in revised conventional articles with jurisdiction vested in a newly created law of the sea authority or whether states should be permitted to prescribe penalties for the commission of the crime or offense of piracy through the utilization of their municipal laws (assuming that they have said legislation).

The next article contained in the report of the Commission is a statement concerning the *acts* which would constitute piracy.

Article 14

Piracy is any of the following acts:

1. Any illegal act of violence, detention, or any act of depredation directed against persons or property and committed for private ends by the crew or the passengers of a private vessel or a private aircraft:

(a) Against a vessel on the high seas other than that on which the act is committed, or

(b) Against vessels, persons or property in territory outside the jurisdiction of any State.

2. Any act of voluntary participation in the operation of a ship or of an aircraft with knowledge of facts which make the ship or aircraft a pirate ship or aircraft.

---

[26] Note the discussion in Chapter III concerning political terrorism. It should be recognized that Article 13 as proposed by the Commission was adopted verbatim as Article 14 of the 1958 Convention on the High Seas and appears as Article 100 of the *Informal Composite Negotiating Text* of 1977 (Appendix 4, Chapter III).

3. Any act of incitement or of intentional facilitation of an act described in paragraph 1 or paragraph 2 of this article.

Comment
The Commission had to consider certain *controversial points* as to the essential features of piracy. . .[27]

In discussing the adoption of Article 14, the summary records disclose only one objection,[28] but clearly show the development of a divergence of opinion among the members of the Commission. There were those members who believed that in connection with both Articles 13 and 14 (and the comments thereto), that the failure to suppress piracy should be considered a crime (Article 13) and that the acts constituting piracy should not be too restrictive.[29] Thus, the members of the Commission reflected the divergent views (for whatever their motives were) of "traditional" wisdom when preparing their draft convention and comments.[30] However, the Commission *compromised* its diverse opinions when formulating their draft articles and comments to a greater extent than the Group did earlier for the purposes of *expediency*. The practical effects of looking forward to obtaining the consent of the Conference States at the 1958 Law of the Sea Conference was beginning to take hold at the meetings of the Committee.

Returning to the discussions, it is observed that contrary to the sole objection to the adoption of Article 14, there was quite a lively debate concerning the drafting of a comment to Article 14.[31] The focus of the debate among the Committee first centered on whether ". . . acts of piracy could be committed by any kind of vessel and not only merchantmen"[32] and on whether it was possible to

[27] 2 Y.B. Int'l L. Comm'n 25 (1955). The complete comment to Article 14 appears in Appendix 3 of this chapter.
[28] 1 Y.B. Int'l L. Comm'n 228 (1955). The objection was as follows: "Mr. Zourek said that the definition of piracy contained in article 13 (renumbered to 14 in the Report that is under consideration) was too restrictive and did not correspond to international law. He maintained his reservations in that respect."
[29] Note that the specific categories of violent acts outlined in the original Harvard Draft, i.e. "rape, wound, enslave," etc.) were replaced by a broader proscription against any "illegal act of violence" in the work of the Commission. This had the effect of broadening the parameters within which an act of piracy could fall.
[30] Note that in some areas the Group adopted a more progressive view than did the Commission. For example, the Group was ready to recognize aircraft as prospective piratical vehicles. The Commission would not go this far. However, it must be recognized that up until 1953 only 17 aircraft hijackings had taken place. As a result, the international community had not, as yet, perceived an act like air hijacking as being conceivably within the definition of piracy. See Joyner, *Aerial Hijacking as an International Crime* (New York: Oceana), 1974, pp. 97-99.
[31] 1 Y.B. Int'l L. Comm'n 266 (1955). These discussions occurred at the 327th meeting, July 5, 1955 and they appear in Appendix 4.
[32] *Ibid.* See the remarks of Mr. Hsu, paragraph 84, Appendix 4.

establish a criterion "... to distinguish between acts committed for private ends and acts committed for political ends."[33] Concerning the private-political ends dichotomy, Sir Gerald Fitzmaurice thought that:

The real antithesis which needed to be brought out was between authorized and unauthorized acts and acts committed in a public or in a private capacity. An act committed in a private capacity could have a political purpose but be unauthorized — as, for example, the seizure of a vessel by the member of an opposition party.[34]

It was also pointed out that the "... controversial question whether a political act could be regarded as piracy had been discussed at great length in the past and had been raised in the Harvard Draft..."[35] As will be elaborated upon more fully later in this study, it is apparent that the "controversial question" regarding politically motivated acts is today the gravamen of the hotly disputed issues from those legal publicists calling for an update in the 1958 conventional articles.

The argument regarding the comment to Article 14 during the 326th meeting (July 4, 1955) was revived at the 330th meeting held July 8, 1955.[36] However, once again certain members of the Committee believed that questions of "... whether parties to a civil war constituted belligerents or not, as well as that of governments which were not universally recognized..."[37] were too complex and controversial to be mentioned in the comments to Article 14 by the Commission. In fact, they represented problems which had never even been discussed by the Commission despite the existence of treaties such as the Nyon Arrangement of September 14, 1937[38] which branded the sinking of merchant vessels by submarines, against the dictates of humanity, as acts of piracy. Thus, the practical effect of this lack of including politically motivated acts within the agreed-upon definition truly limited the thrust of the articles on piracy to acts of piracy that occurred in the past (that is, to moot and nonexistent acts as of 1958). To restrict the "acts" of piracy to "private" ones and later to isolate the geographic locations of these acts to "the high seas or ... any other place

[33] *Ibid.* See the remarks of Mr. Krylov, paragraph 87, Appendix 4.
[34] *Ibid.*, p. 267, emphasis added. See the remarks of Sir Gerald Fitzmaurice, paragraph 92, Appendix 4.
[35] *Ibid.*, p. 266. See the remarks of Mr. François, paragraph 88, Appendix 4.
[36] *Ibid.*, p. 286. These discussions appear in Appendix 5.
[37] *Ibid.* See the remarks of Mr. Hsu, paragraph 5, Appendix 5.
[38] Nyon Arrangement, opened for signature September 14, 1937, League of Nations Document C.409.M.273.1937; U.N. Doc.A/3520.

outside the jurisdiction of any State"[39] greatly hampered the creation of a meaningful convention.

Returning now to the text of the report of the Commission, we continue with the articles and comments which were adopted.[40] According to the summary records Articles 15-20 and the comments thereto were adopted without extensive argument.[41] It was agreed by the Commission that a vessel should *not* lose its national character by the fact of committing acts of piracy: that ". . . a pirate ship should only be regarded as a ship without nationality where the national laws of the State in question regard piracy as grounds for loss of nationality."[42]

The final area of the report discussed by the Commission concerned the "right of visit": entitled the "right of stoppage" at the 321st meeting held June 28, 1955[43] and the "right of inspection" at the 326th meeting held July 4, 1955.[44] The only focus of concern during these discussions involved compensation for an improper visit. It was suggested by Sir Gerald Fitzmaurice that ". . . compensation was justified only where a ship had neither committed any offense nor given any reasonable grounds for suspicion."[45] Thereafter, in the report of the Commission, Article 21 was redrafted.[46] In preparing the comment to Article 21, the summary records disclose primarily that the title was changed to "Right to Visit" in lieu of "Right of Inspection" and that the compensation should be paid for losses sustained rather than providing for severe penalties.[47]

[39] Convention on the High Seas, opened for signature April 29, 1958, 13 U.S.T. 2312 (1962), T.I.A.S. No. 5200, 450 U.N.T.S. 82, Article 14.

[40] 2 Y.B. Int'l L. Comm'n 25-26 (1955). Articles 15-17 and their respective comments appear in Appendix 6.

[41] 1 Y.B. Int'l L. Comm'n 228 (1955). However, in connection with the original Article 18 (listed as Article 17 in the summary record) there was some disagreement. See Appendix 7 for the discussion involving this issue as well as Articles 18-20 and their respective comments.

[42] 2 Y.B. Int'l L. Comm'n 26 (1955). See comment to Article 17, Appendix 7.

[43] 1 Y.B. Int'l L. Comm'n 229 (1955).

[44] *Ibid.*, p. 267. The discussions which surrounded the adoption of Article 20 (Right of Stoppage) at the 321st meeting, June 28, 1955 appear in Appendix 8.

[45] *Ibid.*, p. 229. See the remarks of Sir Gerald Fitzmaurice, paragraph 13, Appendix 8.

[46] 2 Y.B. Int'l L. Comm'n 26 (1955). Article 21 and the comment thereto appear in Appendix 9.

[47] 1 Y.B. Int'l L. Comm'n 267 (1955). The discussions which surrounded the adoption of Article 21 (Right of Inspection) at the 327th meeting, July 5, 1955 appear in Appendix 10.

The Eighth Session (1956)

Thereafter, at its eighth session (1956)[48] the Commission examined the replies from twenty-five governments.[49] These replies were submitted in response to a report issued by Professor J.P.A. François, special rapporteur.[50] The documentation also included a summary of the replies, together with the conclusions of the special rapporteur,[51] which summarized the views with regard, *inter alia,* to piracy.[52] After examining the replies of the states, the Commission discussed the proffered suggestions and then prepared a final report in which some of the points made by the various governments were incorporated.[53]

The discussions of the Commission again reflected the gradual narrowing of the various orthodox and unorthodox views concerning whether to limit or to expand the "traditional" scope of piracy. For example, certain members of the Commission, whose views were exemplified by Mr. Zourek, believed that *acts* of violence and depredation should constitute acts of piracy even when committed (1) for political ends; or (2) by warships or military aircraft; or (3) by aircraft or seaplanes against foreign aircraft; or (4) from the high seas against ships, persons or goods located in the territorial or internal waters or against the land.[54] To the contrary other members of the Commission, whose views were represented by Sir Gerald Fitzmaurice, believed that acts of piracy and their geographic location should be restricted to the "traditional" role of piracy even though (1) the research of the Group disclosed diversity of opinion as to the acts of piracy and location (although the weight of this opinion leaned towards the views of Sir Gerald) and (2) Sir Gerald himself believed in applying "novel" approaches to the problem of the type of craft that could be utilized when committing an act. As he stated, ". . . it would be a pity to delete the reference to private

[48] Report of the International Law Commission, 8th Session (1956), A/CN.4/SER.A/ 1956/Add. 1; 2 Y.B. Int'l L. Comm'n (1956).
[49] A/CN.4/99 and Add. 1 to 9; 2 Y.B. Int'l L. Comm'n 37-101 (1956).
[50] A/CN.4/97 and Add. 2; 2 Y.B. Int'l L. Comm'n 1-13 (1956).
[51] Report of the International Law Commission, 8th Session (1956), A/CN.4/97/Add. 1 to 3 (summary of replies from governments and conclusions of the special rapporteur); 2 Y.B., Int'l L. Comm'n 13-37 (1956).
[52] Excerpts from the replies dealing specifically with piracy appear in Appendix 11 of this chapter.
[53] 1 Y.B. Int'l L. Comm'n 46-48 (1956), from the 343rd meeting, May 9, 1956. The discussions surrounding the adoption of Articles 13-20 on piracy at this meeting appear in Appendix 12.
[54] *Ibid.,* p. 47. See the remarks of Mr. Zourek, paragraph 37, Appendix 12.

aircraft, because the Commission should not disregard an aspect of piracy that was both *novel* and *potentially real . . .*"[55]

Based upon these discussions, the Commission drew up a final report in which it incorporated some of the points made. That part of the Report to the General Assembly[56] dealing with articles on piracy will now be reviewed verbatim in order to see the changes which took place and to compare it with the articles and comments previously cited in the report at the seventh session. Thereafter, a summary of these provisions will be set forth.

The Report to the General Assembly

The first change which transpired occurred in connection with Article 13 and its counterpart in the final report, Article 38. It will be recalled that Article 13 stated that:

All States shall co-operate to the fullest possible extent in the repression of piracy on the high seas."[57]

This article was changed by Article 38 to read:

All States shall co-operate to the fullest possible extent in the repression of piracy on the high seas or in any other place outside the jurisdiction of any State.[58]

The comment to Article 13 was also changed by adopting a new second paragraph. Originally, Article 13, after acknowledging the research conducted by the Group, went on to state in the second paragraph:

Article 13 lays down a sound principle. Any State having an opportunity of taking measures against piracy and neglecting to do so would be failing in a duty laid upon it by international law. Obviously, the State must be allowed a certain latitude as to the measures it should take to this end in any individual instance.[59]

In addition, Article 14 of the report of the seventh session and the accompanying comment were also changed in the report to the General Assembly:

Piracy is any of the following acts:
1. Any illegal act of violence, detention, or any act of depredation directed against persons or property and committed for private ends by the crew or the passengers of a private vessel or a private aircraft:

[55] *Ibid.*, emphasis added. See the remarks of Sir Gerald Fitzmaurice, paragraph 44, Appendix 12.
[56] Report of the International Law Commission to the General Assembly (covering work of its eighth session, April 23-July 4, 1956), A/3159; 2 Y.B. Int'l L. Comm'n 253-303 (1956).
[57] 2 Y.B. Int'l L. Comm'n 25 (1955).
[58] 2 Y.B. Int'l L. Comm'n 282 (1956).
[59] 2 Y.B. Int'l L. Comm'n 25 (1955).

(a) Against a vessel on the high seas other than that on which the act is committed, or

(b) Against vessels, persons or property in territory outside the jurisdiction of any State.

2. Any act of voluntary participation in the operation of a ship or of an aircraft with knowledge of facts which make the ship or aircraft a pirate ship or aircraft.[60]

Article 14 now became Article 39 and read:

Piracy consists in any of the following acts:

1. Any illegal act of violence, detention or any act of depredation, committed for private ends by the crew or the passengers of a private ship or a private aircraft, and directed:

(a) On the high seas, against another ship or against persons or property on board such a ship;

2. Any act of voluntary participation in the operation of a ship or of an aircraft with knowledge of facts making it a pirate ship or aircraft.[61]

The comment was changed in part to reflect the suggested amendments.

Save in the case provided for in article 15, piracy can be committed only by merchant vessels, not by warships.

This was altered to read:

Save in the case provided for in article 40, piracy can be committed only by private ships and not by warships or other government ships;[62]

That provision dealing with the Nyon Arrangement of September 14, 1937 was also changed from:

With regard to point 3 the Commission is aware that there are treaties, such as the Nyon Arrangement of 14 September 1937, which brand the sinking of merchant vessels by submarines, against the dictates of humanity, as piratical acts. But it is of the opinion that such treaties do not invalidate the principle that piracy can only be committed by private vessels. The questions arising in connexion with acts committed by warships in the service of rival Governments engaged in civil war are too complex to make it seem necessary for the safeguarding of public order on the high seas that all States should have a general right, let alone an obligation, to repress as piracy acts perpetrated by the warships of the parties in question. In view of the immunity from interference by other ships which warships are entitled to claim, the seizure of such vessels on suspicion of piracy might involve the gravest consequences. Hence the Commission feels that to assimilate unlawful acts committed by warships to acts of piracy would be prejudicial to the interests of the international community. The Commission was unable to share the view held by some of its members that the principle laid down in the Nyon Arrangement endorsed a new right in the process of development.[63]

[60] *Ibid.*
[61] 2 Y.B. Int'l L. Comm'n 282 (1956).
[62] *Ibid.*, commentary (iii).
[63] 2 Y.B. Int'l L. Comm'n 25 (1955), Article 14, comment 6.

to:

With regard to point (iii), the Commission is aware that there are treaties, such as the Nyon Arrangement of 14 September 1937, which brand the sinking of merchant ships by submarines, against the dictates of humanity, as piratical acts. But it is of the opinion that such treaties do not invalidate the principle that piracy can only be committed by private ships. In view of the immunity from interference by other ships which warships are entitled to claim, the seizure of such ships on suspicion of piracy might involve the gravest consequences. Hence the Commission feels that to assimilate unlawful acts committed by warships to acts of piracy would be prejudicial to the interests of the international community. The Commission was unable to share the view held by some of its members that the principle laid down in the Nyon Arrangement confirmed a new law in process of development. In particular, the questions arising in connexion with acts committed by warships in the service of rival Governments engaged in civil war are too complex to make it seem necessary for the safeguarding of order and security on the high seas that all States should have a general right, let alone an obligation, to repress as piracy acts perpetrated by the warships of the parties in question.

. . . .

(4) In considering as "piracy" acts committed in a place outside the jurisdiction of any State, the Commission had chiefly in mind acts committed by a ship or aircraft on an island constituting *terra nullius* or on the shores of an unoccupied territory. But the Commission did not wish to exclude acts committed by aircraft within a larger unoccupied territory, since it wished to prevent such acts committed on ownerless territories from escaping all penal jurisdiction.

(5) With regard to point (v) the Commission feels that acts committed in the air by one aircraft against another aircraft can hardly be regarded as acts of piracy. In any case such acts committed by a pirate aircraft against a ship on the high seas may, in the Commission's view, be assimilated to acts committed by a pirate ship.[64]

Another change occurred in Article 15 which was changed from:

The acts of piracy committed by a warship or a military aircraft whose crew mutinies are assimilated to acts committed by a private vessel.[65]

to:

The acts of piracy, as defined in article 39, committed by a government ship or a government aircraft whose crew has mutinied and taken control of the ship or aircraft are assimilated to acts committed by a private vessel.[66]

The comment in the report originally stated:

A warship whose crew has mutinied and taken control of the ship must be assimilated to a private vessel, so that acts committed against another vessel can assume the character of acts of piracy.[67]

[64] 2 Y.B. Int'l L. Comm'n 282 (1956).
[65] 2 Y.B. Int'l L. Comm'n 25 (1955).
[66] 2 Y.B. Int'l L. Comm'n 283 (1956), Article 40.
[67] 2 Y.B. Int'l L. Comm'n 25 (1955).

However, it was changed to:

A State ship or State aircraft whose crew has mutinied and taken control of the ship or aircraft must be assimilated to a private ship or aircraft. Acts committed by the crew or passengers of such a ship against another ship can therefore assume the character of acts of piracy. Clearly, the article ceases to apply once the mutiny has been suppressed and lawful authority restored.[68]

Article 16 of the report originally stated:

A ship or aircraft is considered a pirate ship or aircraft when it is devoted by the persons in dominant control to the purpose of committing an act described in the first sentence of article 14, paragraph 1.[69]

This article was changed in Article 41 and read:

A ship or aircraft is considered a pirate ship or aircraft if it is intended by the persons in dominant control to be used for the purpose of committing one of the acts referred to in article 39. The same applies if the ship or aircraft has been used to commit any such act, so long as it remains under the control of the persons guilty of that act.[70]

The comment to Article 16 of the report originally stated only that:

The purpose of this article is to define the terms "pirate ship" and "pirate aircraft" as used in the following articles.[71]

In lieu of the change in the article, the comment (as in the prior sections discussed) became the commentary and stated:

The purpose of this article is to define the terms "pirate ship" and "pirate aircraft" as used in these articles. The mere fact that a ship sails without a flag is not sufficient to give it the character of a "pirate" ship. Two cases of pirate ships must be distinguished. First, there are ships intended to commit acts of piracy. Secondly, there is the case of ships which have already been guilty of such acts. Such ships can be considered as pirate so long as they remain under the control of the persons who have committed these acts.[72]

Article 17 of the report was altered, in part, by taking

... The retention or loss of national character is determined by the law of the State from which it was originally derived.[73]

and stating in Article 42:

[68] 2 Y.B. Int'l L. Comm'n 283 (1956).
[69] 2 Y.B. Int'l L. Comm'n 25 (1955).
[70] 2 Y.B. Int'l L. Comm'n 283 (1956).
[71] 2 Y.B. Int'l L. Comm'n 26 (1955).
[72] 2 Y.B. Int'l L. Comm'n 283 (1956).
[73] 2 Y.B. Int'l L. Comm'n 26 (1955).

. . . The retention or loss of national character is determined by the law of the State from which the national character was originally derived.[74]

Article 18 of the report was modified in part:

On the high seas or in any other place not within the territorial jurisdiction of another State, any State may seize a pirate ship or aircraft or a ship taken by piracy and under the control of pirates and property or persons on board. . .[75]

Article 18 became Article 43 and stated:

On the high seas or in any other place outside the jurisdiction of any State, every State may seize a pirate ship or aircraft, or a ship taken by piracy and under the control of pirates, and arrest the persons and seize the property on board. . .[76]

The comment to Article 18 originally stated:

This article gives any State the right to seize pirate ships (and ships seized by pirates) and to have them tried by its courts. Before this article becomes applicable to a vessel, it must have committed acts of piracy. A ship which has no right to fly any flag but has not committed acts of piracy cannot be assimilated to a pirate vessel.[77]

The commentary to Article 43 was changed to read:

This article gives any State the right to seize pirate ships (and ships seized by pirates) and to have them adjudicated upon by its courts. This right cannot be exercised at a place under the jurisdiction of another State. The Commission did not think it necessary to go into details concerning the penalties to be imposed and the other measures to be taken by the courts.[78]

The wording of Article 20 was practically identical to Article 45:

A seizure on account of piracy may only be carried out by warships or military aircraft.[79]

However, the commentary to Article 45 added another paragraph:

(2) Clearly this article does not apply in the case of a merchant ship which has repulsed an attack by a pirate ship and, in exercising its right of self-defense, overpowers the pirate ship and subsequently hands it over to a warship or to the authorities of a coastal State. This is not a "seizure" within the meaning of this article.[80]

Finally, under the "Right of Visit" provision contained in Article 21, a few changes were made:

[74] 2 Y.B. Int'l L. Comm'n 283 (1956).
[75] 2 Y.B. Int'l L. Comm'n 26 (1955).
[76] 2 Y.B. Int'l L. Comm'n 283 (1956).
[77] 2 Y.B. Int'l L. Comm'n 26 (1955).
[78] 2 Y.B. Int'l L. Comm'n 283 (1956).
[79] 2 Y.B. Int'l L. Comm'n 26 (1955).
[80] 2 Y.B. Int'l L. Comm'n 283 (1956).

(a) That the vessel is engaged in piracy; or[81]

Article 46 now read:

(a) That the ship is engaged in piracy; or[82]

In addition, the comment to Article 21 stated, in part:

The State to which the warship belongs must compensate the merchant vessel
for any delay caused by the warship's action, not only where the vessel was
stopped without reasonable grounds, but in all cases where suspicion proves
unfounded and the vessel committed no act calculated to give rise to suspicion.[83]

The commentary to Article 46 added a sentence to the comment:

. . . This severe penalty seems justified in order to prevent the right of visit
being abused.[84]

The Commission also added a sentence to the last paragraph of the
comment regarding Article 21 which became part of paragraph (4)
of the commentary to Article 46:

. . . The Commission draws attention in this connexion to its comments on
the institution of a contiguous zone for security measures.[85]

This sentence was added to that paragraph in order to show that the
Commission, throughout the entire report, did not wish to include
terms such as "imminent danger" or "hostile acts" and other terms
which could lead to abusive utilization by states.

SUMMARY OF THE WORK OF THE COMMISSION

In summarizing the work of the Commission and comparing it to
the draft convention prepared by the Group, certain areas were
definitively set forth by the Commission. The Group generally
believed, as did most states at that time, that universal jurisdiction
over pirates was vital to insure the safety and passage of vessels
traveling over the high seas. The Group, it will be recalled, believed
that the law of international sea piracy conferred on states a special
basis of jurisdiction which, as set forth in Article 2 of their draft
articles, stated:

[81] 2 Y.B. Int'l L. Comm'n 26 (1955).
[82] 2 Y.B. Int'l L. Comm'n 283 (1956).
[83] 2 Y.B. Int'l L. Comm'n 27 (1955).
[84] 2 Y.B. Int'l L. Comm'n 284 (1956), paragraph (3).
[85] *Ibid.*, paragraph (4).

Jurisdiction

Every state has jurisdiction to prevent piracy and punish persons and to seize and dispose of property because of piracy. This jurisdiction is defined and limited by this convention.[86]

The Commission, on the other hand, merely defined the conditions necessary for the exercise of the jurisdiction and stated in Article 43 that:

On the high seas or in any other place outside the jurisdiction of any State, every State may seize a pirate ship or aircraft, or a ship taken by piracy and under the control of pirates, and arrest the persons and seize the property on board. . .[87]

The purpose of this article was set forth in the commentary which stated, in part:

This article gives the State the right to seize pirate ships (and ships seized by pirates) and to have them adjudicated upon by its courts. . .[88]

Place of Seizure

It will be recalled that the Group, in Article 7[89] of its draft convention permitted a ship to be seized within the jurisdiction of another state if pursuit had been commenced elsewhere and also provided that notice must be given to the coastal state in which the seizure was made. These measures allowed seizure within the territorial jurisdiction of another state under certain conditions. To the contrary, the Commission, after considering the practical implication *that there were few acts of piracy in modern times,* decided not to include this provision but continued to permit states to exercise their unilateral competence in repressing piracy.

Method of Seizure

It will be recalled that the Group, in Article 12 of its draft convention, stated:

A seizure because of piracy may be made only on behalf of a state, and only by a person who has been authorized to act on its behalf.[90]

---

[86] Harvard Draft Convention, *op. cit.*, note 3, p. 768.
[87] 2 Y.B. Int'l L. Comm'n 283 (1956).
[88] *Ibid.*
[89] See Appendix 1, Chapter III.
[90] Harvard Draft Convention, *op. cit.*, p. 846.

The Group stated that although warships may have been the traditional vehicle utilized for capture, it recognized that currently other means, such as police boats, were permissible. Therefore, the Group believed that the state could select the method of seizure but would be held responsible for damages that resulted from the seizures which were made.

To the contrary, the Commission was concerned throughout its entire preparatory work with possible abuses by states and stated, in Article 45:

A seizure on account of piracy may only be carried out by warships or military aircraft.[91]

Although this provision was later modified by Article 21 of the high seas convention,[92] that is, "A seizure on account of piracy may only be carried out by warships or military aircraft, *or other ships or aircraft on government service authorized to that effect*" (emphasis added), the Commission thought that the intended victim could still capture the pirate ship in the exercise of its right of self-defense.

Jurisdiction after Seizure

The jurisdictional competence of the states to prescribe punishment and to apply their laws to the disposition of the property that was taken was left to the states that captured the pirate. If the seizure was without justification, Article 20 of Convention on the High Seas[93] later provided that the seizing state would be liable to the flag state of the seized vessel for any loss or damage sustained because of the seizure.

Therefore, the Commission, under its report to the General Assembly, *inter alia,* defined piracy in terms of "acts" thereby creating an international crime, required only the "private ends" requirement, and set forth the number of vessels required by an act of piracy to exceed one, that is, there would be no single flag requirement included in the definition of piracy. It would remain to be seen if the draft articles that the Commission prepared would be applicable to certain sea incidents which occurred after the 1958 Geneva Conference on the Law of the Sea.

The next step in the development of the international law regard-

---

[91] 2 Y.B. Int'l L. Comm'n 283 (1956).
[92] Convention on the High Seas, *op. cit.,* note 39.
[93] *Ibid.* Note, Articles 14-21 appear in Appendix 1, Chapter I.

ing sea piracy occurred at the Geneva Conference on the Law of the Sea which took place in 1958.[94]

GENEVA CONFERENCE ON THE LAW OF THE SEA, 1958

All of the draft proposals of the International Law Commission, including the articles (Articles 38-45) on piracy, were adopted as a working basis of discussion at the Conference.[95] The articles on piracy which were prepared by the Commission were discussed at the 27th, 29th and 30th meetings of the Second Committee. The controversies which arose at the Conference were no different from those confronted by the members of the Commission and before it, by the Group.

There was the usual complaint that conventional articles regarding piracy were no longer necessary because traditional forms of piracy were no longer problems and that these articles might conflict with other conventions.[96] There was the complaint that the articles on piracy were obsolete because, among other reasons, they failed to take into consideration piratical acts that were politically motivated.[97]

Nevertheless, after considering the various proposals and modifications, the articles, as adopted, were approved by the Conference at the 10th plenary meeting and now appear as articles 14-21 of the Convention on the High Seas.[98]

Since 1958, however, there have been incidents which have occurred where certain states have claimed that "piratical" attacks have been committed upon their vessels. These incidents are illustrative of possible shortcomings in the 1958 conventional articles; and, although they are "political" in nature, they serve to highlight the differences between the "dated" form of swashbuckler-type piracy and the possible terrorist acts which can occur today. The reader shall now review these incidents and, at the same time, keep in mind the question of whether the incidents warrant revising the 1958 conventional articles.

[94] The 1958 Geneva Conference on the Law of the Sea produced the Convention cited above, note 39.

[95] The study was intended for the United Nations Conference on the Law of the Sea to be held pursuant to General Assembly Resolution 1105 (XI) of February 21, 1957; *Official Record*, 11th Session, Suppl. 17 (A/3572), p. 54.

[96] Consider, for example, Uruguay's proposal to delete articles 38 to 45 (A/CONF. 13/C.2/L.78), as cited in Whiteman, *Digest of International Law* (Washington, D.C.: Department of State), 1965, p. 662.

[97] See the Albanian-Czechoslovak proposal (A/CONF.13/C.2/L.46), cited in Whiteman, *op. cit.*, note 96, p. 662.

[98] II U.N. Conference on the Law of the Sea, Plenary Meetings, pp. 21-22, cited in Whiteman, *op. cit.*, p. 662.

APPENDIX 1 TO CHAPTER IV

Regime of the High Seas
Document A/CN.4/L.53

Observations of the Government of Poland, concerning freedom of navigation on the high seas, transmitted by Mr. Jan Balicki, observer of Poland to the Seventh Session of the International Law Commission, 2 Y.B. Int'l L. Comm'n 1-2 (1955)

1. Freedom of navigation, being the most essential element of the principle of freedom of the seas, is one of the basic principles of modern international law. This has been confirmed in numerous judgments of both municipal and international courts, in works of authorities in law and in international documents like the Barcelona Declaration, the Washington Declaration of 1921 and the Atlantic Charter of 1941.

2. The indisputable nature of this principle and its general recognition derive from the significance it has in international relations as a whole. Seas and oceans constituting over 70 per cent of the surface of the globe and being a natural link between continents are predestined to play an essential part in the development of international relations. This significance is reflected, above all, in the field of commercial communication, cultural, technical and other exchange. It would not be erroneous to state that the victory of the principle of freedom of navigation has contributed in a fundamental way to the development of international intercourse and exchange in the course of the last centuries.

3. From this first-rate importance of unhampered navigation on seas and oceans for the life of all nations follows the necessity to safeguard its accessibility to all nations in equal measure, so that one state or a group of states does not extend its jurisdiction over it. Freedom of navigation must be based on the principle of equal rights of all states.

4. From the basic principles of freedom of the seas and freedom of navigation follows the equal right for all states to have their own ships at sea and to participate in maritime exchange. From the principle of freedom of the seas it follows that only the state to which a given ship belongs has the right to extend its jurisdiction over it on the high seas. This concerns merchantmen and men-of-war alike. A merchant ship sailing under the flag of the country she belongs to cannot be stopped by other than warships of her own state. This principle admits very few fairly strictly defined exceptions when a merchant ship on the high seas can be stopped by a man-of-war of another state: (a) in case she commits an international crime — piracy, (b) in the case when a ship which has committed a crime on the territory of another state attempts to escape — the right of pursuit, (c) in cases provided for in international agreements — e.g., suspected smuggling or prohibited liquor trade.

5. In all these exceptional situations action undertaken by men-of-war against foreign merchantmen aims at the protection of the freedom of the seas against criminal activities or against activities recognized by multilateral agreements as harmful, and expresses the concern of various states for the safety and freedom of maritime navigation and trade. They cannot, however, be in any case a justification for any arbitrary action.

6. The exercise of the right of pursuit is confined to the state in whose port or on whose territory a foreign merchantman has committed a crime. Men-of-

war of signatory states are entitled to interference in the case of an infringement of a convention and, only in the case of piracy, which is a heavy common
crime, men-of-war of all states have the right of pursuit.

7. The entire development of international maritime law aims at strengthen-
ing the safety of sea navigation in all its aspects.

8. For some time, however, we have been witnessing the most brutal violation of age-old principles by those who direct hostile activities against vessels of
many states. In the China seas the stopping of merchantmen, the seizure of
their cargoes, the detention of the crews are organized on a wide scale. According to statements by Lloyds, 70 vessels under various flags were subject to
these illegal acts between 23 August 1949 and 16 December 1953. This figure
is not complete, as other vessels were detained at a later time, inter alia, the
Soviet tanker *Tuapse*. Among the seized vessels there were two Polish merchant
ships: *Praca* detained and captured in October 1953, and *Prezydent Gottwald*
in May 1954.

9. The above acts are sufficient proof of the violation in an unprecedented
way of the freedom of navigation in the China seas. It is characteristic that
these acts cannot be justified by any legal arguments. They are simply an
expression of force applied by the use of modern technical means. Foreign
men-of-war assisted by airplanes forced to stop Polish ships maintaining peaceful commercial communication with the Chinese People's Republic. Faced
with the threat of the use of force and with a possible sinking of the ships,
the Polish masters were compelled to submit to orders aimed at bringing the
ships together with their cargoes and crews to Taiwan. These orders were not
justified by anything. None of the Polish ships committed a crime on Chinese
territorial waters or any acts which might be regarded as piratical. None of
the Polish ships violated any provisions of international conventions which
entitle foreign men-of-war to apply means of compulsion. Thus the application
of such means was an act of utter lawlessness. As follows from the above, the
very act of stopping the ships by the use of force was illegal and has no justification whatsoever. In this way the right of the flag, which follows from the
principle of state sovereignty, was violated.

10. It should also be pointed out that the stopping of ships on the high seas
violates the freedom of navigation. Merchantmen carrying cargoes in trade
exchange between countries are seriously endangered and their possibility of
unhampered sailing on sea routes is thus restricted.

11. The acts committed in the China seas constitute a most serious crime —
namely, piracy.

12. The circumstances of the seizure of both Polish ships clearly show that
violence was used against them. On the high seas two Polish merchant ships
were stopped by warships and brought to the island of Taiwan. This was committed under the threat of the use of weapons involving a constant danger to
the lives of the members of the crews. This is thus the main evidence that the
act committed against the Polish vessels has marks of piracy.

13. In these concrete cases there also was *animus furandi* — i.e., the intent
to plunder for gain confirmed by many lawyers as an element of piracy.

14. The seizure of Polish ships which finds no justification in international
law is qualified as piracy, as *delictum jure gentium,* and it should be treated
accordingly. All authorities in international law agree that a crime thus committed on the high seas open to all states must be prosecuted by all states, as
freedom of navigation is not an abstract notion but involves certain rights and
duties. It involves not only the duty for a state not to hamper by its activities

the free use of navigation routes by ships of other states, but also the duty of adopting an active attitude by the state with regard to the observance of that principle.

15. In view of the principles enunciated above, some of the formulations contained in the sixth report on the regime of the high seas cannot but give rise to doubts. Articles 22 and 23 of the draft articles relating to the regime of the high seas are particular cases in point.

16. It seems advisable in article 22 to stress the importance of the general repression of piracy — the first two sentences of the article to read as follows:

"All states are required to co-operate for the more effective repression of piracy and of the slave trade on the high seas. They shall adopt efficient measures to prevent and punish piracy and to prevent the transport of slaves on vessels authorized to fly their colours and the unlawful use of their flag."

17. The formulation of article 23 of the draft is in conflict with established views on piracy. It should be clear that the words "bona fide purpose of asserting a claim of right" cannot be used in connexion with such actions as robbery, rape, wounding, enslavement and killing. It should be clear, for instance, that robbery or enslavement, being by their nature illegal and criminal, could not be committed with a bona fide purpose. Similarly the words "for private ends" should be omitted, since no ends, even when described by the perpetrators as not being "private" (i.e., "public") can justify acts of piracy. The present wording of article 23, if accepted and embodied in an international convention, could be used by pirates to justify any action by maintaining that their action had the bona fide "purpose of asserting a claim of right" and that they were not acting "for private ends."

18. Finally it should be stated that the draft articles do not appear to contain a clear and unambiguous formulation of the acknowledged principle of freedom of navigation on the high seas.

APPENDIX 2 TO CHAPTER IV

International Law Commission: Records of the Seventh Session, 327th Meeting, July 5, 1955: Discussion of Article 13; 1 Y.B. Int'l L. Comm'n 266 (1955)

77. Sir Gerald FITZMAURICE considered that the first sentence in the second paragraph of the comment to article 13 was too categorical: strong arguments could be adduced against the principle laid down in article 13. International law allowed States to take action against pirates irrespective of their nationality and others were required to refrain from interfering. It was a perfectly defensible point of view, endorsed by many authorities, to hold that international law went no further and enunciated no obligation whereby States must suppress piracy. He therefore proposed that the sentence be modified and that the words "laid upon it by international law" be deleted from the second sentence.

78. Mr. FRANÇOIS (Rapporteur) said that he did not altogether agree with the preceding speaker since the Commission had definitely decided that States should co-operate to the fullest possible extent in the repression of piracy.

79. Mr. ZOUREK said that since the Commission had upheld the view that piracy was an international crime something must be said on those lines in the comment.

80. The CHAIRMAN, speaking in his personal capacity, agreed with Sir Gerald Fitzmaurice that failure to suppress piracy was not a violation of international law.

81. Mr. KRYLOV said that the declaration made at the Congress of Vienna in 1815 about the scourge of piracy reinforced the view that it was the duty of States to repress it.

It was agreed to re-draft the first sentence of the second paragraph to read: "Article 13 lays down a sound principle" instead of "Article 13 lays down a principle which cannot be challenged."

APPENDIX 3 TO CHAPTER IV

Report of the International Law Commission to the General Assembly, Seventh Session, Comment to Article 14, 2 Y.B. Int'l L. Comm'n 25 (1955)

The Commission had to consider certain *controversial points* [emphasis added] as to the essential features of piracy. It reached the conclusion that:

1. The intention to rob (*animus furandi*) is not required. Acts of piracy may be prompted by feelings of hatred or revenge, and not merely by the desire for gain.

2. The acts must be committed for private ends.

3. Save in the case provided for in article 15, piracy can be committed only by merchant vessels, not by warships.

4. Piracy can be committed only on the high seas or in a place situated outside the territorial jurisdiction of any State, and cannot be committed within the territory of a State or in its territorial sea.

5. Acts of piracy can be committed not only by vessels on the high seas, but also by aircraft, if such acts are committed against vessels on the high seas.

6. Acts committed on board a vessel by the crew or passengers and directed against the vessel itself, or against the persons or property on the vessel cannot be regarded as acts of piracy.

With regard to point 3 the Commission is aware that there are treaties, such as the Nyon Arrangement of 14 September 1937, which brand the sinking of merchant vessels by submarines, against the dictates of humanity, as piratical acts. But it is of the opinion that such treaties do not invalidate the principle that piracy can only be committed by private vessels. The questions arising in connexion with acts committed by warships in the service of rival Governments engaged in civil war are too complex to make it seem necessary for the safe-guarding of public order on the high seas that all States should have a general right, let alone an obligation, to repress as piracy acts perpetrated by the warships of the parties in question. In view of the immunity from interference by other ships which warships are entitled to claim, the seizure of such vessels on suspicion of piracy might involve the gravest consequences. Hence the Commission feels that to assimilate unlawful acts committed by warships to acts of piracy would be prejudicial to the interests of the international community. The Commission was unable to share the view held by some of its members that the principle laid down in the Nyon Arrangement endorsed a new right in the process of development.

As regards point 4, the Commission considers, despite certain dissenting opinions, that where the attack takes place within the territory of a State, including its territorial sea, the general rule should be applied that it is a matter of the State affected to take the necessary measures for the repression of the acts committed within its territory. In this the Commission is also following the line taken by most writers on the subject.

With regard to point 5, the Commission feels that acts committed in the air by one aircraft against another aircraft cannot be regarded as acts of piracy. In any case such acts are outside the scope of these draft articles. However, acts committed by a pirate aircraft against a vessel on the high seas might, in the Commission's view, be assimilated to acts committed by a pirate vessel.

The view adopted by the Commission in regard to point 6 tallies with the opinions of most writers. Even where the purpose of the mutineers is to seize the vessel, their acts do not constitute acts of piracy.

APPENDIX 4 TO CHAPTER IV

International Law Commission: Summary Records of the Seventh Session, 327th Meeting, July 5, 1955: Discussion of the Comment to Article 14; 1 Y.B. Int'l L. Comm'n 266-267 (1955)

82. Mr. SANDSTROM observed that subparagraph 3 in the first paragraph of the comment was at present in conflict with article 15 and therefore required some modification.

83. Mr. FRANÇOIS (Rapporteur) said that he would be prepared to meet Mr. Sandstrom's point by inserting some such wording as "Save in the case provided for in article 15" at the beginning of subparagraph 3.

84. Mr. HSU considered the distinction drawn in subparagraph 3 to be a false one since *acts of piracy could be committed by any kind of vessel and not only by merchantmen* [emphasis added].

85. It would be remembered that the Nyon Arrangement had been based on the International Treaty for the Limitation and Reduction of Naval Armament signed in London in 1930 which in its turn had been inspired by the Treaty relating to the Use of Submarines and Noxious Gases in Warfare drawn up at Washington in 1922; the purpose of all three had been to outlaw submarine warfare against merchant vessels, and had little connexion with civil war. He therefore felt that the first two sentences of the second paragraph were somewhat irrelevant and should be amended by substituting the words "brand the sinking of merchant vessels by submarines, against the dictates of humanity, as piratical acts" for the words "are inconsistent with the viewpoint adopted by the Commission" and by deleting the words "which in any case are few in number and concerned with the settlement of very special cases," after the words "that such treaties."

86. Mr. FRANÇOIS (Rapporteur) accepted Mr. Hsu's amendments.

87. Mr. KRYLOV proposed deletion of the words "Acts committed for political ends cannot be regarded as piratical acts" after the first sentence in subparagraph 2 *on the ground that it was impossible to establish a criterion*

to distinguish between acts committed for private ends and acts committed for political ends [emphasis added].

88. Mr. FRANÇOIS (Rapporteur) said that the controversial question whether a political act could be regarded as piracy had been discussed at great length in the past and had been raised in the Harvard Draft. He would personally prefer the second sentence of subparagraph 2 to be retained. On the other hand it might be desirable to explain a little more fully what was meant by acts committed for private ends.

89. Mr. SANDSTROM was opposed to modifying subparagraph 2 because it drew an important distinction.

90. Mr. ZOUREK considered Mr. Krylov's proposal to be well-founded. Moreover article 15 implicitly recognized that political acts might be assimilated to acts of piracy.

91. He suggested that the French text of subparagraph 2 might be examined with a view to deciding whether the words *"dans un but personnel"* was an exact rendering of the words "for private ends."

92. Sir Gerald FITZMAURICE said that he could accept Mr. Krylov's proposal, but thought that the Commission should at its next session reconsider the wording of the first sentence in subparagraph 2 so as to find some better expression than "for private ends." *The real antithesis which needed to be brought out was between authorized and unauthorized acts and acts committed in a public or in a private capacity. An act committed in a private capacity could have a political purpose but be unauthorized – as, for example the seizure of a vessel by the member of an opposition party* [emphasis added].

93. Mr. HSU supported Mr. Krylov's proposal.

Mr. Krylov's proposal to delete the second sentence in subparagraph 2 of the first paragraph of the comment was adopted by 5 votes to 3, with 3 abstentions.

94. Faris Be el-KHOURI criticized the confusing manner in which subparagraphs 3, 4 and 5 had been drafted; it could be inferred from the present text that piracy was legal but only on the high seas.

95. The CHAIRMAN felt that the meaning was quite clear. Moreover, the form was customary in legal usage.

96. Mr. FRANÇOIS (Rapporteur) said that he would be unwilling to modify the text for the reasons given by the Chairman.

97. Mr. LIANG (Secretary to the Commission) suggested that subparagraph 3 required amendment since piracy could be committed only by individuals and not by vessels. It would be noted that the article itself referred to acts committed by the crew or passengers.

The comment to article 14 was adopted as amended.

APPENDIX 5 TO CHAPTER IV

International Law Commission: Summary Records of the Seventh Session, 330th Meeting, July 8, 1955: Discussion of the Comment to Article 14; 1 Y.B. Int'l L. Comm'n 286-287 (1955)

1. Mr. FRANÇOIS (Rapporteur) submitted the following amended text for the second paragraph of the comment to article 14:

With regard to point 3, the Commission is aware that there are treaties, such as the Nyon Arrangement of 14 September 1937, which brand the sinking of merchant vessels by submarines, against the dictates of humanity, as piratical acts. But it is of the opinion that such treaties do not invalidate the principle that piracy can only be committed by private vessels. The questions arising in connection with civil war or with acts committed by warships in the service of governments not universally recognized are too complex to make it seem necessary for the safeguarding of public order on the high seas that all States should have a general right, let alone an obligation, to repress as piracy acts perpetrated by the warships of the parties in question. In view of the immunity from interference by other ships which warships are entitled to claim, the seizure of such vessels on suspicion of piracy might involve the gravest consequences. Hence the Commission feels that to assimilate unlawful acts committed by warships to acts of piracy would be prejudicial to the interests of the international community. The Commission was unable to share the view held by some of its members that the principle laid down in the Nyon Arrangement endorsed a new right in the process of development.

2. He had prepared that text in order to meet a point raised by Mr. Hsu [i.e. at the 326th meeting, paras. 84-85]. He understood, however, that Mr. Hsu was satisfied only with the first part of the proposed text and wished the remainder deleted.

3. For his part, he [Mr. François] could not agree to Mr. Hsu's proposal and submitted the whole text to the Commission.

4. Mr. Hsu proposed the following text for the relevant paragraph:

With regard to point 3, the Commission is aware that there are treaties, such as the Nyon Arrangement of 14 September 1937, which brand the sinking of merchant vessels by submarines, against the dictates of humanity, as piratical acts. But it is of the opinion that such treaties do not invalidate the principle that piracy can only be committed by private vessels. The questions arising in connection with civil war or with acts committed by warships in the service of governments not universally recognized are too complex to make it seem necessary for the Commission to enter into them.

5. The question whether parties to a civil war constituted belligerents or not, as well as that of governments which were not universally recognized, were problems far too complex to be mentioned in the paragraph in question. *They were problems which had not been discussed by the Commission*, and there was no necessity to include a reference to them [emphasis added].

6. The Nyon Agreement did not specifically deal with either problem. Its purpose was to condemn unrestricted submarine warfare against merchantmen, as had been done by the Washington Treaty of 1922 and the London Treaty of 1930.

7. Piracy could only be committed by a warship if the crew mutinied and took over control of the ship.

8. Mr. SANDSTROM agreed with the text proposed by the Rapporteur. The Nyon Agreement specifically concerned the case of a civil war; there was, therefore, nothing confusing in the reference to civil war in the paragraph under discussion.

9. Sir Gerald FITZMAURICE said that Mr. Hsu's objection could be partly met if the first two sentences were separated from the rest of the text by dividing it into two paragraphs.

10. Mr. FRANÇOIS (Rapporteur) accepted Sir Gerald Fitzmaurice's suggestion.

11. The CHAIRMAN put the text proposed by Mr. Hsu to the vote.

The text proposed by Mr. Hsu was rejected by 8 votes to 2 with 1 abstention.

12. Mr. LIANG (Secretary to the Commission) suggested that the third sentence of the paragraph proposed by the Rapporteur be amended to read:

The questions arising in connexion with acts committed by warships in the service of rival governments engaged in civil war are too complex to make it seem necessary for the safeguarding of public order. . .

That change would make the meaning of the text clearer. There was really only one problem, and not two separate problems, that of civil war and that of governments not universally recognized.

13. Mr. FRANÇOIS (Rapporteur) accepted that suggestion.

14. Mr. ZOUREK proposed deletion of the penultimate sentence ["Hence the Commission feels . . ."], which appeared to have too wide a scope; he recalled that in article 15 provision had been made for acts of piracy committed by a warship.

Mr. Zourek's proposal was rejected, 5 votes being cast in favor and 5 against, with 1 abstention.

The text proposed by the Rapporteur for insertion in place of the second paragraph of the comment to article 14 was adopted as amended.

APPENDIX 6 TO CHAPTER IV

Report of the International Law Commission covering the work of its Seventh Session, May 2-July 8, 1955, A/2934; 2 Y.B. Int'l L. Comm'n 25-26 (1955)

Article 15
The acts of piracy committed by a warship or a military aircraft whose crew mutinies are assimilated to acts committed by a private vessel.

Comment
A warship whose crew has mutinied and taken control of the ship must be assimilated to a private vessel, so that acts committed against another vessel can assume the character of acts of piracy.

Article 16
A ship or aircraft is considered a pirate ship or aircraft when it is devoted by the persons in dominant control to the purpose of committing an act described in the first sentence of article 14, paragraph 1.

Comment
The purpose of this article is to define the terms 'pirate ship' and 'pirate aircraft' as used in the following articles.

Article 17
A ship or aircraft may retain its national character although it has become a pirate ship or aircraft. The retention or loss of national character is determined by the law of the State from which it was originally derived.

Comment
It has been argued that a vessel loses its national character by the fact of committing acts of piracy. The Commission cannot share this view. Such acts involve the consequences referred to in article 18; even though the rule under which a vessel on the high seas is subject only to the authority of the flag State no longer applies, the vessel keeps the nationality of the State in question, and subject to the provisions of article 18, that State can apply its law in the same way as to other vessels flying its flag. A pirate ship should only be regarded as a ship without nationality where the national laws of the State in question regard piracy as grounds for loss of nationality.

APPENDIX 7 TO CHAPTER IV

International Law Commission: Summary Records of the Seventh Session, 321st meeting, June 28, 1955, 1 Y.B. Int'l L. Comm'n 228 (1955)

Article 17
On the high seas or in any other place not within the territorial jurisdiction of another State, any State may seize a pirate ship or aircraft or a ship taken by piracy and under the control of pirates, and property or persons on board. The courts of that State may pronounce sentence on such persons, and determine the action to be taken with regard to the property, subject to rights of third parties acting in good faith.

The summary records disclose there was some controversy regarding the part of that article which read "on such persons":

7. Mr. Krylov pointed out that the second sentence of the article was ambiguous in its reference to pronouncing sentence "on such persons." The text appeared to suggest that the penalties could be inflicted on the victims of the pirates as well as on the pirates themselves.

This article was referred to the Drafting Committee and appeared in the Report of the Commission as Article 18 as follows.

Report of the International Law Commission Covering the Work of Its Seventh Session, May 2-July 8, 1955, A/2934; 2 Y.B. Int'l L. Comm'n (1955)

Article 18
On the high seas or in any other place not within the territorial jurisdiction of another State, any State may seize a pirate ship or aircraft or a ship taken by piracy and under the control of pirates, and property or persons on board. The

courts of that State may decide upon the penalties to be imposed, and determine the action to be taken with regard to the property, subject to rights of third parties acting in good faith.

Comment
This article gives any State the right to seize pirate ships (and ships seized by pirates) and to have them tried by its courts.

Before this article becomes applicable to a vessel, it must have committed acts of piracy. A ship which has no right to fly any flag but has not committed acts of piracy cannot be assimilated to a pirate vessel.

Article 19
Where the seizure of a ship or aircraft on suspicion of piracy has been effected without adequate grounds, the State making the seizure shall be liable to the State the nationality of which is possessed by the ship or aircraft for any damage caused by the seizure.

Comment
This article penalizes the unjustified seizure of vessels suspected of piracy. The penalty applies to seizure in the circumstances described in article 18 and to all acts of interference committed on the grounds of suspicion of piracy referred to in article 21 [see the comment on article 21].

Article 20
A seizure because of piracy may be made only by warships or military aircraft.

Comment
State action against ships suspected of engaging in piracy should be exercised with great circumspection so as to avoid friction between States. Hence it is important that the right to take action should be confined to warships, since other state-owned vessels do not provide the same safeguards against abuse.

Except for the comments previously discussed in connection with Article 18, Articles 18-20 and the Comments prepared therewith were adopted without further modification.

APPENDIX 8 TO CHAPTER IV

International Law Commission: Summary Records of the Seventh Session, 321st meeting, June 28, 1955, 1 Y.B. Int'l L. Comm'n 229 (1955)

Article 20 (21): Right of Stoppage (Right of Visit)
Except where acts of interference derive from powers conferred by treaty, a warship which encounters a foreign merchant vessel at sea is not justified in boarding her or in taking any further action unless there is reasonable ground for suspecting:
1. That the vessel is engaged in piracy:

2. That while in the maritime zones regarded as suspect in international treaties for the abolition of the slave trade, the vessel is engaged in that trade;

3. That while flying a foreign flag or refusing to show its flag, the vessel is, in reality, of the same nationality as the warship.

In the case provided for in paragraphs 1-3 above, the warship may proceed to verify the vessel's title to fly its flag. To this end, it may send a boat under the command of an officer to the suspect vessel. If suspicion remains after the documents have been checked, it may proceed to a further examination on board the vessel, which must be carried out with all possible consideration.

If the suspicions prove to be unfounded and provided that the vessel boarded has not committed any acts to justify them, it shall be compensated for the loss sustained.

8. Mr. ZOUREK proposed the deletion of the words "or in taking any further action" in the first paragraph.

9. Mr. FRANÇOIS (Special Rapporteur) agreed.

10. He recalled that Mr. Edmonds had proposed the addition of the following words after the words 'reasonable ground for suspecting that the vessel is engaged in piracy or the slave trade,' in the original text of the article:

... or, during times of imminent peril to the security of the State, in activities hostile to the State of the warship. (A/CN.4/L.57).

That proposal had been referred to the *ad hoc* Committee. After due consideration, that Committee had decided that such a provision would lend itself to abuse and should, therefore, not be included in the text. He proposed that the Commission should formally reject the proposed addition.

It was so agreed.

11. Mr. LIANG (Secretary to the Commission) said that the title "Right of Stoppage" was somewhat incongruous. Probably the reference was to the right of verification of flag.

12. In connexion with the final paragraph of the article, in cases where the suspicions proved unfounded, it seemed unnecessary to stipulate in addition that the vessel should not have committed any acts to justify the suspicions. Possibly the intention was to make provision for two alternative possibilities, in which case the words "or if" should be substituted for the words "and provided that."

13. Sir Gerald FITZMAURICE said that the intention was to make provision for two cumulative conditions. If a ship acted in a suspicious manner, it did not deserve compensation even if it eventually transpired that no offence had been committed. Compensation was justified only where a ship had neither committed any offence nor given any reasonable grounds for suspicion. With regard to the title of the article, perhaps "Right of Visit" might be more appropriate.

14. Mr. GARCIA-AMADOR proposed that the paragraphs be numbered in arabic numerals and the subparagraphs of paragraph 1 be lettered (a), (b) and (c), with a consequential change at the beginning of paragraph 2.

15. Mr. FRANÇOIS (Special Rapporteur) agreed.

Subject to final drafting of its title, article 20 (21) was adopted with that amendment.

APPENDIX 9 TO CHAPTER IV

Report of the International Law Commission covering the Work of Its Seventh Session, May 2-July 8, 1955, A/2934; 2 Y.B. Int'l L. Comm'n 26-27 (1955)

Article 21: Right of Visit

1. Except where acts of interference derive from powers conferred by treaty, a warship which encounters a foreign merchant vessel at sea is not justified in boarding her unless there is reasonable ground for suspecting:
(a) That the vessel is engaged in piracy; or
(b) That while in the maritime zones regarded as suspect in international treaties for the abolition of the slave trade, the vessel is engaged in that trade; or
(c) That while flying a foreign flag or refusing to show its flag, the vessel is, in reality, of the same nationality as the warship.

2. In the cases provided for in sub-paragraphs (a), (b), and (c) above, the warship may proceed to verify the vessel's title to fly its flag. To this end, it may send a boat under the command of an officer to the suspect vessel. If suspicion remains after the documents have been checked, it may proceed to a further examination on board the vessel, which must be carried out with all possible consideration.

3. If the suspicions prove to be unfounded and provided that the vessel boarded has not committed any acts to justify them, it shall be compensated for the loss sustained.

The principle of freedom of the seas implies that, generally speaking, a merchant vessel can only be boarded on the high seas by a warship flying the same flag. International law, however, admits certain exceptions to this rule – namely, cases where there is reasonable ground for suspecting:

1. That the vessel is engaged in piracy;
2. That the vessel is engaged in slave trade.

Right of visit was recognized in this latter case by the treaties for the repression of slavery, especially the Brussels Act of 2 July 1890. For purposes of repression this assimilated slavery to piracy, with the proviso that the right in question could only be exercised in certain zones clearly defined in the treaties. The Commission felt that it should follow this example so as to ensure that the exercise of the right of control would not be used as a pretext for exercising the right of visit in waters where the slave trade would not normally be expected to exist;

3. That the vessel is hiding its proper nationality and is in reality of the same nationality as the warship.

In this case it can be presumed that the vessel has committed unlawful acts and the warship should be at liberty to verify whether its suspicions are justified.

In these three cases the warship is authorized to request a ship not flying a flag to show its colours. If the suspicion is not allayed the warship may proceed to check the ship's papers. To this end it must send a boat to the suspect vessel.

As a general rule, the warship may not require the merchant vessel to put out a boat to the warship. That would be asking too much of a merchant ship, and a ship's papers must not be exposed unnecessarily to the risk of getting lost. If the examination of the merchant vessel's papers does not allay the suspicions, a further examination may be made on board the vessel. Such examination must in no circumstances be used for purposes other than those which warranted stopping the vessel. Hence the boarding party must be under the command of an officer responsible for the conduct of his men.

The State to which the warship belongs must compensate the merchant vessel for any delay caused by the warship's action, not only where the vessel was stopped without reasonable grounds, but in all cases where suspicion proves unfounded and the vessel committed no act calculated to give rise to suspicion.

The question arose whether the right to board a vessel should be recognized also in the event of a vessel being suspected of committing acts hostile to the State to which the warship belongs, at a time of imminent danger for the security of that State. The Commission did not deem it advisable to include such a provision mainly because of the vagueness of terms like "imminent danger" and "hostile acts," which leaves them open to abuse.

APPENDIX 10 TO CHAPTER IV

International Law Commission: Summary Records of the Seventh Session, 327th meeting, July 5, 1955, 1 Y.B. Int'l L. Comm'n 267 (1955)

Article 21: Right of Inspection

98. Mr. FRANÇOIS (Rapporteur) said that the words 'right of visit' should be substituted for the words "right of inspection" in the title of article 21 and in the comment.

99. Sir Gerald FITZMAURICE considered that, in the third paragraph of the comment, the first sentence, in which reference was made to severe penalties, did not accurately reflect the provision contained in the article itself and should be deleted. The article merely stated that if the suspicions proved unfounded, and provided the vessel boarded had not committed any acts to justify them, compensation would be made.

100. In the last sentence of the same paragraph the word "and" should be substituted for the words "or where" after the word "where suspicion proves unfounded."

101. Mr. EDMONDS observed that the comment should bring out that compensation must be adequate.

102. Mr. FRANÇOIS (Rapporteur) accepted Sir Gerald Fitzmaurice's second amendment. The word "or" was due to an error.

Sir Gerald Fitzmaurice's proposal for the deletion of the first sentence [It read as follows: "If the suspicions prove to be unfounded, the penalties must be severe."] in the third paragraph of the comment was accepted.

In the same paragraph, it was also decided to replace the full stop after the word "action" by a comma and to delete the words "This applies."

103. Mr. ZOUREK considered that the last sentence in the comment should end at the words "to include such a provision" because other arguments in addition to that mentioned in the remainder of the sentence had been put forward.

104. Mr. FRANÇOIS (Rapporteur) considered that omission to be unnecessary because of the presence of the word "mainly."

The Comment to article 21 was adopted as amended.

Further consideration of the Commission's draft report was adjourned.

APPENDIX 11 TO CHAPTER IV

Summary of Replies from Governments and Conclusions of the Special Rapporteur, A/CN.4/97/Add. 1 to 3, 2 Y.B. Int'l L. Comm'n 18-20 (1956)

Article 13: Piracy

Netherlands (A/CN.4/99/Add. 1):

110. Article 13 refers to piracy "on the high seas" where according to article 14 piracy may also be committed in "territory outside the jurisdiction of any State."

111. The Rapporteur considers that the words "on the high seas" should be deleted from article 13. Piracy is defined in article 14.

Conclusion:

112. The article could be retained, with the amendment indicated above.

Article 14

China (A/CN.4/99/Add. 1):

113. The article defines piracy in the restricted sense only and should be amended to include piracy in the broad sense of the term, according to which any member of the crew or any passenger on board a vessel who, with intent to plunder or rob, commits violence or employs threats against any other member of the crew or passenger and navigates or takes command of the vessel, also commits piracy.

114. The Commission did not wish to adopt the broad definition of piracy advocated by the Chinese Government.

Union of South Africa (A/CN.4/99/Add. 1):

115. On the drafting of article 14 the Union Government makes several comments to which the reader is referred. The Commission did not consider acts committed by one aircraft against another, because it wished to confine its work to maritime law. The Commission only considered warships and private vessels; it did not deal with vessels operated by the State for commercial purposes.

116. The Rapporteur is of opinion that such vessels can in fact be guilty of piracy. The article could be amplified accordingly.

Netherlands (A/CN.4/99/Add. 1):

117. The Netherlands Government would like it to be made clear that article 14 does not refer to warships or to State-owned vessels having a non-

commercial public function. The Netherlands Government points out that in
paragraph 1 (a) only the term "vessel" is used whereas in (b) the words "vessels,
persons or property" are employed. Furthermore, paragraph 1 refers to acts
"against persons or property."

118. The Rapporteur agrees that the drafting could be improved.

United Kingdom (A/CN.4/99/Add. 1):
119. Only drafting amendments are proposed.

Conclusion:
120. The text of the article could be amended to read as follows:

"Piracy is any of the following acts:

1. Any illegal act of violence, detention, or any act of depredation committed for private ends by the crew or passengers of a private vessel or aircraft
or of a vessel or aircraft in commercial service, and directed against:

(a) Vessels, persons or property on the high seas other than the vessel on
which the act is committed;

(b) Vessels, persons or property in territory outside the jurisdiction of any
State."

No change in paragraphs 2 and 3.

Article 15
Belgium (A/CN.4/99):
121. The Belgian Government proposes the following wording:

If the acts referred to in article 14 are committed by a warship or a military
aircraft whose crew has mutinied, then the acts in question are assimilated to
acts of piracy.

122. The Rapporteur accepts this wording.

Netherlands (A/CN.4/99/Add. 1):
123. The Netherlands Government also wishes warships to be assimilated to
State-owned vessels having a non-commercial public function.
124. The Rapporteur supports this proposal.

Yugoslavia (A/CN.4/99/Add. 1):
125. The Yugoslav Government proposes that the words "or any of the ships
mentioned in article 8 of these rules" be inserted after the word "warship."
126. The new wording may perhaps satisfy the Yugoslav Government.

Conclusion:
127. The Rapporteur proposes the following wording:

When committed by a State-owned vessel or aircraft in non-commercial service
whose crew has mutinied, the acts referred to in article 14 are assimilated to
acts of piracy.

Article 16
Belgium (A/CN.4/99):
128. The Belgian Government proposes the following wording:

A ship or aircraft is considered a pirate ship or aircraft if it has committed, or issued or is intended to be used by the persons in dominant control for the purpose of committing, one of the acts referred to in article 14, paragraph 1.

129. The Rapporteur accepts this drafting subject to an amendment by the Netherlands Government.

Netherlands (A/CN.4/99/Add. 1):
130. The Netherlands Government considers that this article could be deleted, or that if it is retained it should refer to the whole of article 14 and not only to paragraph 1 of that article.

Conclusion:
131. The article could be amended as suggested by the Belgian Government, but with the deletion of the final words "paragraph 1."

Article 17
132. No comment.

Article 18
Belgium (A/CN.4/99):
133. The Belgian Government will agree to this article if its proposal concerning article 16 is adopted.

United Kingdom (A/CN.4/99/Add. 1):
134. This article contains no provision concerning the disposal of the pirate ship after seizure. The Commission may wish to consider inserting some provision on this point. The Rapporteur wonders whether a general rule on this matter would not present difficulties, in his opinion it should be left to national courts to decide.

Conclusion:
135. The article can be maintained as it stands.

Article 19
Netherlands (A/CN.4/99/Add. 1):
136. The Netherlands Government asks why the wording differs from that of article 21, paragraph 3. The Rapporteur considers that the wording of article 21, paragraph 3, could also be adopted for article 19.

Norway (A/CN.4/99/Add. 1):
137. The Norwegian Government comments to the same effect.

Conclusion:
138. The wording of this article should be amended to bring it into conformity with article 21, paragraph 3.

Article 20
Union of South Africa (A/CN.4/99/Add. 1):
139. The Union Government asks whether it should not be stipulated that a vessel attacked by a pirate, but which repulses the attack, may seize the pirate vessel pending the arrival of a warship.

140. The Rapporteur considers that such provisional seizure is no more than legitimate self-defence and that it is not necessary to insert a stipulation to that effect.

Conclusion:
141. The article could be maintained as it stands.

Article 21: Right of Visit
Union of South Africa (A/CN.4/99/Add. 1):
142. Paragraph (b) should be extended to cover the high seas generally.
143. This question was discussed at length by the Commission, which came to a conclusion contrary to that of the Union Government. The Commission wishes to prevent suspicion of slave trading from being used as a pretext for searching vessels in parts of the high seas where there is no slave trading.

Netherlands (A/CN.4/99/Add. 1):
144. It is suggested that in the first paragraph the words "at sea" be replaced by the words "on the high seas."
145. The Rapporteur accepts this suggestion.

United Kingdom (A/CN.4/99/Add. 1):
146. Paragraph 3 should refer to "any" loss sustained.
147. The Rapporteur agrees.

Conclusion:
148. The article could be adopted with the above amendments.

APPENDIX 12 TO CHAPTER IV

International Law Commission: Summary Records of the Eighth Session, April 23-July 4, 1956, A/CN.4/SR, 343rd meeting, May 9, 1956, 1 Y.B. Int'l L. Comm'n 46-48 (1956)

Article 13: Piracy
19. Mr. FRANÇOIS, Special Rapporteur, said that the Netherlands Government had proposed the deletion of the words "on the high seas." He would accept that amendment.
20. Mr. KRYLOV concurred.
21. Mr. PAL asked whether, if that proposal were adopted, a State in whose territorial waters an act of piracy was committed would allow the vessels of another State to intervene.
22. The CHAIRMAN pointed out that an essential condition of piracy was that it should be committed outside the jurisdiction of any State. A vessel so captured would be subject to the jurisdiction of the State of the vessel effecting the capture.
23. Sir Gerald FITZMAURICE observed that in article 14, paragraph 1 (b), the intention had been to cover the case of piracy committed on desert islands, which were not under the jurisdiction of any State. If that were so, the Netherlands proposal was logical.

24. Mr. AMADO said that international co-operation could be ensured only on the high seas, so that in one sense the phrase "on the high seas," while adding precision to the article, was redundant.

25. Mr. SANDSTROM urged that it was surely an obligation of States to suppress piracy wherever it was committed.

26. Mr. SPIROPOULOS suggested the addition of the phrase "or in any other place not within territorial jurisdiction of another State," to be found in the first sentence of article 18.

27. Mr. PAL pointed out that, as drafted, the phrase "on the high seas" might refer not to the place of piracy, but to the situs for measures of co-operation. The phrase "on the high seas" should be retained, but expanded to cover all cases of piracy. Mr. Spiropoulos' proposal would meet that requirement.

Article 13, as amended by Mr. Spiropoulos, was adopted.

Article 14

28. Mr. FRANÇOIS, Special Rapporteur, said that the Netherlands Government had proposed that it should be made clear that the article did not refer to warships or state-owned vessels having a non-commercial public function.

29. Mr. KRYLOV said that he would maintain the position he had taken up when the article was discussed at the seventh session [A/CN.4/SR.330, paragraph 36].

30. Mr. LIANG, Secretary to the Commission, said that since the previous session the question of the interpretation of paragraph 1 (b) had arisen in connexion with the question of slavery. The problem was whether acts referred to in article 14 were to be regarded as acts of piracy when committed on land outside the jurisdiction of any State. He himself had read paragraph 1 (b) to imply a definite connexion between the act of piracy and the high seas, but it might be advisable to clarify further the phrase "territory outside the jurisdiction of any State."

31. Sir Gerald FITZMAURICE thought that point had been made clear in paragraph 1 by the reference to "a private vessel or a private aircraft."

32. Mr. SPIROPOULOS, while agreeing, quoted the case of the crew of a ship landing in "no man's land" and committing an act of piracy 100 miles from the coast. It would be impossible in an article of that kind to cover all possible contingencies.

33. He emphasized that the text was only a *minimum* definition of piracy. States had the right to punish other acts of piracy than those mentioned, as could be seen from a comparison between the article and the piracy legislation of individual States [emphasis added].

34. Mr. AMADO, while appreciating the Secretary's point, suggested that the question of territory outside the jurisdiction of any State be left to the Sub-Committee.

35. Mr. SPIROPOULOS, concurring, said it should be made clear in the comment on the article that the territory referred to was some such place as a desert island or shoal, and not some remote spot in the hinterland.

36. Mr. LIANG, Secretary to the Commission, said that in the case he had quoted his own interpretation of article 14 — namely, that "piracy" means acts committed on the high seas or from vessels on the high seas — was partly based on the first part of paragraph 1, referred to by Sir Gerald Fitzmaurice. However, the phrase "or a private aircraft" might provide some basis for a different interpretation, if the sense of the article were not further clarified.

37. Mr. ZOUREK said that he would take his stand on the reservations that he had made in the discussions on the definition of piracy at the seventh session [A/CN.4/SR.321, paragraph 4]. *He considered, in particular, that the acts of violence and depredation referred to in article 14 constituted acts of piracy even when committed (a) for political ends; (b) by warships or military aircraft; or (c) by aircraft or seaplanes against foreign aircraft or seaplanes, unless, in those three cases, the acts in question were acts of aggression committed, (d) from the high seas against ships, persons or goods situated in territorial waters or internal waters, or against the land* [emphasis added].

38. The Secretary's point was linked with the South African comment. The question of aircraft in general in relation to piracy was an interesting one which had various aspects, such as the question whether acts of violence committed by an aircraft taking off from a desert island or some other place not within the territorial jurisdiction of a State could be regarded as acts of piracy. The analogy between vessels and aircraft was close, and intention and violence were elements common to such acts committed by both.

39. Mr. SPIROPOULOS *suggested that the Commission should restrict its consideration to acts of piracy committed by vessels. He wondered whether any cases were known of acts of piracy committed by aircraft. It would be a mistake further to complicate an already controversial subject.* In that connexion, subparagraph 5 of the first paragraph of the comment on the article (A/2934) would require reexamination [emphasis added].

40. Mr. PAL proposed that in the opening sentence the word "is" be replaced by the word "includes," and that in paragraph 1 the words "or a private aircraft" be deleted.

41. He further pointed out that in paragraph 1 (a) the words "on which" were somewhat confusing. The intention was not to exclude the vessel "on which" piracy was committed, but the vessel "from which" it was committed. An act of piracy "against" a vessel would normally be committed on that vessel. It should be made clear,that the intention was to exclude the pirate vessel from which the act of piracy might be committed "against," "in" or "on board" another vessel.

42. Sir Gerald FITZMAURICE urged that a precise definition of piracy was required because it gave warships of all nations a right of visit and seizure.

43. *Mr. Spiropoulos was correct in pointing out that the definition of piracy would vary from one country to another. Nevertheless, for cases outside the territorial waters of a State, the jurisdiction of its vessels was limited by the definitions of piracy in international law* [emphasis added].

44. *With regard to Mr. Pal's second proposal, it would be a pity to delete the reference to private aircraft, because the Commission should not disregard an aspect of piracy that was both novel and potentially real.* Ships could be controlled by aircraft in war; aircraft were also used for fishery protection patrols in territorial waters. It was not difficult to conceive of piracy being committed by an aircraft, particularly a flying-boat [emphasis added].

45. Mr. PAL admitted the force of Sir Gerald Fitzmaurice's argument for a precise definition of the term "piracy."

46. Mr. SPIROPOULOS, referring to private aircraft, said that he had merely adduced a point, and had not made a formal proposal. His only desire was to avoid unnecessary complications. While accepting Sir Gerald Fitzmaurice's argument, he was still of opinion that subparagraph 5 of the comment should be revised.

47. In reply to Mr. KRYLOV, Mr. FRANÇOIS, Special Rapporteur, said that deletion of the reference to private aircraft would obviously facilitate the task of the Sub-Committee. Sir Gerald Fitzmaurice's arguments were, however, compelling and the draft would be enriched by the retention of the reference to private aircraft.

48. Mr. AMADO suggested that subparagraph 4 of the first paragraph of the comment should be taken as a basis for reviewing the text of paragraph 1 (b).

49. Mr. KRYLOV and Mr. ZOUREK wished to place on record their opposition to the article in its existing form.

Subject to drafting changes in the light of the discussion, article 14 was adopted.

Article 15

50. Mr. FRANÇOIS, Special Rapporteur, said that the Government of the Netherlands had made the same proposal as for article 14 — namely, the assimilation of warships to State-owned vessels having a non-commercial public function. The other proposals were drafting amendments only.

51. Mr. KRYLOV said that the text should be retained and the Netherlands proposal rejected as quite unrealistic.

52. Sir Gerald FITZMAURICE, while sharing Mr. Krylov's dislike of modifying an adopted text, felt that the Commission was bound to give serious consideration to a proposal of substance raised by a government.

53. The Commission's conception had been that piracy was essentially an act committed by a ship's company or persons acting on their own authority, thereby excluding warships. There had come into existence, however, a new class of vessel which, though not a warship, was nevertheless acting under the authority of the State. The Netherlands proposal, therefore, had some force. The case contemplated in article 15 was admittedly exceptional. If, however, that was possible in the case of a warship, was it not much more likely to occur in the case of other kinds of government-owned vessels? The question should be ventilated in the Sub-Committee.

54. Mr. PAL supported Sir Gerald Fitzmaurice's last suggestion; precision in such a matter was of the utmost importance.

55. On a point of drafting, he would draw attention to the fact that, whereas article 14, paragraph 1, referred to acts committed "by the crew or the passengers of a private vessel," article 15 referred merely to acts committed by the vessel itself. It should be made clear that the meaning intended was that the acts were committed by persons.

Subject to drafting changes in the light of the discussion, article 15 was adopted.

Article 16

56. Mr. FRANÇOIS, Special Rapporteur, said that the government comments related only to points of drafting.

57. Mr. SANDSTROM noted that the Special Rapporteur appeared to accept the Belgian Government's amendment, which would have the effect of removing the limitation on the period during which a ship or aircraft would be considered a pirate.

58. Mr. FRANÇOIS, Special Rapporteur, suggested that the point might be referred to the Sub-Committee.

59. Mr. SANDSTROM said he would have no objection.

It was agreed to refer article 16 and the point raised by Mr. Sandstrom to the Sub-Committee.

Article 17
Article 17 was adopted without comment.

Article 18
60. Mr. FRANÇOIS, Special Rapporteur, said that he saw no need to insert a provision concerning the disposal of the pirate ship after seizure, as suggested by the United Kingdom Government. It was undesirable for the Commission to go into too much detail and the matter could be left to national legislation.

61. Sir Gerald FITZMAURICE, while not dissenting, from the Special Rapporteur's view, pointed out that the United Kingdom Government was anxious to make it clear that the word "property" in the second sentence included the vessel itself, since the present text might be misconstrued as meaning that the State seizing a pirate ship could take action only with regard to the property on board.

62. Mr. SANDSTROM considered that the United Kingdom Government was right in thinking a provision was needed concerning the disposal of a pirate ship after seizure, particularly as confiscation was not always justified – for example, in cases where the crew had mutinied.

63. Mr. SCHELLE agreed with Sir Gerald Fitzmaurice.

64. Mr. PAL thought the text was obscure and should be revised so as to make it clear that the State seizing a pirate ship or a ship taken by piracy could take action to dispose of either or both vessels.

65. Mr. PADILLA-NERVO suggested that Sir Gerald Fitzmaurice's point might be met by inserting the words "ships, aircraft or" after the words "action to be taken with regard to the" in the second sentence.

Mr. Padilla-Nervo's amendment was accepted. Article 18, thus amended, was adopted.

Article 19
66. Mr. FRANÇOIS, Special Rapporteur, said that the government comments were confined to drafting points: he agreed that the wording of the article should be amended to bring it into line with that of article 21, paragraph 3.

Subject to that amendment article 19 was adopted.

Article 20
67. Mr. FRANÇOIS, Special Rapporteur, said that the Government of the Union of South Africa had asked whether it should not be stipulated that a vessel which had repulsed the attack of a pirate might seize the pirate vessel pending the arrival of a warship. As he had stated in paragraph 140 of the addendum to his report [A/CN.4/97/Add. 1], such a stipulation was unnecessary because provisional seizure of that kind was no more than legitimate self-defence.

68. Mr. SCHELLE agreed with the Special Rapporteur. Moreover, the text as it now stood went further than the rules of municipal law concerning legitimate self-defence, since it allowed a vessel which had repulsed the attack of a pirate to exercise provisionally the police powers of a warship, a situation which concorded entirely with his theory that in the absence of public authorities their functions should be discharged by someone else who was in a position to do so.

69. The CHAIRMAN wondered whether, in view of the restriction imposed in article 20, it should not be made clear in the comment that private vessels were only authorized to effect provisional seizure in legitimate self-defence.

70. Sir Gerald FITZMAURICE agreed that the point could be covered in the comment and the article itself retained without change.

It was agreed that a sentence should be inserted in the comment on the lines of the statement in paragraph 140 of the addendum to the Special Rapporteur's report (A/CN.4/97/Add. 1).

Article 20 was adopted without change.

Article 21: Right of Visit
71. Mr. FRANÇOIS, Special Rapporteur, observed that the proposal of the Union of South Africa to extend the application of paragraph 1 (b) to the high seas generally, instead of limiting it to the maritime zones regarded as suspect in connexion with the slave trade, had been rejected by the Commission after long discussion because such extended application would be open to abuse and might be used as a pretext for searching vessels in areas where there was no slave trading [A/CN.4/SR.288, paragraphs 12-54; A/CN.4/SR.289, paragraphs 2-42 and 54-66]. He proposed that the Commission should adhere to the decision taken at the previous session.

It was so agreed.
The Netherlands amendment substituting the words "on the high seas" for the words "at sea" in paragraph 1 was adopted.

72. Sir Gerald FITZMAURICE explained that the reason for the United Kingdom amendment substituting the words "any loss" for the words "the loss" in paragraph 3 was that there might in fact have been no loss.

73. Mr. PAL believed that the effect of the United Kingdom amendment would be nullified unless the word "sustained" were deleted.

74. Sir Gerald FITZMAURICE, while not believing that there was much force in that objection, wondered whether Mr. Pal would prefer the phrase "any loss that may have been sustained."

Sir Gerald Fitzmaurice's wording was adopted.

75. Mr. AMADO asked whether the word "loss" in English was the precise equivalent of the word "dommage" in French, which he would have thought was wider in scope.

76. Mr. PADILLA-NERVO thought the text should be made more comprehensive by referring to both damage and loss.

77. Sir Gerald FITZMAURICE agreed that it would be desirable to refer to loss or damage in paragraph 3, particularly as an act of piracy might not necessarily cause damage, but could result in loss if a vessel were delayed.

It was agreed to insert the words "or damage" after the word "loss" in paragraph 3.
Article 21 as amended was adopted.

CHAPTER V

A REVIEW OF CERTAIN "PIRATICAL" ACTS
OCCURRING AFTER THE CONVENTION WITH A VIEW
TOWARD CHANGING THE 1958 CONVENTIONAL
ARTICLES ON PIRACY

Commencing in 1958, certain incidents took place which have led legal publicists to believe that perhaps political motivations (together with the private ends requirement) should have been included in the 1958 conventional articles on piracy. The main disturbances where the word "piratical" has been utilized are the Guatemalan-Mexican incident, 1958;[1] the Boatwright case (1960);[2] the *Santa Maria* (1961);[3] and the *Mayaguez* incident (1975).[4] The key issue is whether these recent incidents warrant changing the 1958 conventional articles on piracy or whether new or revised conventional articles should be prepared and utilized in order to cover acts of terrorism on the seas. It will be recalled that in Chapter I of this study, we examined the testimony found in a trial which took place in the 1600's in order to see the traditional type of swashbuckler piracy. Let us now examine a contemporary incident in order to see how the passage of time has affected, if at all, our conception of piracy in the current affairs of today.

The case of the *Santa Maria* tested the validity of Article 15 of the 1958 Geneva Convention as applied to the take-over of a ship on the high seas.

---

[1] The Guatemalan-Mexican incident of 1958 involved a dispute over fishing rights. Guatemala, angered by the repeated incursion of Mexican fishing vessels into Guatemalan territorial waters, instituted "Operation Drake" which called for machine-gun and rocket attacks against such foreign fishing vessels by Guatemalan F-51 aircraft. It was the position of the Guatemalan government that such fisheries violations constituted piracy. See Whiteman, *Digest of International Law* (Washington, D.C.: Department of State) 1965, pp. 663-665.

[2] The Boatwright case involved the murder of the captain of the *Muriel III*, anchored off the Bahamas, by two United States nationals who had been shipwrecked on the island. After the murder the two killers sailed the vessel, of American registry, to Cuba. See Whiteman, *op. cit.*, p. 665.

[3] The *Santa Maria* incident is discussed in detail in the text. See also Fenwick, *Piracy in the Caribbean*, 55 Am. J. Int'l L. 410 (1961), and Green, The Santa Maria: *Rebels or Pirates?*, 37 Brit. Y.B. Int'l L. 496 (1961).

[4] The S.S. *Mayaguez* was a United States merchant ship seized on May 12, 1975 by Cambodian naval vessels on the high seas. See *Contemporary Practice of the United States*, 69 Am. J. Int'l L. 875-878; U.S. Digest, ch. 14, section 1.

[In retrospect, this is true. At the time of the incident (January-February, 1961), the Convention on the High Seas was not yet in force. Ratification did not occur until September 30, 1962.] Admittedly, the position of the *Santa Maria* in international law has not been clearly discerned. Authoritative writers in international law, such as Charles Fenwick, assert that the seizure of the *Santa Maria* constituted an act of piracy, though he does not cite conclusive evidence to support his contention. Whiteman, on the other hand, indicates

"Since the ship was taken over by certain of its own passengers (apparently for private ends), and not by another ship, as at first reported, it was considered that for this, if for no other reason, Article 15 of the 1958 Convention was inapplicable."

A detailed analysis of the seizure of the *Santa Maria* reveals the tangled nexus of legal, social, economic, and political complications which serve to point up the need for a more precise application of the term "piracy" with respect to international law.

On January 23, 1961, a group of seventy men led by Captain Henrique Galvao, a former Portuguese commissioner and a prominent opponent of the Salazar government, seized the 20,900-ton Portuguese liner, the *Santa Maria*. The vessel was captured in the West Indies shortly after having left the port of Curaçao in the Netherlands Antilles. The *Santa Maria*, a pleasure cruising vessel, belonged to the Portuguese Colonial Navigation Company (*Companhia Colonial de Navegaçao*), and carried over 600 passengers. Included among the men, women, and children were passengers of Portuguese, Dutch, Venezuelan, Spanish and American descent.

Although the vessel was expected to land at Port Everglades, Florida, before its return to Lisbon, Portugal, its voyage was radically changed after the seizure. It appears that Galvao had attempted to follow an east-southeast direction, probably steering towards West Africa. In a special announcement from the vessel on February 2, 1961, Galvao proclaimed that

". . . the coup was a declaration of political war on Salazar, envisaging 'a revolutionary objective: the reconstruction of Portuguese society on new bases' which would 'open up also overseas the doors of liberty, progress, and independence.'"

Before becoming a political exile, Galvao had received a commission in 1947 from the Portuguese government to give an "on-the-spot" report of the conditions of two Portuguese colonies, Angola and Mozambique. According to the Salazar sources, Galvao's report was too unfavorable for publication. When the National Assembly to which Galvao was a member refused to print his account of the colonial maladies, Galvao began his open opposition to the Salazar regime. Although imprisoned in 1951, he escaped eight years later and fled to South America to join General Humberto Delgado, who had been defeated by Salazar in the 1958 Portuguese presidential election.

Soon after the seizure of the *Santa Maria*, Galvao's suppressed report of the sordid conditions in Mozambique and Angola appeared in the January 29, 1961 edition of the London newspaper, *The Observer*. In this publication, Galvao reported severe cases of undernourishment, a high mortality rate, especially among children, and a drastic lack of health facilities. Galvao claimed that the labor forced upon the African population verged upon slavery.

Thus, in his first radio announcement to the outside world on January 24, 1961, Captain Galvao proclaimed that he had captured the *Santa Maria*

". . . in the name of the Independent Junta of Liberation led by the General Humberto Delgado, the legally elected President of the Portuguese Republic, who has been fraudulently deprived of his rights by the Salazar Administration."

He acknowledged that all passengers were safe and that most of them had favorably accepted his take-over as a political act. One wonders under those conditions what might have occurred had the passengers strongly objected to Galvao's seizure. The crew, however, did not fare so well as the passengers. The day before his announcement, Galvao had docked briefly at Castries, St. Lucia, in the British West Indies. Here he placed ashore a lifeboat containing eight wounded crewmen and the body of Third Officer Costa. [The crewmen on deck were wounded by hand grenades and machine-guns discharged by Galvao's men.] Although most of Galvao's men had boarded ship at Curaçao and had been disguised as passengers, it was also thought that some of Galvao's men were among the original 300 crew members of the *Santa Maria*.

Immediately after the seizure, the Portuguese government requested that American, British, and Dutch ships help search for the *Santa Maria* and recapture her "in accordance with the well-defined terms of international law governing piracy and insurrection on board ship."

When the *Santa Maria* was sighted in international waters by both British and American naval vessels, Galvao radioed that he would be willing to bring the *Santa Maria* to port provided that both he and his crew receive guarantees that they would be treated as political insurgents. Following Galvao's announcement, Rear-Admiral Allen Smith, commander of the U.S. Navy destroyer *Gearing*, went aboard the *Santa Maria* to speak with Galvao. During his talk, Galvao reaffirmed his position that he would peacefully surrender the ship and its crew only if he received assurances that he would be treated as an insurgent.

After the *Santa Maria* was securely anchored in Recife, Brazil, the U.S. State Department announced that the United States had acted under the international laws against piracy. Although General Delgado had proclaimed that the seizure was a political act carried out on his orders, the State Department denied any knowledge of Delgado's demand or Galvao's insistence that the ship be recognized as an international belligerent against Portugal. Regardless of the position taken by the United States, Galvao was immediately granted political asylum by the new President of Brazil, Janio Quadros. [Had Great Britain and the United States not been sympathetic towards the revolution which Galvao and his followers proposed, the two nations would not have been so concerned about harboring the *Santa Maria* in a Brazilian port and would have delivered it directly to the Portuguese government in Lisbon.]

While the case of the *Santa Maria* conformed with the Portuguese definition of piracy, it fell far short as an incidence of piracy on the high seas as prescribed by the 1958 Geneva Convention. [The Portuguese Government defined piracy as ". . . forcible seizure of a ship . . . the commission of acts of violence, damages or thefts on any such ship . . . the pursuance on board of activities directly against the Portuguese state." The two-vessel requirement in Article 15 of the Geneva Convention is noticeably absent from the Portuguese municipal concept of piracy.] According to Jacobson, "the facts of the seizure revealed that it was made with the intention of sparking political consequences in Portugal and not for the purpose of private gain."

Certainly, all of the action took place aboard a single ship, and the capture of the *Santa Maria* rendered it an academic question as to whether or not Galvao and his followers may have intended to commit future acts of piracy directed against other vessels on the high seas. It is interesting to note, however, that China had sought expansion of Article 15 of the 1958 Geneva Convention to include the taking over of navigation or command of a ship by a person or persons aboard. Such a provision would definitely have applied to the seizure of the *Santa Maria* incident and subsequent aircraft hijacking a moot issue.[5]

It is observed that the *Santa Maria* incident deals primarily with political problems relating to, *inter alia,* insurgency, belligerency and political asylum. It will be recalled that the Group and certain members of the Commission did not really want to involve themselves with anything other than acts committed by individuals for private ends. Both believed that these were the acts akin to "traditional" notions regarding sea piracy. It is also noteworthy to mention once again that the word "piracy," in modern usage, could be utilized by states in order to describe some sort of villainous deed in order to gain public backing for the course of action taken by the particular state. Bearing this in mind, another recent incident involved the seizure of a Japanese freighter, *Sheiro Maru,* in a Philippines port in September, 1975 by a revolutionary group which sought to overthrow the government of the Philippines.[6] This seizure was also regarded as "piracy" which resulted in the Philippine government intervening and recapturing the vessel. Again, these acts dealt with *individuals* and not *states.*

An example of an alleged act of piracy committed by a *state* is the seizure of the United States merchant vessel, *Mayaguez,* by a Cambodian patrol boat in the Gulf of Siam in May, 1975. The seizure took place more than sixty miles off of the coast of Cambodia[7] and the President of the United States officially declared the act to be piratical and ordered remedial action. The *Mayaguez* was not a "private" ship in pursuit of "private ends." The Cambodian vessel was a warship. But, the United States had not recognized the Cambodian government, that is, the *Khmer Rouge,* that had ordered the seizure of the U.S. merchant vessel.

---

[5] This discussion of the *Santa Maria* incident is taken from the excellent description contained in Nancy D. Joyner, *Aerial Hijacking as an International Crime* (New York: Oceana), 1974, pp. 106-113. Footnotes are omitted in this study but can be found in the original text.

[6] *New York Times,* September 30, 1975, p. 3, column 1, as appears in Crockett, *Toward a Revision of the International Law of Piracy,* 26 De Paul L. Rev. 78 (1976), p. 80.

[7] *New York Times,* May 13, 1975, p. 1, column 8; see also *New York Times,* May 17, 1975, p. 17, column 2.

In a recent article calling for revision of the laws of piracy, Professor Crockett deals with the rather sensitive area of "State piracy"[8] and gives some examples which

... may indicate the breadth of the private ends exception as applied to cases involving acts associated with a State.

Case I: The naval forces of State A attack a merchant vessel of State B in order to prevent non-innocent passage through A's territorial sea. The attack, however, due to a mistake, is made on the high seas, there is no justification for the act. Under these circumstances the act of State A would not be piracy under traditional pre-1958 law or the Geneva Convention.

Case II: State A, in order to lay claim to offshore mineral deposits, regularly attacks merchant vessels on the high seas which stray within a three-mile radius of the site of the deposits.

Case III: The President of State A issues orders to vessels under State control to seize on the high seas any vessels flying the flag of State B, C, or D. The objective may be revenge or gain.

In Cases II and III, it would be difficult to conclude that the attacks and seizures were for private gains. Yet, the threat to the freedom of the high seas is sufficiently severe in these cases to justify the exercise of the common jurisdiction. Thus, under the traditional theory of piracy, Cases II and III would be piracy.[9]

Professor Crockett further stated that

... it is suggested that appropriate provisions could be drawn to distinguish various cases which contain an element of State involvement.[10]

Professor Sundberg discusses piracy and state responsibility and states that:

... the more important obligation to fight piracy is not the tone relating to the high seas, but the one relating to the states' *territorial waters*. To suppress piracy within a state's territorial jurisdiction is considered to be an international law obligation, not based upon the Geneva Convention but on general international customary law. "If a State should fail to do so or should associate itself persistently with piratical ventures, it would certainly violate this rule" says Schwarzenberger. He adds: "It is liable for the commission of an international tort and, in an extreme case, may even forfeit its own international personality and be treated as an international outlaw." It is not difficult to see behind that statement the plight of China in the nineteenth century which was forced by means of treaties with European powers to undertake to fight the pirates in the Chinese waters. From a practical point of view, such destruction of base areas for the pirates may be even more important than hunting them on the high seas. But it would also seem to follow that this obligation cannot extend to forms of piracy other than those defined in the Geneva Convention.[11]

---

[8] Crockett, *op. cit.*, note 6.
[9] *Ibid.*, p. 91.
[10] *Ibid.*, p. 92.
[11] Sundberg, *Piracy: Air and Sea*, 20 De Paul L. Rev. 337 (1970), p. 385, emphasis added.

However, the problems connected with the so-called "acts of piracy" that are committed within the territorial waters of a coastal state are numerous. First, outside of the few newspaper articles that have been reported on piracy within this geographical area,[12] there are no statistics available to support the number of incidents that could be referred to as piratical in nature which occur in territorial waters. Possibly, this lack of important information is due to the fact that no state is willing to admit: (1) that such an act has occurred within its jurisdiction, and (2) that the state is unable or too disinterested to resolve the problem. Secondly, although many persons are willing to believe that acts of piracy still occur in certain, relatively remote, coastal waters (for example Indonesia, the South China Sea; and Africa), they perceive no threat of piracy in most areas. This view is incorrect. For example, in the Bahamas acts of piracy occur which involve the hijacking of private yachts by criminals in order to utilize their services in connection with smuggling drugs or other contraband into various countries. The sad problem is that there are no statistics available either to support or challenge these beliefs.

Thirdly, under the 1958 conventional articles, the acts of piracy which constitute an international crime occur only on the high seas. Therefore, if the coastal state does not have municipal legislation dealing with the particular kind of transgression involved, the culprits cannot be tried as "pirates" (assuming that other states do not have concurrent jurisdiction).

Lastly, one would think that, although statistics are not available from public sources, perhaps private sources, such as insurance carriers, would have records available in order to determine the amount of premium to charge to their clients. To the contrary, piracy, at least in the United States, is not insured by a casualty organization but, instead, by marine insurance underwriters. The premium for said coverage is included within the war and strikes risk premium. However, there does not exist any actuarial procedure to develop premium reserves for an eventual piracy (or war) loss.[13] Damage to an insured hull (or to insured cargo) is investigated and adjusted just as would any other hull or damage loss. Further no statistics are available either from underwriters or from the

---

[12] See the reports excerpted from the *South China Morning Post* and the *Hongkong Standard* in Appendix 2 to Chapter II. An account of a recent pirate attack which occurred off the coast of Nigeria appears in Appendix 1 of this chapter.

[13] Personal communications from Arthur E. Brunk (Vice-President, Scor Reinsurance Company, December 2, 1977), and E.M. Lindley (Ropner Insurance Services Ltd., Lloyd's insurance and reinsurance brokers, October 6, 1977).

Lloyd's information service. They simply do not keep any records on piracy cases.[14] There are no specific piracy clauses in existence. Acts of piracy, in the private sphere, either fall under the war clauses (American War Clauses in the United States) or else are covered under the hull form as in the case of barratry, and so on.

Thus, the current incidents that are reported concern both individuals and states regardless of geographic location. When dealing with the acts of individuals that are politically motivated, we are confronted with problems regarding, *inter alia,* insurgency, belligerency, political asylum, and extradition. When dealing with the acts of state, we are dealing with questions of whether the acts of alleged piracy are connected with the same political considerations as are those committed by an individual or, placed in a different context, whether the states are actively or passively involved in piratical acts. In addition, we are confronted with the same practical problem facing the Group and Commission, namely: Can states really be expected to permit their sovereignty to be impugned in any manner? Would states readily agree to incur liability for these acts under conventional law? And the ultimate question is: Do these current incidents really warrant changing the 1958 conventional articles on piracy?

Let us now examine some suggestions for possible approaches to the recent occurrences. It will be recalled that while the various publicists called our attention to problems that could need reviewing, none of them (except in the case of air piracy) *proposed any method* of dealing with the alleged necessity for change. Nevertheless, it is submitted to the reader that in the opinion of the author, there are some suggestions which could be utilized depending upon the receptability of the Conference States. The purpose of setting forth some possibilities will be discussed in the next chapter; but, it is believed that *if* there is to be any development in this area, a fresh look at the various problems is necessary instead of attempting to adopt dated governing concepts and traditional terms to a current area of discontent. In other words, in the next chapter, we are dealing with possible recommendations, but we are also very much concerned with suggesting new *approaches* to current (and possibly future) problems – the progressive development of international law.

---

[14] "Why a Big Surge in 'Boatnapping'," *U.S. News & World Report,* February 27, 1978, p. 41. This article appears in Appendix 2 of this chapter.

APPENDIX 1 TO CHAPTER V

"Pirates in Nigeria Attack Danish Ship," The Miami Herald, Wednesday, November 23, 1977, p. 5-A

Copenhagen, Denmark — Pirates boarded the Danish ship *Lindinger Ivory* anchored outside the Nigerian port of Lagos, killed the captain and wounded all 14 crew members, the ship's owners said Tuesday.

The Lindinger Line said that Capt. Sonnich Kromann Frederiksen, 44, was shot and thrown overboard and the rest of the crew were seriously wounded when about 20 pirates boarded and attacked the ship Monday morning while it was anchored outside the harbor waiting for a berth.

APPENDIX 2 TO CHAPTER V

"Why a Big Surge in 'Boatnapping'," U.S. News & World Report, February 27, 1978, p. 41

A major battle against fast-increasing boat theft is under way. But police are finding it's a crime that is difficult to prevent.

A nationwide wave of boat thefts — capped by outright piracy of yachts on the high seas — has touched off an urgent campaign to curb such crime.

Hundreds of law-enforcement officials in agencies such as the Coast Guard, Federal Bureau of Investigation and local police are mustering forces for a joint assault on growing numbers of "boatnappers" who are stealing an estimated 20,000 vessels per year. Americans now own about 10 million boats, ranging from canoes to yachts, double the total a decade ago.

Two main reasons are cited for increased boat theft: the high price of yachts — many worth from $50,000 to 1.5 million dollars — and lack of security arrangements on most vessels.

Observes Lawrence G. Mallon, deputy counsel of the House Merchant Marine and Fisheries Committee: "It's three times easier to steal a boat than a car because a boat is harder to identify and easier to license."

Some countermeasures. Among recent developments:
A task force to combat yacht hijacking has been formed under the supervision of the Coast Guard in Washington, D.C.
Interagency cooperation, sometimes haphazard in the past, is increasing in the sharing of information on boat thefts and in the pursuing of thieves in all states. Investigations routinely will include Interpol, the international police-liaison agency.
Legislation is under consideration in Congress to tighten laws on boat registration, making it harder to sell vessels after they are stolen. The proposal also calls for the training of more marine law-enforcement officers.

Much of the impetus for a crackdown comes from "yacht-jacking": seizure of large luxury boats with the owners or crew aboard. Such crimes are relatively few — only six verified cases in the past seven years, according to the Coast

Guard. But any kidnapping is a matter of such serious concern that demands by boat owners for more protection are being widely heeded.

One case attracting international attention was that of the U.S. yacht *Imamou* which sailed from Colombia in 1973 with two Americans and two foreign crewmen aboard.

The vessel was reported overdue, and a search of the Caribbean was started. In 1974, the boat was found at the island of Guadeloupe, where authorities said two Frenchmen claimed the Americans had given them the yacht. The Americans were not located, and the Frenchmen were charged with unlawful possession of a vessel.

In another incident, the U.S. yacht *Kamalii* was hijacked at gunpoint by three men at a berth in Honolulu in 1971. The vessel headed out to sea, where the three-man professional crew was set adrift on a life raft without food or water.

The raft was spotted by an Italian freighter and the crew was rescued. The Coast Guard, notified by radio, located the fleeing *Kamalli,* boarded the yacht and arrested three men.

"Too easy." Often, however, the hijackers are not caught. Observes Representative Mario Biaggi (D-N.Y.), who headed a congressional investigation of marine crime: "It is too easy, in many instances, to seize an ocean-going yacht and its crew; to elude predictable Coast Guard search-and-rescue efforts; to sail to a cooperative country like Mexico, Colombia, Indonesia, or some North African country where vessel documentation is either nonexistent or may be conveniently purchased. The yacht may then be resold on the legitimate market."

Less spectacular but far more numerous are cases of boat thefts with no kidnappings involved. In some areas such as the beach communities of south Florida, police dockets are sometimes more crowded with reports of stolen boats than stolen cars. The Insurance Company of North America reports that losses from boat thefts jumped from 2 percent to 14 percent of its claims payments from 1972 to 1975.

Investigators say most vessels are stolen simply to get from one place to another. Rarely are thefts linked to other crimes such as drug trafficking or piracy to seek political asylum in Cuba or elsewhere.

"People involved in drug smuggling can afford to buy their own boats," asserts FBI Special Agent James P. Tucker of Miami. "It doesn't make sense to double the risks by stealing boats, too."

Work of "the mob"? Some investigators say the increase in boat thefts is partly the result of efforts by organized-crime groups.

Explains Mallon of the House Merchant Marine and Fisheries Committee: "They steal to order. A boat disappears in Florida one day and shows up later in New York." He says at least four groups are engaged in such trafficking, although other authorities believe the crimes are largely the work of unco-ordinated individuals.

Many officials believe that better law enforcement and tougher legislation will help to cut boat theft considerably, but some risks are expected to remain.

"It's practically impossible to protect a boat absolutely," concludes Mallon. "All we can do is make boat theft as difficult as possible."

CHAPTER VI

POSSIBLE APPROACHES CONCERNING REVISING
THE LAW OF INTERNATIONAL SEA PIRACY

INTRODUCTION

Before considering possible suggestions concerning revising the law of international sea piracy, it would be appropriate to observe first some thoughts of Professor Bassiouni in relation to the creation of a new international crime (as distinguished from the progressive development of conventional law):

... The late Professor Donnedieu de Vabres [who was France's judge on the International Military Tribunal at Nuremberg and one of the world authorities on international criminal law], believed that an act could become an international crime only if it so offends the common morality of mankind that it would be universally condemnable...[1]

Although Professor Bassiouni was reviewing an article concerning the creation of the crime of air piracy,[2] his ideas reveal a possible analogy to the development of the law of international sea piracy or the possible creation of a crime or offense of international terrorism at sea:

... Is unlawful seizure of aircraft the same as piracy on the high seas and, therefore, by analogy also an international crime, or is it a different type of offense equally deserving of being considered an international crime, but for other reasons? Have such acts risen in the common morality of mankind to the level of universal condemnation likely to merit recognition as an international crime? Have the member states of the world community recognized, with some degree of uniformity such acts as reprehensible and, therefore, likely to warrant the conclusion that their condemnation is a generally accepted principle of international law? ...[3]

These comments are very important. The problem with which we are confronted in this study is whether the incidents, which have

---

[1] Bassiouni, *Introduction to a Symposium on Issues in Aero-Space Law*, 20 De Paul L.R. 337 (1970), p. 236.
[2] Sundberg, *Piracy: Air and Sea*, 20 De Paul L.R. 337 (1970).
[3] Bassiouni, *op. cit.*, p. 326.

occurred in the past twenty years or which could possibly occur in the future warrant a revision in the 1958 conventional articles regarding piracy. It is rather ironic that the legal publicists interested in the development of the crime of air piracy always utilize a discussion of the law of international sea piracy in order to demonstrate its applicability and nonapplicability to the creation of the crime of air piracy.[4] Professor Bassiouni discusses the necessary standard and continues:

> ... Professor Sundberg surveys the history of piracy on the high seas and seeks to show that the unlawful seizure of aircraft is but the same crime accomplished by other means.... The 1958 Geneva Convention on the Law of the Sea analogizes the two types of "piracy" and labels both as the crime of "piracy." The contemporary standards of the common morality of mankind are, however, taken for granted by the author without regard to the opinions of some publicists who still refute the notion that air piracy is a crime, *jure jus gentium.* The case for air piracy as an international crime still needs to be made by more publicists like Professor Sundberg so that it can gain wider recognition in legal doctrine to be manifested by the "writings of the most high qualified publicists" [which are another source of international law].
>
> *The unlawful seizure of aircraft must be established as an international crime and be so recognized by the world community because it constitutes a threat not only to commercial interests common to most countries of the world, but also because it represents a real danger to mankind. This is demonstrated by such acts regardless of their nationality or status . . .*[5]

It is again observed that for years legal publicists had called for the creation of a crime of air piracy. Now that various conventions concerning air piracy have been created,[6] it is necessary to utilize the ideas for creating these conventions on air piracy in order to justify and to explain why the 1958 conventional articles on international sea piracy need to be updated. In other words, we must turn to the incidents which have occurred recently in order to ascertain whether there is constituted a

> ... threat not only to commercial interests common to most countries of the world, but also because it represents a real danger to mankind. . . .[7]

Having reviewed the laborious efforts of the Group and the adaptability of its draft convention to the practical and political considerations which confronted the Commission in the entire law of the

---

[4] See for example, Joyner, *Aerial Hijacking as an International Crime* (New York: Oceana), 1974, pp. 13-115.

[5] Bassiouni, *op. cit.,* pp. 326-327.

[6] See for example, Convention on Offenses and Certain Other Acts Committed on Board Aircraft, signed at Tokyo on September 14, 1963, 704 U.N.T.S. 10106 (1969); 58 Am. J. Int'l L. 566 (1964); 20 U.S.T. 2914, and: Convention for the Suppression of Unlawful Seizure of Aircraft (Hague Convention), opened for signature December 16, 1970, 22 U.S.T. 1643 (1971), T.I.A.S. No. 7192, effective October 14, 1971.

[7] Bassiouni, *op. cit.,* p. 327.

sea area and the Commission's resulting report to the General Assembly which contained the provisions on piracy,[8] let us now discuss some possible approaches and alternatives with a view toward answering the questions posed at the beginning of and during the course of this study.[9]

MAINTAIN THE STATUS QUO BY LEAVING THE 1958 CONVENTIONAL ARTICLES INTACT

Proponents of maintaining the status quo could point to that portion of Article 14 which limits the geographic location of piracy to "the high seas or in any other place outside the jurisdiction of any state."[10] In support of this view, one argument would state that the total areas falling outside the territorial jurisdiction of states, where piratical acts could be committed under conventional law, is *diminishing*. According to Robert D. Hodgson:

... if all base points, which are valid for the measuring of the territorial sea, are used for the creation of a 200-mile economic zone, we find that approximately 36 and one-half percent of the world's surface would be included within an economic zone of one state or another ...[11]

Relating the percentage figure to total mileage, the 118 independent coastal states (after various adjustments) would be allocated 26,632,400 square nautical miles of continental shelf and adjacent seabed.[12] The average state allocation would be 208,100 square nautical miles;[13] the mean state allocation would be 61,000 square nautical miles.[14] The following chart shows allocation of seabed areas (in square nautical miles) to coastal states according to the 200-nautical-mile proposal for maritime jurisdiction in effect at the time of the study:[15]

[9] Note the questions posed by the author on pp. 2-4. See also the discussion of the issue raised by Professor Joyner in note 8, Chapter II.

[10] Convention on the High Seas, *op. cit.*, note 8.

[11] Personal communication from Robert D. Hodgson, Director of the Office of the Georgrapher, Department of State, May 4, 1977.

[12] The Geographer, *Theoretical Aerial Allocations of Seabed to Coastal States Based on Certain U.N. Seabeds Committee Proposals*, Office of the Geographer, Bureau of Intelligence and Research, Washington, D.C. (International Boundary Study, Series A, Limits in the Seas, No. 46), August 12, 1972, p. 4.

[13] *Ibid.* "Average" is determined by adding the total allocations of all coastal states and dividing by their number, i.e., 118.

[14] *Ibid.* "Mean" is defined as the figure which represents the middle of the states, i.e., 59 have areas greater and 59 have areas less than this figure.

[15] *Ibid.*, p. 35.

	Total	200 nautical miles
Atlantic (includes Arctic Ocean)	31,040,000 (100%)	11,668,000 (37.59%)
Indian	21,842,000 (100%)	7,064,000 (32.34%)
Pacific	52,385,000 (100%)	19,013,000 (36.29%)
Total	105,267,000 (100%)	37,745,000 (35.89%)

The proponents of maintaining the status quo could argue further that although high seas freedoms and laws are preserved in the economic zone under the composite text (1977), states could conceivably treat piracy as a threat to this zone and thereby claim "exclusive jurisdiction" or utilize other jurisdictional concepts created under Part XV of the composite text, Article 295,[16] in order to cope with these piratical acts under Articles 100-107[17] of the *ICNT*:

... The implication that high seas freedoms and high seas law are not preserved in the economic zone is contradicted by a close reading of the text, and even more importantly by the basic assumptions surrounding the negotiation of the economic zone. Yet that implication could prove to be a temptation for coastal states to seek to alter the balance of the economic zone. A 200-mile territorial sea claimant might conveniently refuse to ratify the new "contract," yet point to the "decision in principle" that the area within 200 miles of the coast is not high seas. If supple, it might concede freedom of navigation in principle but then impose restraints that would not be permissible were it a party to the "contract." The fact that current 200-mile territorial sea claimants are among the most vociferous opponents of high seas status for the economic zone cannot be overlooked.[18]

The proponents of maintaining the status quo could proffer the above-stated argument together with the view, expressed by certain nations, that traditional piracy is a moot point. Further it is contended that even if the incidents occurring after the 1958 high seas convention were acts of piracy, they are too few in number and too political in nature to warrant any change in the 1958 conventional articles. These proponents could argue that if states are confronted

[16] Part XV of the *ICNT* deals with settlement of disputes. Article 295 is concerned with the finality and binding force of decisions. See the *Informal Composite Negotiating Text*, U.N. Doc. A/CONF.62/WP.10/CORR.1 (1977), Part XV, reproduced in Appendix 3 to Chapter II.

[17] *ICNT, op. cit.*, pp. 62-63. See Appendix 4 to Chapter III.

[18] Oxman, *The Third United Nations Conference on the Law of the Sea: The 1976 New York Sessions*, 71 Am. J. Int'l L. 247 (1977), p. 265. See also, Burke, *Submerged Passage Through Straits: Interpretations of the Proposed Law of the Sea Treaty*, 52 Wash. L. Rev. 193 (1977), pp. 200-215.

with terrorist activities outside their jurisdictional boundaries, it would be desirable to enact separate conventional articles to deal with that particular problem. They could utilize the various air piracy conventions and demonstrate the various strengths and weaknesses thereof in order to prepare new conventional articles.[19]

POSSIBLE APPROACHES CONCERNING REVISING THE 1958 CONVENTIONAL ARTICLES

It should come as no surprise to the reader that this study on the law of international sea piracy has been utilized by the author as a vehicle by which certain old and new concepts of international law could be discussed in order to aid in the progressive development of international jurisprudence.[20] Piracy was a rather stable area to choose in order to create a framework and reference within which to make certain suggestions. As in any discussion regarding the development of new concepts in international law it becomes necessary to reexamine the traditional norms and governing concepts regarding the law of the sea in order to keep pace with modern developments and perhaps be fortunate enough to provide some foresight for problems which are "unique" or "novel."[21] Piracy is a good topic for examining the so-called "traditional" views because, as had been emphasized throughout the text, there really was no "traditional" uniform wisdom. There were at least two diverse opinions on each of the draft articles prepared and commented on by the Group. The so-called "better" views were placed in their draft convention and the practicalities were later ironed out by the Commission. By this continuing process the law of the sea developed further.

One problem area is the fact that over a period of time, states tend to perceive these conventions as "traditional" views and governing concepts. This belief is fallacious. The conventions are, at best, of a temporary nature in the long run. The 1958 conventional articles represent an understanding regarding problems that may have been relevant at the time the discussions took place. The international lawyer should be interested in developing the law with the ultimate

---

[19] See for example: Green, *Piracy of Aircraft and the Law,* 10 Alberta L.R. 72 (1972); Sundberg, *op. cit.,* note 2. It would be ironic if this type of argument were utilized because legal publicists have been discussing the 1958 conventional articles on sea piracy in order to create a special jurisdiction on crimes of air piracy.

[20] Note the discussion of the purposes of this work on pp. 10-11.

[21] 1 Y.B. Int'l L. Comm'n 47 (1956). See the remark of Sir Gerald Fitzmaurice, paragraph 44, Appendix 12 to Chapter IV.

goal of world stabilization. Uniform prescriptions should be created but not with the attitude or view that they can remain static without being examined, updated, and revised, as necessary.

In connection with sea piracy (and keeping in mind that the foregoing statements do not mean to imply necessarily that the 1958 conventional articles need to be revised), let us now examine some possible suggestions for revision.

SOME SUGGESTIONS FOR DEVELOPING THE LAW OF INTERNATIONAL SEA PIRACY

Geographic Location of Piratical Acts

One concern today is that some coastal states may be incompetent to cope with acts of piracy conducted within their territorial waters. As stated in the last chapter, statistics on acts of piracy occurring within territorial waters are impossible to obtain because coastal states are not anxious to demonstrate that they do not have the resources to evaluate such a situation. Acts of piracy occurring in the Bahamas, off the coast of Africa, Indonesia and other parts of Asia are commonplace and are recognized by persons who have lived in these areas as representing a serious threat to navigation, human life, and commercial interests.[22] Yet, these acts of piracy, although subject to the municipal laws of the nations involved, persist. Contrary to earlier days, the high seas are not geographic areas of high risk. To the contrary, it would appear that most incidents occur within the geographic areas of internal and territorial waters and exclusive economic zones because many coastal states do not maintain a navy or coastguard of sufficient strength to deal with this type of problem. Therefore, it is recommended that the international crime of sea piracy be extended to include areas outside the "normal baselines."[23]

For the purpose of discussion, let us, therefore, divide the conventional geographic areas of waters involved into zones. Zone *A* represents the 1958 conventional definition of the high seas area. Zone *A* can be viewed, for this discussion, as an international zone. It is also the zone of lowest risk of piratical attacks to commercial

---

[22] Appendix 2 to Chapter I contains an account of some incidents involving piratical activities.

[23] Article 5 of the *ICNT, op. cit.,* note 16, defines the term "normal baseline" as follows: "Except where otherwise provided in the present Convention, the normal baseline for measuring the breadth of the territorial sea is the low-water line along the coast as marked on large-scale charts officially recognized by the coastal State."

shipping as it is the furthest zone from the coast from which pirates or terrorists could be expected to embark on their missions. Zone *B* is the exclusive economic zone that is currently being proposed at the various law of the sea conferences. Its distance is generally 200 miles from the baseline (i.e., the point where the coastal state measures seaward its territorial waters). Zone *C* represents the territorial waters which, for the purpose of discussion, shall be 12 miles. Zone *D* represents the internal waters, (waters on the landward side of the baseline), as defined by conventional law, and the land of the coastal state.

The competing claims and interests in connection with this discussion will be, *inter alia*, the principle of state sovereignty versus the interest of the international community in preventing and controlling sea piracy and terrorism. We know that the acts of piracy can occur in either zones *A* or *B* under conventional law. Acts of piracy occurring in zones *C* and *D* are supposedly covered under the municipal jurisdiction of the coastal state. Nevertheless, we can have occurrences which commence in zone *A* (an international zone of high seas) and continue into *B* and *C* and even *D*. We can also have situations where the piratical acts commence in zones *D* and *C* and extend into zones *B* and *A*.[24] We can also have many combinations of these occurrences in various geographic areas with the individual or state vessel going from one zone to another. We are aware of the fact that the coastal state is under a minimum duty pursuant to customary and conventional international law to attempt to suppress piracy.[25]

Jurisdiction to Enforce Prescriptive Penalties Could Be Given to a Dispute Settlement Mechanism

Currently, under conventional law, acts of piracy are defined, but the enforcement of penalties comes within municipal laws of the various nations (assuming that they have said legislation).[26] Possibly, jurisdiction could be placed within the competence of a dispute settlement mechanism.[27] Dispute settlement could be of a com-

[24] Article 101 of the *ICNT, op. cit.,* note 16, states that piracy consists of "... any ... acts committed ... on the high sea ... or ... in a place outside the jurisdiction of any state." The article is reproduced in full in Appendix 4 to Chapter III.

[25] *Ibid.,* Article 100. See Appendix 4 to Chapter III.

[26] Article 105 of the *ICNT, op. cit.,* puts the determination of penalties for piratical acts within the purview of the courts of the capturing state.

[27] For a discussion of the operation of the dispute settlement mechanism proposed by the Law of the Sea Conference see Adede, *Settlement of Disputes Arising Under the Law of the Sea Convention,* 69 Am. J. Int'l L. 798 (1975), and Sohn, *Settlement of Disputes Arising out of the Law of the Sea Convention,* 12 U. of San Diego L. R. 495 (1975). Articles 279-297 of the *ICNT* on the settlement of disputes appear in Appendix 3 to Chapter II.

pulsory nature requiring the signatory Conference States to submit
to the jurisdiction of the convening body. The draft articles contained in the Composite Text[28] could be adapted to cover any
revision in the 1958 conventional articles. In this regard, the international tribunal would be given jurisdiction to prescribe penalties
and could utilize Article 38 of the ICJ rules[29] as a guideline in
arriving at their decisions. They could therefore (1) determine if an
act of piracy has occurred, (2) evaluate the seriousness of the
offense, and (3) prescribe penalties for the offender depending upon the seriousness of the act. It would also be possible to give this
body the power to grant political asylum. Obviously, the ultimate
goal would be the elimination of the competence of municipal law
to prescribe and enforce penalties regarding the law of international
sea piracy (and acts of terrorism). In addition, if the coastal state
were somewhat reluctant to act under the current or possibly
revised conventional laws because of a fear of reprisal (for example,
by any terrorist organization), an international dispute settlement
mechanism, pertaining to law of the sea, could allay these fears
by exercising its jurisdiction over the matter.

Expanding the 1958 Conventional Law to Include Provisions for Current and Future Incidents

The private ends requirement under current conventional law[30]
could be eliminated and replaced with a provision which would
permit the political, as well as private, motivations of *individuals*
to be considered. As a practical matter, perhaps the various "active"
or aggressive acts of piracy committed by *states* would not be
permitted.[31] Certainly it would be best if those acts were included
in revised conventional articles on piracy as it would be better to
have all such acts defined under the revised articles as piracy rather
than treated as an act of war. It is believed that this treatment would
lead to the suppression of the incident rather than having it explode
into further aggressive hostilities. The 1958 conventional law could
not be expanded to cover politically motivated activities by individuals and states without the introduction into the conventional
articles of some kind of compulsory dispute settlement mechanism

---

[28] *ICNT, op. cit.*

[29] See note 170, Chapter III.

[30] Article 101 of the *ICNT, op. cit.*, defines piracy as an act committed "for private ends."

[31] Professor Crockett analyzes these issues in *Toward a Revision of the International Law of Piracy*, 26 De Paul L. 78 (1976), pp. 87-99.

that pertains uniformly and exclusively to conventional sea controversies. Therefore, what we must be concerned with is the development of a uniform set of prescriptions that would be applied to the Conference States. This uniform scheme would be effectuated by the body or mechanism as previously discussed. The result would be that municipal legislation would no longer be utilized either in defining or prescribing penalties for piracy or terrorism occurring in geographic areas seaward of the baselines.

Assuming we adopt politically motivated acts in a definition of the law of international sea piracy, it would be a better approach to categorize the penalty according to the seriousness of the offense (for example mere robbery is not so serious an offense as murder). This approach could assist in eliminating the indiscriminate labelling of certain acts as "piracy" in order to incite the masses into a favorable frenzy for supporting further aggression.[32]

Examples of How These Revisions Would Interplay with Other Conventional Articles

Assuming that an act of piracy occurred in zones *A* or *B*, it could be possible to allow for the expansion of the doctrine of hot pursuit in order to permit the offended state the opportunity of giving chase and pursuing the alleged international criminal at least as far as zone *C*.[33] But assume further that the offended state could not capture the alleged pirate in zone *C* and the pirate went into zone *D*. At that point, the coastal state would be compelled to place the alleged pirate in an international jail to await the further disposition of the case by the dispute settlement body.[34] Justification of the extension of the doctrine of hot pursuit could be based upon the fact that the alleged pirate is really an international criminal subject to the jurisdiction of the international community.[35] The community, through the dispute settlement mechanism, could, for example, utilize its jurisdictional competence to decide, *inter alia,*

---

[32] Note the discussion of the effect of Article 15 of the 1958 Convention on the High Seas (Appendix 1 to Chapter I) in Crockett *op. cit.,* pp. 93-96.

[33] The present definition of the permissible extent of hot pursuit is contained in Article 23 of the 1958 Convention on the High Seas (Appendix 1 to Chapter II).

[34] See Paust, *A Survey of Possible Legal Responses to International Terrorism: Preventing, Punishment, and Cooperative Action,* 5 Ga. J. Int. and Comp. L. 431 (1975); Smith, *The Probable Necessity of an International Prison in Solving Aircraft Hijacking,* 5 Int. Lawyer 269 (1971).

[35] The subject of hot pursuit is extensively discussed in Poulantzas, *The Right of Hot Pursuit in International Law* (Leiden: A.W. Sijthoff), 1969, pp. 345-348, and Moore, *Digest of International Law* (Washington, D.C.: Government Printing Office), 1906, vol. 2, p. 985.

whether said acts really did constitute piracy; to decide the penalty, if any; to decide if the offender should be given political asylum; to decide if said acts were really acts committed by insurgents or belligerents; and, if so, to determine whether the offender should or should not be punished because of the circumstances of the case. Even if the 1958 conventional articles are not amended, it is envisaged that the extension of the hot pursuit doctrine, in certain instances, would pose little potential for abuse by states. The offended state giving chase could be required to check with the coastal state regarding whether it shall be permitted to proceed with the pursuit. If no response is given to the request, the offended state should be permitted to enter zone C in order to capture the offender. If the coastal state stated that it would apprehend the alleged pirate, then it would have the obligation to turn over the fugitive to the international tribunal (via the international jail). Suppose, however, that the coastal state does not respond to the request for capture and the alleged pirate proceeds into zone D. At this point, the offended nation would be confronted with the option of seeing the alleged pirate go unapprehended or of violating the sovereignty of the coastal state. If there is a compulsory dispute settlement, the international body would have jurisdictional competence to hear such a case. Appropriate sanctions could be placed on the coastal state for failure to capture the alleged pirate (i.e., a passive, nonaggressive act). Alternatively, the offended nation could risk greater hostilities by entering zone D and capturing the alleged pirate (an international fugitive).

At this stage, there are many hypothetical situations which could arise. If the Conference States agree upon adoption of uniform international rules regarding acts of piracy and the enforcement of sanctions (thereby removing piracy from municipal law altogether), perhaps the offended state would be justified, under the revised conventional articles, in entering zone D to capture the alleged pirate. Again, possible justification is that the alleged pirate is an international fugitive; that the coastal state is aiding and abetting an international fugitive and is thereby passively violating international law by failing to assist in the suppression of piracy;[36] that there is an "international zone" created surrounding and following the alleged international fugitive because of the international crime which was committed against a member of the international community; and therefore, the principle of sovereignty would not be

---

[36] See Bassiouni's discussion of *delicta juris gentium* which appears in Appendix 4 to Chapter II.

applicable to the coastal state – thus permitting the offended nation to proceed into the international zone (the geographic area where the location of the pirate is found to be).

We have been assuming that the above-stated factual situations transpire from the extension of the hot pursuit doctrine. But what if there is no hot pursuit, the alleged pirate is located within zone D, and the coastal state is not taking any action (that is, it is aiding and abetting the alleged international villain and is therefore liable to the international community for the commission of an international crime).[37] At this point, the matter could be submitted to the jurisdiction of a dispute settlement mechanism for further determination.

Thus, it would seem that any viable recommendation really requires the creation of a dispute settlement mechanism which has the competence to act pursuant to a uniform scheme contained within the conventional articles. Said scheme would include a wider definition of the acts of piracy, as well as provision for the prescribing of punishment. This approach would entail having states submit themselves to the jurisdiction of a newly created international body. Because of the highly political issues which occur today, perhaps the Conference States will not be so hesitant to submit to this jurisdiction if it means not having to apply their own municipal laws and thereby becoming involved in entanglements in which they may not have any interest.

Thus, some of the areas which will warrant further development relate to (1) the geographic location of piratical acts; (2) jurisdiction to enforce prescriptive penalties given to a dispute settlement mechanism; (3) expansion of the conventional law to cover current and future conditions; and (4) examples of how these revisions would interplay with other conventional articles. With the possible exception of extending the doctrine of hot pursuit under current conventional law, all possibility for change would seem to depend upon the willingness of the Conference States to create an international body or mechanism that would have jurisdictional competence to prescribe a newly created uniform scheme. Therefore, the same question confronts the international community today as it did when both the Group (1932) and the Commission (1950's) prepared their draft conventions – Have the nations of the world reached a point in their evolution in international relations where they can agree upon a procedure to cope with political problems without having to resort to acts of war?

[37] See Bassiouni's discussion of the universality principle which appears in Appendix 4 to Chapter II.

BIBLIOGRAPHY

I. BOOKS

A. General

Brierly, James L. *The Law of Nations*, 6th ed. Oxford: Oxford University Press, 1963.

Brownlie, Ian. *Principles of Public International Law*, 2nd ed. Oxford: Oxford University Press, 1973.

Fenwick, Charles S. *International Law*, 3rd ed. New York: Appleton-Century-Crofts, 1948.

Hyde, Charles C. *International Law*, vol. 1, 2nd ed. Boston: Little, Brown, 1945.

O'Connell, D.P. *International Law*, 2nd ed. London: Stevens and Sons, 1970.

Oppenheim, Lassa F.L. *International Law, A Treatise*, ed. by Hersch Lauterpacht. London: Longman's, Green, 1947.

Schwarzenberger, Georg. *A Manual of International Law*, 5th ed. London: Institute of World Affairs, 1967.

Whiteman, Marjorie. *Digest of International Law*. Washington, D.C.: Department of State, 1965.

B. Special

Bishop, William W., Jr. *International Law: Cases and Materials*. Boston: Little, Brown, 1962.

Brierly, James L. *The Basis of Obligation in International Law*. Oxford: Oxford University Press, 1958.

Colombos, Constantine, D. *International Law of the Sea*, 6th rev. ed. New York: David McKay, 1967.

Erickson, Richard. *International Law and the Revolutionary State*. New York: Oceana, 1971.

Garcia-Mora, Manuel R. *International Law and Asylum as a Human Right*. Washington, D.C.: Public Affairs Press, 1956.

Gilmore, Grant and Charles L. Black, *The Law of Admiralty*. New York: Foundation Press, 1975.

Greig, D.W. *International Law*. London: Butterworth's, 1976.

Gross, Philip. *The History of Pirates*. London: Longman's, Green, 1932.

Grotius, Hugo. *The Freedom of the Seas*, trans. by Ralph Magoffin. New York: Oxford University Press, 1916.

Hall, William E. *A Treatise on International Law*. Oxford: Oxford University Press, 1924.

Hackworth, Green Haywood. *Digest of International Law*. Washington, D.C.: Government Printing Office, 1940-1944.

Halleck, Henry W. *International Law*, vol. 1, 3rd ed. Philadelphia: G.S. Appleton, 1866.

Healy, Nicholas J. and David J. Sharpe. *Cases and Materials on Admiralty*. St. Paul, Minnesota: West Publishing, 1974.

Ivamz, E.R. Hardy. *Casebook on Shipping Law*. London: Butterworth's, 1970.

Jessup, Philip. *A Modern Law of Nations*. New York: Macmillan, 1950.

Joyner, Nancy Douglas. *Aerial Hijacking as an International Crime*. New York: Oceana; Leiden: A.W. Sijthoff, 1974.

Kelsen, Hans. *Principles of International Law*, 2nd ed. New York: Rinehart, 1966.

Lauterpacht, Hersch, *Recognition in International Law*. Cambridge: Cambridge University Press, 1947.

Lucas, Jo Desha. *Cases and Materials on Admiralty*, 2nd ed. New York: Foundation Press, 1978.

Matte, Nicholas M. *Aerospace Law*. London: Sweet and Maxwell, 1969.

McDougal, Myres S., and William T. Burke. *The Public Order of the Oceans*. New Haven, Connecticut: Yale University Press, 1962.

Moore, John Bassett. *Digest of International Law*. Washington, D.C.: Government Printing Office, 1906.

Oppenheim, Lassa F.L. *International Law*, 2nd ed. London: Longman's, 1905.

Poulantzas, Nicholas M. *The Right of Hot Pursuit in International Law*. Leiden: A.W. Sijthoff, 1969.

Rienow, Robert. *The Test of the Nationality of a Merchant Vessel*. New York: Columbia University Press, 1937.

Shearer, Ivan A. *Extradition in International Law*. New York: Oceana, 1971.

Smith, Herbert A. *The Law and Custom of the Sea*. London: Stevens, 1959.

Wheaton, Henry. *Elements of International Law*, ed. by George G. Wilson. Oxford: Oxford University Press, 1936.

II. ARTICLES

Adede, A.O. "Settlement of Disputes Arising Under the Law of the Sea Convention." *American Journal of International Law* 69 (1975) 305-311.

Aggarwala, Narindes. "Political Aspects of Hijacking." *International Conciliation* 585 (November 1971) 7-27.

"Aircraft Piracy: The Hague Hijacking Convention." *International Law* 6 (July 1972) 642.

"Air Piracy." *Insurance Counsel Journal* 42 (October 1973) 540-559.

"Anti-Hijacking Act of 1974 – A Step Beyond the Hague Convention." *South Texas Law Journal* 16 (1975) 356-370.

Bassiouni, M. Cherif. "International Extradition in the American Practice and World Public Order." *Tennessee Law Review* 36 (1969) 1.

—. "Introduction to a Symposium on Issues in Aero-Space Law." *De Paul Law Review*, 20 (1970) 326.

Bingham, Joseph. "Piracy: An Introduction." *American Journal of International Law* 26 (1932) 749-760.

Boutrous-Ghali. "The Addis Ababa Charter: A Commentary." *International Conciliation* 546 (1964) 25-32.

Brodsky, John A. "Terry and the Pirates: Constitutionality of Airport Searches and Seizures." *Kentucky Law Journal* 62 (1974) 623-680.

Brownlie, Ian. "International Law and the Activities of Armed Bands." *International and Comparative Law Quarterly* 7 (1958) 729.

—. "The Use of Force in Self Defense." *British Yearbook of International Law* 37 (1961) 183-252.

Burke, William T. "Submerged Passage Through Straits. Interpretations of the Proposed Law of the Sea Treaty Text." *Washington Law Review* 52 (1977) 193.

Bynkershock. "Quaestiones Juris Publici." *American Law Journal* 3 (1810) 258.

Cheng, Bin. "Crimes on Board Aircraft." *Current Legal Problems* 12 (1959) 177-207.

Crockett, Clyde H. "Toward a Revision of the International Law of Piracy." *De Paul Law Review* 26 (1976) 78-99.

Deen, Arthur H. "The Geneva Convention on the Law of the Sea: What Was Accomplished." *American Journal of International Law* 58 (1958) 608-628.

Deere, Lora L. "Political Offenses in the Law and Practice of Extradition." *American Journal of International Law* 27 (1933) 247-270.

Dickinson, Edward D. "Is the Crime of Piracy Obsolete?" *Harvard Law Review* 38 (1924-1925) 334-351.

Fairman, Charles. "A Note on Re Piracy *Jure Gentium*." *American Journal of International Law* 29 (July 1935) 508-512.

Fenston, John, and Hamilton de Saussure. "Conflict in the Competence and Jurisdiction of Courts of Different States to Deal with Crimes Committed on Board Aircraft and Persons Involved Therein." *McGill Law Journal* 56 (1952) 66-83.

Fenwick, Charles. "Piracy in the Caribbean." *American Journal of International Law* 55 (1961) 410-426.

Finch, George A. "Piracy in the Mediterranean." *American Journal of International Law* 31 (1937) 659-665.

Forman, Benjamin. "International Law of Piracy and the *Santa Maria* Incident." *Judge Advocate-General Journal* (October-November 1961) 143.

Gehring, Robert W. "Defense Against Insurgents on the High Seas: the Lyla Express and the Johnny Express." *Judge Advocate-General Journal* 27 (Summer 1973) 317-348.

Glickman, Stephen K. "Enforcement Mechanisms of the Law of the Sea Treaty." *Suffolk Transnational Law Journal* 1 (1976-1977) 1-23.

Green, L.C. "Piracy of Aircraft and the Law." *Alberta Law Review* 10 (1972) 72.

—. "The Santa Maria: Rebels or Pirates?" *British Yearbook of International Law* 37 (1961) 496.

—. "The Nature of Political Offenses." *Solicitor Quarterly* 3 (1964) 213.

—. "Recent Trends in the Law of Extradition." *Current Legal Problems* 6 (1953) 284-287.

Gutteridge, J.A.C. "The Notion of Political Offenses and the Law of Extradition." *British Yearbook of International Law* 31 (1954) 430.

Harvard Research in International Law. "Draft Convention on Extradition and Comments." *American Journal of International Law* 29 (1935) 16-434.

Harvard Research in International Law. "Draft Convention on Piracy with Comments." *American Journal of International Law,* 26, supplement (1932) 749-1002.

Henkin, Louis. "Force, Intervention, and Neutrality in Contemporary International Law." *Proceedings of the American Society of International Law* (1963) 154.

Horlick, Gary N. "The Developing Law of Air Hijacking." *Harvard International Law Journal* 12 (Winter 1971) 33-70.

Kirchheimer, Otto. "Asylum." *American Political Science Review* 53 (December 1959) 985-1016.

Kirsch, Arthur I., and David Fuller. "Aircraft Piracy and Extradition." *New York Law Forum* 16 (Spring 1970) 392-419.

"International Law: Convention on Offenses and Certain Other Acts Committed on Board Local Aircraft: The Tokyo Convention." *De Paul Law Review* 20 (Winter 1970) 485.

Jacobsen, Peter M. "From Piracy on the High Seas to Piracy in the High Skies: A Study of Aircraft Hijacking." *Cornell International Law Journal* 5 (1972) 161-187.

Janis, Mark W. "Dispute Settlement in the Law of the Sea Convention: The Military Activities Exception." *Ocean Development and International Law* 4 (1977) 51-65.

Jessup, Philip C. "International Law Moot Court Competition: Case Arising out of an Aerial Hijacking Incident." *American Journal of International Law* 65 (September 1971) 392.

Johnson, D.H.N. "Piracy in Modern International Law." *Transactions of the Grotius Society* 43 (1957) 63-85.

Knauth, Arnold. "Crime in the High Air: A Footnote to History." *Tulane Law Review* 25 (1951) 446.

Lenoir, James J. "Piracy Cases in the Supreme Court." *Journal of Criminal Law, Criminology and Political Science* 25 (1934) 532-553.

McMahon, John P. "Air Hijacking: Extradition as a Deterrent." *The Georgetown Law Journal* 58 (1970) 1135-1152.

McWhinney, Edward. "New Developments in the Law of International Aviation: The Control of Aerial Hijacking." *American Journal of International Law* 55 (1971) 71-75.

"S.S. *Mayaguez* Incident." *American Journal of International Law* 69 (1975) 875-879.

de Montmorency, J.E.G. "The Barbary States in International Law." *Transactions of the Grotius Society* 4 (1918) 87-94.

— "Piracy and the Barbary Corsairs." *Vanderbilt Quarterly Review* 35 (1919) 133-141.

Morrison, Stanley. "A Collection of Piracy Laws of Various Countries." *American Journal of International Law* 26, supplement (1932) 887-1013.

O'Higgins, Paul. "Disguised Extradition: The Soblen Case." *Modern Law Review* 27 (1964) 521.

Oxman, Bernard H. "The Third United Nations Conference on the Law of the Sea: The 1976 New York Sessions." *American Journal of International Law,* 71 (1977), no. 2, pp. 247-270.

"Panel: New Developments in the Law of International Civil Aviation: The Control of Aerial Hijacking." *Proceedings of the American Society of International Law* 65 (September 1971) 71-96.

BIBLIOGRAPHY

Partridge, Eric. "History of Pirates." *Quarterly Review* 26 (1934) 142-153.
Paust, Jordan, J. "A Survey of Possible Legal Responses to International Terrorism: Prevention, Punishment, and Cooperative Action," *Georgia Journal of International Comparative Law* 5 (1975) 431-469.
"In Re Piracy *Jure Gentium*." *American Journal of International Law* 29 (1935) 140-508.
Poulantzas, Nicholas M. "Hijacking or Air Piracy?" *Nederlandse Juristenblad* 566 (1970) no. 20.
"Prospects for the Prevention of Aircraft Hijacking Through Law." *Columbia Journal of Transnational Law* 9 (Spring 1970) 60.
Roxburgh, R.F. "Submarines at the Washington Conference." *British Yearbook of International Law* 3 (1923) 150-155.
Schwarzenberger, Georg. "The Problem of an International Criminal Law." *Current Legal Problems* 3 (1950) 263-269.
Shubber, S. "Is Hijacking of Aircraft Piracy in International Law?" *British Yearbook of International Law* 43 (1968-1969) 193.
"Skyjacking and Refugees: The Effect of the Hague Convention Upon Asylum." *Harvard International Law Journal* 30 (Winter 1975) 93-112.
"Skyjacking: Problems and Potential Solutions – A Symposium." *Villanova Law Review* 18 (June 1973) 985-1085.
Smith, Chester Lee. "The Probable Necessity of an International Prison in Solving Aircraft Hijacking." *International Lawyer* 5 (April 1971) 269-278.
Sohn, Louis B. "Settlement of Disputes Arising Out of the Law of the Sea Convention." *University of San Diego Law Review* 12 (1975) 495-515.
Spooner, Robert H. "The *Mayaguez* Incident." *Orange County Bar Journal* 2 (Winter 1975) 706-711.
Sundberg, John W. "Piracy: Air and Sea." *De Paul Law Review,* 20 (Winter 1970) 337-435.
"Symposium on Hijacking." *Journal of Air Law and Commerce* 37 (Spring 1971) vii.
Van Alstyne, A. "American Filibustering and the British Navy: A Caribbean Analogue of Mediterranean 'Piracy'." *American Journal of International Law* 32 (1938) 141.
Van Panhuys, Haro F. "Aircraft Hijacking and International Law." *Columbia Journal of Transnational Law* 9 (Spring 1970) 1-22.
Volpe, John A. and John T Steward. "Aircraft Hijacking: Some Domestic and International Responses." *Kentucky Law Journal* 59 (Winter 1970) 273-318.
Whang, Paul K. "Anti-Piracy Measures." *China Weekly Review* 66 (September 2, 1933) 24.
Whatley, A.T. "Historical Sketch of the Law of Piracy." *Law Magazine and Review* 3 (1874) 536-618.
Wilson, George "Insurgency and International Maritime Law." *American Journal of International Law* 1 (1907) 46-60.
Woolsey, L.H. "Closure of Parts by the Chinese Nationalist Government." *American Journal of International Law* 44 (1950) 350-354.
Zwanenberg, Van. "Interference with Ships on the High Seas." *International and Comparative Law Quarterly* 10 (1961) 785.

III. PUBLIC DOCUMENTS

Convention on the High Seas, opened for signature April 29, 1958, 13 U.S.T. 2312 (1962), T.I.A.S. No. 5200, 450 U.N.T.S. 82.

Convention on Offenses and Certain Other Acts Committed on Board Aircraft (Tokyo Convention). Signed September 14, 1963, 20 U.S.T. 2941, 704 U.N.T.S. 10106 (1969), *American Journal of International Law* 58 (1964) 566.

Convention for the Suppression of Unlawful Acts Against the Safety of Civil Aviation (Montreal Convention). Opened for signature September 23, 1971, 2 U.S.T. 1641 (1971), T.I.A.S. No. 7570, effective January 26, 1973.

Convention for the Suppression of Unlawful Seizure of Aircraft (Hague Convention). Opened for signature December 16, 1970, 22 U.S.T. 1643 (1971), T.I.A.S. No. 7192, effective October 14, 1971.

Convention on the Territorial Sea and the Contiguous Zone. Opened for signature April 29, 1958, 15 U.S.T. 1606 (1964), T.I.A.S. No. 5639, 516 U.N.T.S. 205.

Convention on the Status of Refugees. Adopted in 1951, 189 U.N.T.S. 137.

European Convention on Mutual Assistance in Criminal Matters. Signed in Strasbourg, April 20, 1959, 472 U.N.T.S. 195.

European Convention on the Suppression of Terrorism. Opened for signature January 27, 1977, *International Legal Materials* 15 (November 1976) no. 6, p. 1272.

International Law Commission. 1 *Yearbook of the International Law Commission* (1955). 2 *Yearbook of the International Law Commission* (1955).

—. Report of the International Law Commission, 7th Session (1955), A/CN. 4/79, 1 *Yearbook of the International Law Commission* (1955) 69.

—. Observations of the Government of Poland, A/CN.4/L.53, 2 *Yearbook of the International Law Commission* (1955) 1.

—. Summary records of the seventh session, May 2-July 8, 1955, A/CN.4/SER. A/1955, 1 *Yearbook of the International Law Commission* (1955).

—. 1 *Yearbook of the International Law Commission* (1956).

—. 2 *Yearbook of the International Law Commission* (1956).

—. Report of the International Law Commission covering the work of its eighth session, April 23-July 4, 1956, U.N. Doc. A/3159 (1956), 2 *Yearbook of the International Law Commission* (1956) 253-303.

—. Summary of replies from governments and conclusions of the special rapporteur, A/CN.4/97/Add. 1 to 3, 2 *Yearbook of the International Law Commission* (1956) 13-37.

Nyon Arrangement. Adopted September 14, 1937, U.N. Doc. A/3520. League of Nations C.409.M.273.1937.

Report of the League of Nations Committee of Experts for the Progressive Codification of International Law (1926). League of Nations Doc. C.196. M.70.1927.V., pp. 116-119.

—. Professor M. Matsuda, "Projet de dispositions pour la repression de la piraterie," p. 119.

—. Reply of Rumania to questionnaire 6 on piracy, p. 202.

Third United Nations Conference on the Law of the Sea. *Informal Single Negotiating Text*, U.N. Doc. A/CONF.62/WP.8/Part I-III and SD. Gp/2nd Session/No. 11, Rev. 5 (1975).

Third United Nations Conference on the Law of the Sea. *Revised Single Negotiating Text*, U.N. Doc. A/CONF.62/WP.8/Rev.1/Part I-III and A/CONF.62/WP.9/Rev.1 (1976).
—. *Informal Composite Negotiating Text*, U.N. Doc. A/CONF.62/WP.10 (1977).

IV. LEGAL CITATIONS

The Ambrose Light, 25 F. 408 (S.D.N.Y. 1885).
Bonnet's Trial, 5 George I. A.D. 1718, pp. 1234-1237, 15 How. St. Tr. 1231 (1718).
Dawson's Trial, 8 William III. A.D. 1696, 13 How. St. Tr. 455 (1697).
In Re Piracy *Jure Gentium*, [1934] A.C. 586.
United States v. The Pirates, 5 Wheat. (U.S.) 184 (1820).
United States v. Smith, 5 Wheat. (U.S.) 153 (1820).

V. OTHER SOURCES

The Geographer. *Theoretical Aerial Allocations of Seabed to Coastal States Based on Certain U.N. Seabeds Committee Proposals*, Office of the Geographer, Bureau of Intelligence and Research, Washington D.C. (International Boundary Study, Series A, Limits in the Seas, No. 46) August 12, 1972.
Hongkong Standard. Thursday, August 11, 1977, p. 8: "Sabah's War on Pirates Paying Off?" by Colin Bickler.
S.S. *Mayaguez* Incident. "Contemporary Practice of the United States." *American Journal of International Law* 69 (1975) 875-878; *U.S. Digest*, ch. 14, section 1, p. 875 (1975).
The Miami Herald, Wednesday, November 23, 1977, p. 5-A: "Pirates in Nigeria Attack Danish Ship."
New York Times. May 13, 1975, p. 1, column 8.
—. May 17, 1975, p. 17, column 2.
South China Morning Post. Tuesday, August 9, 1977 (Business News), p. 11: "Sea Corridors Curb Pirates and Smugglers," by Colin Bickler.
U.S. News & World Report. October 31, 1977, pp. 23-24: "Is the Tide Turning Against Terrorists?"
—. February 27, 1978, p. 41: "Why a Big Surge in 'Boatnapping'."

INDEX

advisory penalties   75
aircraft   52, 55, 57, 73, 74, 87, 122, 152, 155

belligerents   7, 149
Boatwright case   146
Bonnet, Trial of   38, 93, 94

characteristics of piracy   41
conference states (see also U.N. Conference on Law of the Sea (1958))   2, 4, 38, 40, 54, 57, 68, 77, 86-89, 108, 123
contiguous zone   15, 16, 106
continental shelf   106
Convention on the High Seas (1958)   2, 4, 5, 6, 8, 17, 47, 51, 52, 57, 58, 62, 69, 83, 88, 104, 146, 151, 159, 164
  −Appendix 1 to Chapter 1   11
    −Article 14   11
    −Article 15   11
    −Article 16   11
    −Article 17   11
    −Article 18   12
    −Article 19   12
    −Article 20   12
    −Article 21   12
    −Article 1   17
    −Article 23   18
  Appendix 1 to Chapter 2   24-25
Convention on the Territorial Sea and the Contiguous Zone   15
  −Articles 1 and 2   15, 16
  −Article 3   16
  −Article 24   16
  −Article 23   19

Dawson's Trial   1
dispute settlement   4, 15, 20, 21, 22, 78, 161, 163, 169

exclusive economic zone   4, 19, 20
expediency (see also practicality   78, 89, 104, 107

geographic limitations   151, 157-161
Guatemalan-Mexican incident   146

Harvard Research Group   3, 9, 10, 37-102, 103, 104, 109, 149, 156
  −Draft Articles and Comments   47, 102
  −Appendix 1 to Chapter 3 (Draft Convention on Piracy with comments)   90-93
high seas   15, 85, 106, 119
Hongkong Standard   5
  −Appendix 2 to Chapter 1   13, 14
hostis humanic generis   42, 45
hot pursuit   77, 165

immunity   62, 65
individuals   7
informal composite negotiating text   4, 5, 16, 22, 158
  −Article 86   17, 18
  −Article 111   19
  −Articles 55-75   19
  −Articles 61-68   20
  Appendix 2 to Chapter 2
  −Articles 55-60   25-27
  −Articles 73-75   27
  Appendix 3 to Chapter 2
  −Articles 279-297   28-34
  Appendix 4 to Chapter 3
  −Articles 100-107   95-96
insurance   151-152
insurgents   7, 149
internal waters   18
international court of justice   21, 89, 162
international crime   75
international jail   163
international law commission   3, 9, 10, 37, 39, 40, 68, 69, 86, 89, 104-123, 149, 156
  −7th session (1955)   109-113
  −8th session (1956)   114-120